Readings in the Sociology of Religion

BY

JOAN BROTHERS, B.A., Ph.D.

PERGAMON PRESS

OXFORD · LONDON · EDINBURGH · NEW YORK
TORONTO · SYDNEY · PARIS · BRAUNSCHWEIG

Pergamon Press Ltd., Headington Hill Hall, Oxford
4 & 5 Fitzroy Square, London W.1

Pergamon Press (Scotland) Ltd., 2 & 3 Teviot Place, Edinburgh 1

Pergamon Press Inc., 44–01 21st Street, Long Island City, New York 11101

Pergamon of Canada, Ltd., 6 Adelaide Street East, Toronto, Ontario

Pergamon Press (Aust.) Pty. Ltd., 20–22 Margaret Street,
Sydney, New South Wales

Pergamon Press S.A.R.L., 24 rue des Écoles, Paris 5ᵉ

Vieweg & Sohn GmbH, Burgplatz 1, Braunschweig

Printed in Great Britain by Watmoughs Limited, Idle, Bradford; and London

Contents

PREFACE   vii

ACKNOWLEDGEMENTS   ix

PART I Introduction

Introduction   3
By JOAN BROTHERS

PART II What is the Sociology of Religion?

What is the Sociology of Religion?   29
By P. H. VRIJHOF

The Sociology of Religion in England   61
By J. A. BANKS

PART III Religion and Sociological Theory

The Theoretical Development of the Sociology of Religion   71
By T. PARSONS

Weber's Sociological Theory and the Modern Dilemma of
Value and Belief in the Social Sciences   89
By LORD SIMEY

Objectivity in Research in the Sociology of Religion   115
By E. VOGT

PART IV Types of Research

1. *Religious Sociology*

Religious Sociology and Science of Religions   129
By G. LE BRAS

Religious Sociology and its Aims   151
By E. POULAT

The Role of Reference Groups in the Integration of
Religious Attitudes   167
By H. CARRIER, S.J.

2. *Institutional Analysis*

The Urban Parish as a Social Group   189
By J. H. FICHTER, S.J.

3. *Religion and Society*

Religion in a Secularized Society   201
By W. HERBERG

Religion's Impact on Secular Institutions   217
By G. LENSKI

BIOGRAPHICAL NOTES   237

Preface

THIS is one of a series of volumes to be published by the Pergamon Press. Each will consist of a collection of articles on a specialized aspect of sociology, together with an introduction designed to relate the selected Readings to the state of sociological knowledge and research in the field in question. Each volume of Readings has been prepared by a distinguished scholar who has specialized in the area. The individual editors have worked closely with an editorial board of international repute.

A characteristic feature of the series is the inclusion in each volume of a number of articles translated into English from European and other sources. English-speaking scholars and students will have an opportunity of reading articles which would not otherwise be readily available to them. Many important contributions to sociology made by European and other writers will be given a wider circulation in this way. It is hoped that the series will contribute to an international cross-fertilization of sociological theory and research.

York University, ANTHONY H. RICHMOND
Toronto *General Editor*

THE COMMONWEALTH AND INTERNATIONAL LIBRARY

READINGS IN SOCIOLOGY

Forthcoming Volumes

S. N. Eisenstadt, *Social Change and Development*

Clifford Jansen, *Migration*

Kurt Danziger, *Parent–Child Relations and Socialization*

R. E. Pahl, *Urban Sociology*

Acknowledgements

ACKNOWLEDGEMENT is due to the publishers, editors and authors whose material has been reprinted in this volume. The article by Emile Poulat, "La Sociologie religieuse et son objet", has been previously published by Editions De Minuit, Paris, in No. 118 of the journal *Critique*. The article by H. Carrier, S.J., "Le Rôle des groupes référence dans l'intégration des attitudes religieuses", was published in *Social Compass*, Vol. 8, No. 2, by the International Federation of Catholic Institutes for Social Research (FERES), The Hague. The material by P. H. Vrijhof, "Was ist Religions-soziologie?" and that by E. Vogt, "Über das Probleme der Objektivität in der Religionssoziologie-Forschung", have been published by Westdeutscher Verlag GmbH, Opladen, in the publication *Kölner Zeitschrift für Soziologie und Sozialpsychologie*, No. 6 (Probleme der Religionssoziologie). "Religion in a Secularized Society", by Will Herberg, was originally published in the *Review of Religious Research*, Vol. 3, No. 4, and Vol. 4, No. 1, Copyrighted 1962 by the Religious Research Association Inc., as was "Religion's Impact on Secular Institutions", by Gerhard Lenski. Lord Simey's work was published as "La Obra de Max Weber y el Porvenir de la Sociologia" in *Atlantida*, Vol. 2 (1964), pp. 594–615, by Ediciones R.I.S.L.P., S.A., Madrid. "The Sociology of Religion in England", by J. A. Banks, was published in *Sociologische Gids* by J. A. Boom & Zoon C.V., Te Meppel. Talcott Parsons's article, "The Theoretical Development of the Sociology of Religion", has been published by the *Journal of the History of Ideas*, New York, in Vol. 5, No. 2, April 1944. "Sociologie religieuse et sciences de religions", by Gabriel Le Bras, originally appeared in the journal *Archives de Sociologie des Religions*, No. 1, June 1956, published by Centre National de la Recherche Scientifique, Paris. The article by J. H. Fichter originally appeared as "La paroisse urbaine comme groupe sociale" in *Paroisses Urbaines, Paroisses Urbaines,* Actes du 5ᵉ Conférence Internationale de Sociologie Religieuse, Casterman, Paris, 1954.

The editor is indebted to the authors of the articles reproduced in this volume for their co-operation, and especially for the general comments and references several of them gave. She wishes to thank Professor A. H. Richmond (General Editor of the Series), C. K. Ward and M. B. Gaine, who read the Introduction in draft and offered many useful comments and references; she is particularly indebted to Professor Lord Simey for his invaluable advice and encouragement. She would also like to express her appreciation of the help given by the staff of Pergamon Press throughout the preparation of this volume.

Although every effort has been made to give full documentation, it has not been possible in the case of some references.

PART I

Introduction

Introduction

Joan Brothers

Because of its relevance to theoretical and methodological issues, the sociology of religion has been one of the most influential areas of sociology, and in recent years it has been prolific. Yet even the student of sociology has usually only a fleeting acquaintance with its scope and literature, perhaps because it has been so diversified; to the general reader the subject can suggest a variety of things: analyses which will explain religious phenomena in purely social terms, an aid to ecclesiastical decisions, and so on.

So much work has been done that a short volume cannot aim to survey it all; the specialist journals will provide plenty of references.[1] What is more important is to indicate the main issues in the subject, and to show what kind of work has been done. All the articles included in this volume have already been published. Some authors, like the famous American sociologist, Talcott Parsons, will be well known to readers for their general contributions to sociological theory and research. Others will be less familiar because they have developed a specialized sphere of research. In so short a volume not all the major writers in the subject could be included; there are some, for example, whose main ideas are contained in book rather than article form, while others have extended their contribution to the sociology of religion over a number of works.

The selection concentrates upon comparatively recent theories, concepts and studies. Only one article, Talcott Parsons's analysis

---

[1] *Archives de Sociologie des Religions* (Paris), *Social Compass* (The Hague and Brussels), the American *Review of Religious Research*, the Italian *Sociologia Religiosa*, etc.

of the theoretical development of the sociology of religion, is more than ten years old. Why have the contributions of Durkheim, Max Weber, Troeltsch,[2] and the like been omitted? It is, after all, for their classical studies that the sociology of religion is usually known.

The failure to include excerpts from such works does not imply any slight upon their stature. But sociology, having few founders, has been over-ready to show respect for them and the result has been the incarceration of the dynamic concepts and themes of these men in historical museums. Max Weber's analysis of the relationship between Protestantism and Capitalism,[3] for instance, is all too often handed to students without requiring them to give consideration to subsequent historical research which casts doubt upon the validity of the thesis as it stands. It pays no real tribute to a scholar's work to revere his theories uncritically or to see them as being simply of historical interest. If Durkheim and Weber and other early writers have anything meaningful to contribute to the development of sociological thought now—and there are many reasons for concluding that they have[4]—then they must be used rather than enshrined. It is for this reason that evaluative analyses are included in this volume, not extracts from the writers themselves.

The selections fall into three sections. First of all (Part II) there is the question of what the sociology of religion is, dealt with by the Dutch sociologist, Vrijhof, and by Banks. Following on from this, Part III tackles the significance of the sociology of

[2] As Troeltsch is mentioned only briefly in this volume, it is worth referring to the work of Jean Séguy, Ernst Troeltsch et ses Soziallehren, *Archives de Sociologie des Religions* **11**, 7–14 (1961) and Ernst Troeltsch et sa sociologie du Christianisme, *Cahiers du Cercle Ernest Renan* **32** (4) (1961). There is a recent edition in English (New York, 1960) of Troeltsch's *Die Soziallehren der christlichen Kirchen und Gruppen*, Tübingen, 1912.

[3] *The Protestant Ethic and the Spirit of Capitalism*, New York, 1930. Reprinted 1950.

[4] See, for instance, Talcott Parsons's Introduction to Weber's *The Sociology of Religion*, Boston, 1963. Cf. Capitalism and Religion, in S. Andreski, *Elements of Comparative Sociology*, London, 1964.

religion for sociological thought, with articles by Parsons and Simey on the implications for theory, while Vogt considers the problems concerning objectivity in socio-religious research. Part IV of the book considers the main types of research which have been undertaken: *religious sociology*, which includes papers by Le Bras, Poulat and Carrier; *institutional analysis*, illustrated by an article of Fichter's; and finally *religion and society*, dealt with by two American sociologists, Herberg and Lenski. These divisions are necessarily arbitrary ones, and papers overlap considerably. Thus Vrijhof's article, for instance, is extremely relevant to the discussion of the implications of the sociology of religion for sociological theory, while Le Bras's article might well have been included in the section which deals with definitions of the subject.

These articles give some idea of what has been achieved in the way of empirical research, on the one hand, and in the field of theory, on the other. Emphasis is placed upon the dominant trends in research and upon work which indicates the failures and omissions of the sociology of religion to date.

Because sociologists have chosen to study many different types of religious groups,[5] particularly in the United States,[6] it would be hard to reproduce a balanced selection of representative denominations or groups from these analyses. Accordingly, the stress in this volume is upon theoretical and methodological issues.

WHAT IS THE SOCIOLOGY OF RELIGION?

This is the title of the first paper, written by the Dutch sociologist Vrijhof, and he describes the manifold and baffling problems involved in trying to answer this question, amongst these

---

[5] Cf. B. Johnson, Church-Sect Typology. A Critical Appraisal, *American Sociological Review* **22** (1) 88–92 (1957); P. L. Berger, Sectarianism and Religious Sociation, *American Journal of Sociology* **64** (1) 41–4 (1958).

[6] To take a few at random: L. Pope, *Millhands and Preachers*, New Haven, 1942; M. Sklare (ed.), *The Jews. Social Patterns of an American Group*, Glencoe, 1958; J. L. Thomas, *The American Catholic Family*, Englewood Cliffs, N.J., 1956; B. Y. Landis, *Rural Church Life in the Middle West*, New York, 1922, etc.

being the definition of "religion" itself. Some of the controversial areas covered by the sociology of religion are indicated in this analysis, which introduces the reader to some of the main contributors to the development of the subject, from Weber, Troeltsch and Wach,[7] to contemporary writers like Schelsky, Yinger and Goldschmidt.

One of the basic issues in the sociology of religion is the question of the status and definition of religion itself. Is religion essentially a personal, individual matter and should sociology therefore be concerned only with its secondary characteristics, its social consequences? Or are religious beliefs themselves to be subjected to sociological analysis and are its personal manifestations in individual life merely epiphenomena? Have they any reality or meaning outside their social context? Can they be explained wholly in terms of the social functions they perform? It is with these sorts of questions that Vrijhof is concerned, and he deals with some of the answers that have been given in the brief history of sociology. The differences of opinion which have arisen have been very much influenced by the approach of individual sociologists, their personal beliefs, and the ideology of the group to which they belong. For instance, as Vrijhof points out, Roman Catholic writers in the sociology of religion have tended to be unwilling to submit the content of belief to examination; in their work certain ideas are taken as given.

The article makes it plain that the sociology of religion is not a clearly demarcated field[8] which has only one acceptable approach. Of the sociologists dealing with religion perhaps more than any other branch of sociology it is true to say *quot sunt homines, tot sunt sententiae*. The approach to religious phenomena involves the individual sociologist's philosophy and "life view". (The implications of this are taken up in Vogt's article in Part III of the selections.) Some seem well aware of this and

[7] Cf. J. Séguy, Joachim Wach, sociologue des religions, *Archives de Sociologie des Religions* **14**, 27–34 (1962).

[8] Cf. E. Vogt, Religion et idéologie, faussent-elles la sociologie des religions? *Archives de Sociologie des Religions* **12**, 75–80 (1961).

state their value position clearly at the outset, or let it be revealed plainly in the course of their writings; but others seem to believe it possible to be entirely objective, and it is only in their conclusions (if at all) that their value premises are revealed, and then as one version or another of positivism. There is a tendency today for the latter view to overshadow the former so deeply that it is sometimes forgotten or disbelieved that there can be any other definition of religion than the positivist.

As Goldschmidt has pointed out (cited in Vrijhof's article), the emphasis has changed in the sociology of religion from studying how religion affects social behaviour to the analysis of how religious behaviour is socially determined.

Like a number of writers in the sociology of religion, however, Vrijhof is concerned with religious beliefs in themselves as well as with their social consequences—thus, he considers theological definitions of religion as well as the sociological. He considers how far sociology and theology might interact, a theme which has attracted the attention of theologians as well as sociologists.[9] Many of those who are engaged in research in the sphere of religion are interested in the consequences of their work for religious groups. Some want their findings to be immediately available for ecclesiastical action[10] (this is discussed later), but when writers like Vrijhof and Simey[11] call for the interaction of theology and sociology, they are thinking in terms of fundamentally reconstructing our religious ideas and beliefs in the light of

[9] As, for instance, Schillebeeckx, Theological reflections on religio-sociological interpretations of modern "Irreligion", *Social Compass* **10** (3), 257–84 (1963), an article by a Catholic theologian complemented by a Protestant approach in R. Mehl's Sociologie du christianisme et théologie, in the same number. See, also, B. Häring, *Macht und Ohnmacht der Religion*, Salzburg, 1956, and Spiegel-Schmidt, Theologie und Soziologie, in *Studium Soziale: Festschrift für Karl Valentin Müller* (ed. K. G. Specht, R. G. Rasch, H. Hofbauer), 1963.

[10] This has led to a great deal of writing on sociology as a pastoral tool, for instance, E. R. Wickham, *Encounter with Modern Society*, London, 1964. See, also, J. Laloux, Sociologie et Pastorale, *Revue Diocésaine de Namur* **13** (3) (1959).

[11] Simey, The Church of England and English Society, *Social Compass* **11** (3–4) 5–11 (1964). Cf. C. Vereker, The Church and Social Studies, *Christian Frontier* **5** (4) (1957).

sociological theory and research and of a better understanding of the social environment in which they are expressed. From the theological point of view this involves a restatement and perhaps an amplification of the doctrine of the incarnation.

Continental work might lead one to conclude that the division between those who want their work to be of immediate and direct use to the churches and those who are interested in a much more long-term contribution to religious life is a confessional one. But when the work carried out in the United States, and to a lesser extent in Britain, is taken into account, it becomes clear that this is more a matter of professional approach on the part of both sociologists and theologians than denominational persuasion.

J. A. Banks contributes a short article on the tendency of recent British work to be divorced from the characteristically different approach to religion of earlier writers like Spencer, Tylor, Malinowski and Frazer; this continues the discussion as to the nature of the sociology of religion. A recent survey of a Roman Catholic parish[12] falls as much under the general heading of the sociology of organization as under that of religion, argues Banks, whereas the earlier tradition in the social sciences in Britain was unconcerned with this kind of institutional analysis, having in mind broader notions about the functions of religion in relation to life's crises such as birth and death.

A good deal of contemporary research in the sphere of religion, in the United States as well as in Britain (where in any case the studies are so few that it is hard to generalize[13]), does in fact deal

[12] C. K. Ward, *Priests and People*, Liverpool, 1961. See, also, Ward's Some Aspects of the Social Structure of a Roman Catholic Parish, *The Sociological Review* **6** (1) 75–93 (1958). Cf. M. B. Gaine's contribution The Social Setting of the Modern Parish, in *The Parish in the Modern World* (ed. Davis), London, 1965.

[13] A few recent studies include: B. Wilson, *Sects and Society*, London, 1961; J. Highet, *The Scottish Churches*, London, 1960; E. R. Wickham, *Church and People in an Industrial City*, London, 1957; R. H. T. Thompson, *The Church's Understanding of Itself*, London, 1957; *Anglican–Methodist Relations* (ed. W. S. Pickering), London, 1961; J. Brothers, *Church and School*, London, 1964; Gould and Esh, *Jewish Life in Modern Britain*, London, 1964, etc. Other references can be found in an article by the present writer, Recent Developments in the

with the analysis of social organization, role performance, relationships and the like, and it is true to say that the findings of this kind of research are relevant to the general discussion of roles, and the like. Whether or not this is a limitation, however, is another matter. A later contribution to this volume, that of the American sociologist, J. H. Fichter, deals with this type of work. The emphasis in this approach has been upon empirical work leading to what Merton has called "theories of the middle range",[14] rather than to all-embracing theories which generalize about the functions of religious beliefs. Fichter's typology of parishioners and its subsequent modifications by authors like Ward are characteristic of these middle-range theories.

RELIGION AND SOCIOLOGICAL THEORY

It has been pointed out that the sociology of religion has attracted the attention of some of the outstanding figures in the social sciences. Amongst these has been the American sociologist Talcott Parsons. In the article included in this volume, he describes the development of a conceptual framework to deal with religious phenomena as part of a social system. Both analytical and predictive, the article shows how the theoretical development of the sociology of religion has been a case study of sociology in general.[15]

Using his own framework and vocabulary, Parsons shows that progress has been made in a theoretical approach to religious phenomena "within the basic structural scheme with which

Sociology of Religion in England and Wales, *Social Compass* 11 (3–4) 13–19 (1964). Earlier documentation can be found in N. Burnbaum, Soziologie der Kirchengemeinde in Grossbritannien, in *Soziologie der Kirchengemeinde* (ed. D. Goldschmidt, F. Greiner, H. Schelsky), Stuttgart, 1960; and C. K. Ward, Sociological Research in the Sphere of Religion in Great Britain, *Sociologia Religiosa* (3–4) 79–94 (1959).

[14] R. K. Merton, *Social Theory and Social Structure*, Glencoe, 1949. Revised 1957.

[15] Cf. the comments of J. Milton Yinger in *Religion, Society and the Individual*, New York, 1957.

'rationalistic positivism' started". Reviewing the contributions of Pareto, Malinowski, Durkheim and Max Weber, he indicates how sociological theory in general has been built up through their analyses of religion.

The influence of positivist thought has persisted in the approach of many sociologists to the present time, and few have attempted analyses of the ways in which social developments have been affected by religious thought and ideas. Amongst those who took a different line the most notable is Tawney in his classic analysis of the influence of religious beliefs upon economic development.[16] It is interesting that he believed that Max Weber was concerned not with the social behaviour of Puritans, but with their theological doctrines.[17]

As Parsons points out in the article which is included in this volume, the sociology of religion has played a crucial part in the development of general theory in sociology. In discussing sociological approaches to religious beliefs and phenomena, the difficult problem of the status of values arises. Ought the sociologist to be concerned only with what "is", leaving the "ought" out of his conceptual framework? Is this position possible? The distortion of Max Weber's *wertfrei* approach to sociological situations, now reappraised,[18] led many sociologists to the conclusion that values are not proper objects of study, a conclusion reached by some members of religious bodies, though for different reasons. They consider values ought not to be included in their analyses, not because their meaning and relevance transcends empirical investigation, as many Christians and others would maintain, but because values have no validity except in so far as they affect actual situations.

---

[16] *Religion and the Rise of Capitalism*, London, 1926.

[17] Cf. R. K. Merton, Puritanism, Pietism and Science, in *Social Theory and Social Structure*, Glencoe, 1949. Revised 1957.

[18] W. L. Kolb, Values, Positivism and Functional Theory, in Yinger, *op. cit.*; Simey, Weber's Sociological Theory of Value: An Appraisal in Mid-Century, *The Sociological Review* **13** (1) (1965), etc.

As Kolb has pointed out,[19] such a view can produce a great problem for the individual sociologist concerning his responsibilities to speak out on the question of values. Issues concerning the logical status of values in the social sciences are returning to the fore, and it is with these kinds of problems that Simey's article is concerned. Dealing initially with the social sciences in general, like Talcott Parsons he sees the sociology of religion as the crucial area where these issues come to a head. The theoretical significance of this branch of sociology is therefore very considerable, not only because of the role it has played in the history of sociological theory but also because recent writers are examining the general methodological problems it highlights.

Contrary to the usual view, Simey maintains that Weber's approach to religion and values was based on the assumption that religion can be in itself a cause of social change. For the discipline of sociology to develop, the influence of ideas and beliefs needs to be studied, as well as the more usual approach of considering how far human behaviour is socially conditioned.

Another of the general issues in sociology which is prominent in the study of religion is the question of objectivity. How far is it possible for a sociologist to study processes of which he himself is a part?[20] More difficult still, how far can he analyse the content of values and ideas without becoming partisan and allowing the findings of his research to be influenced accordingly? These issues, interwoven with the theme of Simey's article, are the concern of Vogt's contribution. Like the previous writer, the Norwegian sociologist considers that it is unreal to separate facts from values in the social sciences.

The beliefs and affiliations of individual sociologists are very much apparent in the type of work they carry out, though some of them seem less conscious of this than others and their positions are not learned from their own statements but by implication from the kind of conclusion they reach about the influence of

[19] *Loc. cit.*

[20] Cf. the present writer's Perception in Socio-Religious Research, *Sociologia Religiosa* **7** (9–10) 65–70 (1963).

values upon social situations or about the extent to which religious beliefs and institutions are socially conditioned. Vogt's emphasis upon the relevance of the sociologist's own background, ideology, social status and similar factors to his research indicate yet another problem area of methodology which is highlighted in the sociology of religion.

The growth of the sociology of religion, then, has been crucial in the general development of sociological thought, because within it a number of methodological issues have been raised in a critical form. For this reason it is one of the most significant and controversial areas in sociology.

TYPES OF RESEARCH

1. *Religious Sociology*

In continental Europe, in addition to extensive contributions to the sociology of religion as it is ordinarily understood, there has developed a prolific discipline known as *sociologie religieuse*,[21] usually translated as "religious sociology", a term which conveys rather unfortunate overtones to sociologists in Britain and the United States. This movement originated in 1931,[22] when a French canon lawyer, Gabriel Le Bras, finding the legal categories which attempted to provide for all sections of the population were inadequate to describe human situations,[23] made a notable appeal for historians, archivists, clergy and the like to co-operate in an effort to understand the religious position in France. For

[21] For a brief description, see J. Labbens, *La Sociologie Religieuse*, Paris, 1959. Cf. G. Le Bras, F. Boulard, J. Labbens, M.-D. Chenu, J. Folliet, F. Dumont, *Sociologie et Religion*, Paris, 1958; A. Birou, *Sociologie et Religion*, Paris, 1959, etc.

[22] G. Le Bras, Statistique et histoire religieuse. Pour un examen détaillé et pour une explication historique de l'état du Catholicisme dans les diverses régions de la France, *Revue d'histoire de l'église de France* **17**, 425–49 (1931). Reprinted in *Études de sociologie religieuse*, 2 vols., Paris, 1956.

[23] See Le Bras's own remarks in Sociology of Catholicism in France, *Lumen Vitae*, English edition, **7** (1–2) 13–24 (1951); also reprinted in Le Bras, *Études de sociologie religieuse*.

some years Le Bras worked almost alone, producing numerous articles; the positivist philosophy with which sociology was originally associated made acceptance of sociology as a positive science slow in ecclesiastical circles. Eventually, collaboration came from Canon Fernand Boulard who was responsible for collecting a great deal of material on religious observance in rural France.[24] Soon surveys based upon Le Bras's approach were being produced throughout France. Religious statistics of various kinds were rapidly compiled by both clergy and laity, concentrating mainly upon demographic studies of religious observance. Those who have been involved in this kind of research, originally a movement within French Catholicism but now considerably extended both to other countries and to other confessions, have been concerned primarily with the practical application of their findings to pastoral work.[25]

Gradually socio-religious research institutes were set up in other countries in Europe, modelled on Le Bras's work. Catholic in origin, the methods of religious sociology have since been adopted in Protestant circles.[26] As the movement spread, so have the kinds of survey developed. The earlier studies differed in their precise aims, but tended to collect background data about the area being considered, taking into account historical factors, following Le Bras's example, and then to study intensively demographic features in particular groups;[27] typically, a study might be concerned with a survey of those actually present in church on a particular Sunday (either on a parochial or a

[24] Through the publication of this writer's *Premiers itinéraires en sociologie religieuse* (Paris, 1954) in English (translated M. Jackson, London, 1962), religious sociology has become known in some circles in Britain.

[25] E.g. F. Houtart, La Sociologie religieuse auxiliaire de la pastorale, extrait des Collectania Mechlinensia, March, 1955; J. Newman, *Change and the Catholic Church*, Baltimore and Dublin, 1965, etc.

[26] Cf. F. G. Dreyfus, Vocation et limites d'une sociologie du protestantisme en France, *Social Compass* 7 (2) (1960).

[27] Cf. J. Labbens, *Les 99 autres . . . ou l'église aussi recense*, Lyons and Paris, 1954.

diocesan level), including information on the age, socio-economic background, occupational status and family structure and the like.[28] Because of the limited methods and aims of the early surveys there has been a tendency in some sociological circles to dismiss such analyses as mere headcounting; this is a superficial judgement which ignores recent work which has considerably wider aims and has, through the interpretation of data, contributed a great deal to the understanding of the influence of religious beliefs and institutions in certain areas.[29] As these surveys have developed, so has the scope of their inquiries, and the interpretation of these statistics has contributed considerably to our knowledge of religious behaviour.[30]

Numerous socio-religious research institutes now exist all over the continent of Europe to collect sociographic information. One of the most important is the Belgian *Centre de Recherches Socio-Religieuses*, originally in Brussels, now in Louvain, with several branches throughout Belgium. Such institutes are usually at the disposal of the bishops and undertake research with the aim of providing information which is intended to be directly useful to ecclesiastical administrators. Work of this kind has recently spread far afield, notably to Latin America, where the Director of the Belgian Centre, Canon François Houtart, one of the most notable figures in religious sociology who has produced a large number of studies,[31] has been responsible for directing surveys.

[28] Cf. P. Virton, *Enquêtes de sociologie paroissiale*, Paris, 1953.

[29] For instance, E. Pin, *Pratique religieuse et classes sociales dans une paroisse urbaine, St. Pothin à Lyon*, Paris, 1956.

[30] For example, it is to this kind of study that we owe our knowledge of the phenomenon that, as far as Roman Catholics are concerned, as the standard of education increases, so does the observance of religious duties; see, for instance, Centre de Recherches Socio-Religieuses Rapport No. 59, *Étude socio-religieuse de l'agglomération de Namur*; Namur, 1960; Y. Daniel, *Aspects de la pratique religieuse à Paris*, Paris, 1952; J. Labbens et R. Daille, *La Pratique dominicale dans l'agglomération Lyonnaise*, Lyons, 1956, etc. Cf. J. Kerkhofs, *Godsdienstpraktijk en sociaal milieu*, Brussels, 1953.

[31] For instance, *L'Église et la pastorale des grandes villes*, Brussels, 1955; *Aspects sociologiques du catholicisme américain*, Paris, 1957; Les Variables qui affectent le rôle intégrateur de la religion, *Social Compass* **1** (1960).

Some of the research centres, like the Protestant and Catholic Institutes in the Netherlands,[32] have extended their analyses to wider social problems and have developed their methodological approach from the predominantly demographic to more sociological analyses.

In 1948 a group of Catholics from France, Belgium and Holland met at Louvain and founded the *Conférence Internationale de Sociologie Religieuse*,[33] which has since developed its range, by including work of a more strictly sociological nature, on the one hand, and by its attention to other religious groups, on the other.[34] A smaller body, the Colloquium on the Sociology of Protestantism, places its emphasis upon sociology rather than upon demography.

Demographic material of the kind widely collected on the Continent has been accumulated for some time by the Roman Catholic Newman Demographic Survey, which came into being in 1953 to collect information about Roman Catholics in England and Wales.[35] Its director, A. E. C. W. Spencer, has since joined with Leslie Paul[36] and David Martin[37] to form an independent ecumenical research agency, S.R.R.S. (Socio-Religious Research Services), their first project being an ecumenical census service.[38]

[32] Cf. W. Goddijn, The Sociology of Religion and Socio-Religious Research in the Netherlands, *Social Compass* **7** (4) (1960). See, also, R. Vekemans, La Sociographie du catholicisme aux Pays-Bas, *Archives de Sociologie des Religions* (3) 129–37 (1957).

[33] J. Labbens, Le Rôle de la conférence internationale de sociologie religieuse, *Social Compass* **7** (1) (1960).

[34] See, for instance, the scope of the papers of its meeting at Königstein, Germany, in 1962, and at Barcelona in 1965.

[35] A. E. C. W. Spencer, The Newman Demographic Survey, 1953–1964, *Social Compass* **11** (3–4) 31–40 (1964).

[36] Author of the controversial study *The Deployment and Payment of the Clergy of the Church of England*, London, 1964.

[37] The Denomination, *British Journal of Sociology* **13** (1) 1–14 (1962).

[38] A study in religious sociology in Britain has been produced by a Belgian, Vanni Bressan, *La Structure sociale d'une paroisse urbaine*, Louvain, 1961. Work largely based upon the methods of religious sociology has also been started in the Anglican diocese of Southwark, under the direction of the Rev. Leslie Harman.

Religious sociology has rapidly become specialized. For instance, recruitment to the priesthood and religious communities has been made the object of research of this kind, and numerous detailed studies have been produced.[39] Because the early development of religious sociology has already been adequately documented[40] and its aims clearly described elsewhere, and since the present spate of publications makes it impossible to produce an account which will remain up to date,[41] it has been possible to present only a slight indication of what has been done. An excellent bibliography of the sociology of religion in all its forms, including religious sociology, is published regularly in *Archives de Sociologie des Religions,* and this will enable anyone who is interested to keep in touch with recent developments. *Social Compass,* too, publishes articles and bibliographies from all over the world. In both journals accounts are given regularly of the current state of religious sociology in various European countries.

Instead of documenting the development of religious sociology, then, or selecting a typical sociographical analysis, the inclusion of an evaluative review seems more worth while. Accordingly, an article written by Le Bras himself dealing with the relationship of religious sociology to other disciplines studying religious phenomena has been included. It was a paper published at a critical point in the development of the study of religion, in the first number of *Archives de Sociologie des Religions.* It illustrates how at times some Continental writers use the sociology of religion and religious sociology as synonymous terms. In Britain, on the other hand, religious sociology is often entirely disregarded by professional sociologists. It seems to the present writer that the best

[39] See the very full bibliography by J. Dellepoort, N. Greinacher and W. Menges, Bibliographie annotée pour une sociologie du clergé, *Social Compass* **8** (4) 355–65 (1961).

[40] E.g. F. Houtart, État present de la sociologie religieuse, *La Revue Nouvelle* **14** (10) 333–41 (1951); C. K. Ward, *op. cit.,* Chapter 1, etc.

[41] A notable bibliography has recently appeared, H. Carrier and E. Pin, *Sociology of Christianity,* Rome, 1964.

approach is to treat religious sociology as a branch of the sociology of religion.

The limitations of the methods of religious sociology are admirably described in Poulat's article. He indicates some of the major problems the discipline faces[42] and suggests ways in which it may develop. Because of the light this article throws upon attempts to grasp religious realities meaningfully, its relevance to the whole study of religion, not just religious sociology, is considerable.

Repetition of surveys of the established pattern rather than studies embodying fresh directions in their aims and methods has been one of the main weaknesses in religious sociology. It should, however, be emphasized that this has had one important compensatory element which has been conspicuously lacking in most social research in other fields. Evidence to support certain trends has been accumulated systematically, and as a result it has been possible to describe certain religious phenomena with more assurance that the results are widely valid than has ever been true of other areas of research.

Some of the limitations in religious sociology have been the result of a desire for the findings to be immediately available for pastoral decisions. There has also been a tendency to take for granted the pastoral aims for which research is being provided. The preoccupation with the immediate end of obtaining information on a particular pastoral problem, the analysis of urban development to locate a parish, for instance, has resulted in the failure to examine basic questions like the role and function of a religious community in a particular *milieu*. Research of a more strictly sociological nature should lead those who are concerned with the consequences of their findings to a more fundamental consideration of values and purposes.

The superficiality of demographic analyses and their inadequacy in indicating the religious life of a community have

[42] Further limitations of religious sociology are discussed by the present writer in Sociology and Religion in *Uses of Sociology* (ed. J. D. Halloran and Joan Brothers), London, 1966.

naturally been the target for criticism. Most critics have tended
to assume that only a more truly sociological approach can overcome this limitation, and have not attempted a reconciliation of
methods within the subject. Recently, however, such an attempt
has been made with considerable success by the French-Canadian
writer, Carrier. In his survey of the relevance of social psychology
to socio-religious studies he has indicated a conceptual framework
which may overcome some of the basic limitations of religious
sociology;[43] the article which is included in this volume summarizes some of the writer's ideas on this. His approach has
already been received with enthusiasm on the Continent and it is
probable that a good deal of future socio-religious research in
Europe will be influenced by his work. It is a particularly
attractive approach in that it indicates not only how a more
profound knowledge of social situations may be given than has
hitherto been the case in religious sociology, but also how the
findings and concepts of social psychology may be utilized to
understand the attitudes and values which are responsible for
religious behaviour, a task which the sociology of religion in
general has failed to accomplish so far.

The three articles on religious sociology included in this volume,
then, indicate its relationship to other disciplines studying
religion; analyse its failures; and finally indicate a conceptual
framework which may enable it to overcome these limitations and
move on to a more adequate approach to the analysis and understanding of religious behaviour in its social context.

2. *Institutional Analysis*

One of the most important aspects of the sociological approach
has been the empirical study of how institutions work. Religious
institutions have been considered in this kind of way;[44] this is

[43] *La Psycho-sociologie de l'appartenance religieuse*, Rome, 1960. English edition
The Sociology of Religious Belonging, London, 1965.

[44] See, for instance, B. Y. Landis, *Rural Church Life in the Middle West*, New
York, 1922, etc.

especially true of the United States where a general study of an
area will usually include the analysis of religious communities.[45]
(This is in marked contrast with surveys in Britain which usually
omit the question of religion.) Within the context of institutional
research the obvious starting point has been the study of the
parish, the local unit of the Christian churches, and the sociology
of the parish has developed rapidly.[46]

The methods used to study parochial structures have varied
somewhat. The extremes are illustrated in two recent studies of
Roman Catholic parishes in England. The sociographical
approach described in the previous section has been used by a
Belgian writer studying a London parish;[47] analysing the education, occupation, age and marital status of church attenders, it
approaches the parish as a demographic unit. In great contrast,
C. K. Ward's survey of a Liverpool parish is an example of
British empirical work.[48] Considering both observable structures
and events in parochial life, the working of organizations and the
like, it also produces the findings of interviews with parishioners
who describe their part in parochial life and how their lives are—
or are not—affected by membership of the parish.

Parochial studies on the Continent, such as Pin's notable work
in Lyons,[49] one of the best examples of this trend, have tended to

[45] E.g. R. Lynd and H. Lynd, *Middletown. A Study in American Culture*, New
York, 1929, etc.

[46] E.g. C. J. Nuesse and T. J. Harte, *The Sociology of the Parish*, Milwaukee,
1951; J. B. Schuyler, *Northern Parish*, Chicago, 1960; A. M. Greeley, Some
Aspects of Interaction between Religious Groups in an Upper Middle Class
Roman Catholic Parish, *Social Compass* 9 (1–2) 39–61 (1962); Thompson, *op. cit.*;
P. H. Vrijhof, Soziologie der Pfarrer, *Anstosse*, April, 1963; P. H. Vrijhof and
W. Eicholtz, Ways in which the Churches had reacted to Changes in Urban
Structure, *Sociologisch Bulletin* 17 (4) 96–108 (1963); J. Brothers, Two Views of
the Parish, *The Furrow* 16 (8) 471–8 (1965); M. J. Jackson and P. H. Mann,
Anglican–Methodist Relations in Two Urban Parishes, in Pickering (ed.)
op. cit.; M. M. Abbot, *A City Parish Grows and Changes*, Washington, 1953, etc.

[47] Bressan, *op. cit.*

[48] Ward, *op. cit.*

[49] *Op. cit.*

be of the former kind, and as such fall under the heading of religious sociology.

In the United States, on the other hand, the kinds of studies which have been produced have had more in common with analyses of other institutions than with Continental work on religion.[50] Surveys have been produced of religious institutions of various kinds, and consider the social relationships which arise within such systems.[51] Prominent in this field has been the American sociologist, J. H. Fichter, whose work is represented in this volume. The author of numerous surveys on religious institutions, the short extract included in this volume deals with his approach to the Catholic parish as a social institution. He has also produced a major study of a parochial school,[52] and other work includes a recent survey of relationships between priests and people in American Catholicism,[53] all representing the same type of methodological approach.

What is particularly important about Fichter's work is the way in which the observation and analysis of religious structures are accompanied by the development of theory. For instance, his typology of parishioners—nuclear, modal, marginal and dormant —has grown out of his empirical investigation of parochial life. Used and refined by subsequent writers, this typology has been a very useful analytical tool in institutional research in the sphere of religion.

Role theory has also been relied on in this kind of research, because those engaged in this type of investigation are concerned with the relationships which arise out of participation in a

[50] Cf. the Yankee City Series, e.g. W. Lloyd Warner and P. S. Lunt, *The Social Life of a Modern Community*, Yale, 1941.

[51] Cf. T. F. O'Dea, Five Dilemmas in the Institutionalization of Religion, *Social Compass* **7** (1) (1960).

[52] *The Parochial School; A Sociological Study*, Notre Dame, 1958. See, also, *Social Relations in the Urban Parish*, Chicago, 1954; *Southern Parish*. Vol. I. *The Dynamics of a City Church*, Chicago, 1951.

[53] *Priests and People*, New York, 1965.

religious system.[54] Thus, for instance, the role of the priest in the parochial system has become an important area for research.[55]

There are special methodological advantages in this kind of work; for instance, the examination of how a religious institution such as a parochial community or a school works can be carried out by anyone trained in sociological techniques. Although it is clearly necessary to know something about the development of the parish as an ecclesiastical unit and to have some idea of its social and legal relevance in a church, at the same time it does not involve a special knowledge of the content of religious beliefs that some kinds of research require. It is probably the easiest type of research for the investigator who has no prior knowledge of the group through his own membership (though most people engaged in this kind of investigation are in fact members of the church bodies they study). It is also likely that it is the area where subjective evaluation matters least; anybody can study factors such as the socio-economic background of membership of an organization. Its security lies in its similarity to other branches of sociology.

But at the same time there are criticisms to be made of this approach, from two sides. Firstly, some members of religious groups find it hard to accept that religious communities can be studied in the same sort of way as other institutions. There is, they believe, more to the working of a religious community than the ordinary factors of organization, status hierarchy and the like. One of the major contributions of Fichter[56] has been to demonstrate, through empirical research instead of the assertions other writers often make on the subject, that religious institutions are susceptible to sociological investigation without their ideologies being undermined. Sociological analysis may reveal that beliefs

---

[54] A German study of thirty-four Lutheran parishes is interesting in this context, G. Wurzbacher, K. M. Bolte, R. Klaus-Roeder, I. Rentdorff, *Der Pfarrer in der modernen Gesellschaft*, Hamburg, 1960.

[55] E.g. Paul, *op. cit.*; C. K. Ward, Priests and People: A Study of Parish Visitation in an English City, *Sociologia Religiosa* 5 (7) 79–84 (1961); J. Brothers, Social Change and the Role of the Priest, *Social Compass* 10 (6) 477–91 (1963).

[56] In *Social Relations*.

produce conflict in everyday life; it may reveal that the behaviour of participants in a religious community has little relation to the values they profess (as, for instance, in professing egalitarian beliefs while practising discrimination against other people). It cannot evaluate the ultimate truth or falsity of values, nor indeed is that its aim, but it can demonstrate that an ideology gives rise to certain characteristic stresses and strains, and possesses specific administrative or political advantages or disadvantages in an institutional setting.

The second major criticism of research into religious institutions of the type illustrated by the work of Fichter is contained in Banks's article: namely, that the sociology of religion should be concerned more with the role of ideas and beliefs rather than with the operation of institutions. Writers such as Fichter have a different approach from that to be found in the works of early authors like Frazer and Malinowski. But they *are* concerned in their analyses with the impact of ideas upon behaviour, though this may be disguised by the fact that their immediate aim is a more limited one. Rather than taking the basic ideas that people have about the world, life and death, as some of the earlier writers did, they consider the more mundane values people have in relation to other members of a religious institution. This may be a more limited approach, but it does provide a solid empirical foundation for future theories which we hope will emerge on a larger scale.

3. *Religion and Society*

One of the major limitations of institutional analysis in relation to religion has been the concentration upon religious communities as though they were self-contained units, to the neglect of relationships with the wider society, both formally in terms of official interaction of one institution with others and informally through the everyday contact of members with those outside the group. Concentration upon the minutiae of organization within a religious system can be responsible for disregarding the functions of religious institutions in the general society and the influence of membership of a religious group in ordinary living. It is this general weakness in the sociology of religion that is largely over-come by the approach of two American sociologists, Lenski and Herberg.

The theme of Herberg's analysis is the experience of minority groups as they become assimilated into the middle classes and are seen as acceptable within the American way of life.[57] His analysis illustrates how religious beliefs can be absorbed by a community and made to fulfil functions unrelated to the religious sphere.[58] Acting as a means whereby people can be assimilated into society in a way comprehensible to all,[59] the dominant religious communities, Protestantism, Catholicism and Judaism, have contributed to the secular order, as the author sees it, in unexpected ways. Identification with one of the three major reference groups in the United States may be the passport to social acceptability. Like Carrier,[60] Herberg uses the findings of a great many surveys on religion;[61] from these he develops a theoretical framework. Through the insight this analysis gives into the general working of social systems, his contribution to the understanding of social processes in general is considerable.

The broader kinds of study of religion have often tended to assume that because a church or sect teaches a certain doctrine, this automatically reacts upon the behaviour of members. Thus, for instance, there are crude assumptions that because Roman Catholics have access to an institutional way of getting rid of guilt feelings through the sacrament of confession, they are likely to be free from guilt feelings, an assumption which does not always appear to be borne out by the facts. We do not know to

[57] Cf. R. J. Kennedy, Single or Triple Melting Pot? Intermarriage Trends in New Haven, 1870–1940, *American Journal of Sociology* **49** (3) 331–9 (1944).

[58] Cf. E. Rosenthal, Acculturation Without Assimilation? The Jewish Community in Chicago, Illinois, *American Journal of Sociology* **66**, 275–88 (1960).

[59] Cf. J. Milton Yinger, *Sociology Looks at Religion*, New York, 1963.

[60] *Op. cit.*

[61] *Protestant–Catholic–Jew*, Garden City, 1955.

c

what degree formal beliefs or ideologies are actually accepted in a given community. Assumptions involving descriptions of the formal content of belief are used too often to explain behaviour unsatisfactorily. We should be less naïve when we consider the evidence that certain formal values receive only notional assent from members of a community;[62] many groups, for example, have shown themselves adept in re-interpreting doctrines about the equality of men to justify slavery, apartheid and social and political discrimination.[63]

In his work in Detroit,[64] Lenski sought to discover how far beliefs and membership of a religious group were a factor in determining reactions to political, economic and social issues. His analysis reveals that religion is as strong an influence as social class in affecting behaviour. These findings challenge the conceptual framework of many writers in the sociology of religion. Religion, it seems, can be an important causal factor in social situations, and is an essential analytical tool without which they cannot be understood.

But not only does religion affect social behaviour in anticipated sorts of ways—certain formal values are accepted and produce the kind of behaviour one would expect—it also has unintended

[62] In this context, it is worth noting that in commenting on the failure of Thomas and Znaniecki (*The Polish Peasant*, 5 vols., Boston, 1918–21) to make valid predictions about marriage amongst the families of Polish immigrants, an American writer has observed:

"The inability to take into account the subjective aspect of religion and its strength in shaping the attitudes of the individual is one of the great weaknesses of their approach. They seem to have been satisfied with considering religion as an external institution which exerts pressure in much the same way as does any other. . . .

"Second, although they rightly insisted on the necessity of considering the subjective factors in social change, they oversimplified reality by not recognizing the manifold 'values' forming an 'attitude' and by underestimating the possibility of a conflict of 'attitudes' resulting in an ambivalence which rendered prediction well-nigh impossible."

J. L. Thomas, Marriage Prediction in *The Polish Peasant*, *American Journal of Sociology* **55** (6) 572 (1950).

[63] Cf. E. Franklin Frazier, *The Negro Church in America*, Liverpool, 1964.

[64] *The Religious Factor*, Garden City, 1961.

consequences. The influence of subgroups within religious communities enters into the question here. The complex subcultures which develop within religious communities can exert considerable influence upon general attitudes and behaviour and make religion a particularly powerful force in determining social behaviour.

The significance of Lenski's work lies in the way he has introduced a new dimension into the sociology of religion; by analysing the effect of beliefs in a social context, he considers not only the content and form of ideologies but also their relationship to actual situations. Whatever the limitations of a particular survey, it is this kind of approach which seems to promise most for the future development of the sociology of religion.

Here, then, are some of the main themes and research fields in the sociology of religion. With its origins in the earliest of sociological writings, it has been one of the most controversial fields in the subject. Historically it has been important in the development of general sociological theory, but what makes it an even more interesting and exciting discipline is that the kinds of issues which are highlighted in it make it a case study for the future development of sociology in general.

The limitations of individual studies produced so far have been considerable, but recent developments make it clear that some writers are very conscious of the theoretical and methodological weaknesses of the subject and are attempting to develop our understanding of how ideas, beliefs and values affect the way we live.

PART II

What is
the Sociology of Religion?

What is the Sociology of Religion?

P. H. Vrijhof

The title of this article sounds pretentious, and raises hopes which cannot be fulfilled. Its formulation is nevertheless deliberate. The intention implicit in it is not to analyse what the sociology of religion is, or might be, or should be. The aim is rather to explain why the question of the sociology of religion *is* a question and will remain so for the time being. In its present state much depends on defined and relevant questions being asked in regard to its theme and its object. It is to this debate that the writer hopes to contribute.

I. THE THEME OF THE SO-CALLED "CLASSICAL" SOCIOLOGY OF RELIGION

The sociology of religion is a young science, still at an early stage of development, and as yet with little assurance as to its subject matter and methods. Such a statement, almost obligatory in any general consideration of sociology or any of its subdivisions, is in remarkable contrast to the common opinion on the sociology of religion which, more or less consciously, appears to obtain among many sociologists engaged in this field. This common opinion can be put in approximately the following terms: the sociology of religion is not a religious science, but a sociological one, namely the scientific study of human beings and their group relationships; religion itself is relevant to this study only in so far as it permits conclusions to be drawn about human relationships. This statement includes the question concerning the impact of religion on human society and its reverse. In other words: the sociology of religion has the interrelationship and interaction of

29

religion and society as its subject matter. This definition suggests that religion and society are independent, separate elements which (may) interact with each other. Religion is not a factor which goes without remainder completely into human relations or into society, nor can it be deduced or "explained" either from human relations or from society. Religion is a meta-social phenomenon, which surpasses man and society.

Such, broadly speaking, was the concept of the older workers in the field (Max Weber, Troeltsch, Sombart, etc.), the exponents of what Helmut Schelsky called the "now almost classical sociology of religion".[1] There are, however, some differences in their views, which cannot be neglected. For Ernst Troeltsch the focal point was the sociologically relevant effects of religious phenomena. Christianity, he considers, "just like every other phenomenon, such as sex, instinct, art, science, earning a living, or like every pastime or fleeting aim, has a sociological effect".[2] Troeltsch examines first "the particular sociological concept of Christianity and its development and organization". He comes next to his central inquiry into "the relationship of this sociological development to social issues, i.e. the state, social economy and family". He is primarily concerned with "the real effects of the socio-religious background on other areas of life", but he also reviews, on the other hand, "the effects of political and social education upon religious communion". Finally he considers "to what extent this has had an inward, penetrating effect, and to what extent it has led to an inner unity of community life".[3] Troeltsch limited his investigation to the historico-sociological analysis of Christianity. Nevertheless, there is, in the formulations just quoted, clear evidence of the theme of interrelationship and

[1] H. Schelsky, Ist die Dauerreflektion institutionalisierbar? Zum Thema einer modernen Religionssoziologie. In: *Zeitschrift f. evangelische Ethik* 1957, No. 1, 153–74. Cf. Discussion of this article: *ibid.*, 254–90, and 1959, No. 4, 193–220.

[2] E. Troeltsch, *Die Soziallehren der christlichen Kirchen und Gruppen*, Tübingen, 1912; 3rd ed., Tübingen, 1923. Translation: *The Social Teaching of the Christian Churches*, New York, 1960, p. 5.

[3] *Ibid.*, p. 14 f.

interaction between religion (i.e. Christianity) and society. In spite of his historical approach, Troeltsch sees Christianity as an independent, autonomous phenomenon, which, as such, influences man and society.

Max Weber does not explicitly formulate the question of relationships between religion and society. He sees the "understanding of social behaviour" as the principal task of sociologists. For him, therefore, the sociology of religion is concerned not with the "essence" of religion, but with the conditions and effects of a defined kind of social action which can only be understood from the subjective experiences, ideas and aims of the individual— from the sense giving meaning motivation—since the external manifestations follow so varied a course. Originally, the orientation of religiously or magically motivated behaviour is "this wordly".[4] This much-quoted formulation is a scientific,descriptive maxim, not a judgement on religion or a religious phenomenon as such. For Weber the influence of religion is not an effect of a supernatural phenomenon on man and society, but a human sense giving of the supernatural, and as such he leaves it out of account.

The works of Troeltsch and Weber are of a general historical nature. Dietrich Bonhoeffer can therefore reproach the sociology of religion that it "has studied almost only religious history in its general historical or political economic aspects".[5] It has no systematic sociological frame of reference. Troeltsch and Weber had, however, other aims. Troeltsch aimed ultimately at ascertaining the true essence of Christianity, by analysing the forms it takes in different societies. Weber was basically concerned with studying the particular character and development of European culture, and in doing this he took religion as one of its

[4] M. Weber, Wirtschaft und Gesellschaft. In: *Grundriss der Sozialökonomik*, Teil II, Abteilung 3, especially Chapter IV, Religionssoziologie (Types of religious community), Tübingen, 1921; 4th ed. (by J. Winckelmann), Tübingen, 1956, p. 227.

[5] D. Bonhoeffer, *Sanctorum Communio. A Dogmatic Study of the Sociology of the Church*, 3rd ed., Munich, 1960, p. 14.

most significant factors. In his comparative historical studies his aim was to investigate this factor and its past, present and future role in European culture. His observations on the sociology of religion therefore form the fourth main division in the second part of his work *Economy and Society*. For him, as for the other exponents of the classical school, the sociology of religion is not a sub-division of general sociology. Religion, art, politics, etc., are simply aspects of one indivisible social reality, the true essence and significance of which has to be grasped and understood.

With their historical approach and their comparative view-points, Troeltsch and Weber have assumed, more or less as self-evident, religion to be a formative social force in society. At the time when they were both planning their works, religion and the church were still generally recognized, influential factors. These two authors also found—in contrast to the psychological theories of Tylor, Freud and others, and the sociological concepts of Comte, Marx and others—that "religion was an integrating element in social life, which clearly could not be dispensed with in any society".[6] Writers in this school accordingly took as their broad subject "the derivation of the modern world from Christianity, the discovery of the religious roots of rationalism in finance, capitalist production, industry and labour, and in the concepts of state, legislature, etc.".[7] According to Dietrich Goldschmidt, the common denominator was "study of the religious conditioning of social behaviour".[8] In studying the relationship between religion and society, it is religion that is of primary importance. Its influence on society must be tracked down; and be understood as a part of social reality.

---

[6] D. Goldschmidt, Zur Religionssoziologie in der Bundesrepublik Deutschland. In: *Archives Soc. Relig.* **4**, 1959, No. 8, 53–70; and *ibid.* **5**, 1960, No. 9, 153–4, p. 54. And Standort und Methoden der Religionssoziologie. In: *Soziologie und moderne Gesellschaft: Verh. 14. Deutschen Soziologentages*, Berlin, May 1959, Stuttgart, 1959, p. 140.

[7] Schelsky, *op. cit.*, p. 153.

[8] Goldschmidt, *op. cit.*, p. 57 and p. 143.

In an attempt to systematize the work of his predecessors and contemporaries, Joachim Wach formulated the theme of the sociology of religion very broadly as "the interrelation of religion and society and the forms of interaction which take place between them".[9] He sees religion as an integrating factor in human society, expressing itself in myth, dogma, cult and religious grouping. The last-named is of particular importance for the sociology of religion, which has therefore to pay special attention to a "typology of religious groups".[10] Yet Wach puts special emphasis on "the tremendous fomenting and integrating power possessed by religion". He quotes with approval the well-known saying of Bacon: "*religio praecipuum humanae societatis vinculum*".[11] The influence of religion is seen in all walks of society. Wach's observations are thus also of a general cultural and historical nature. His more systematic analyses seem insufficiently grounded and rounded off. In his case, too, there can be no talk of the sociology of religion as an independent subdivision of sociology.

II. THE CURRENT THEME OF THE SOCIOLOGY OF RELIGION

In general it can be said that the approach and subject matter of the sociology of religion at present reflect the profound changes that have taken place in the position and significance of religion and the church in modern society. The influence of modern dynamic society on religion and the church can clearly be seen everywhere. As Goldschmidt puts it, "the earlier formulations of Weber and Troeltsch (which studied how social behaviour was conditioned by religion) have been converted into study of the

[9] J. Wach, *Sociology of Religion*, Chicago, 1944, London, 1947. German translation, *Religionssoziologie*, from 4th ed., trans. by H. Schoeck, Tübingen, 1951, pp. 6, 11, 384. See, also, *Sociology of Religion in Twentieth Century Sociology* (eds. G. Gurvitch and W. E. Moore), New York, 1945, pp. 433 ff.

[10] Wach, *Sociology of Religion*, p. 384.

[11] *Ibid.*, p. 6.

ways in which contemporary religious behaviour and even content are socially determined".[12] Friedrich Fürstenberg speaks in similar vein of the "worldly aspects of religious social behaviour and the religious institutions" which form the real subject matter of the sociology of religion.[13]

Schelsky finds that the central theme of the sociology of religion today is "the ways in which religion or Christianity adapt to modern society". He confines "adaptation" as "changes in the social forms of Christianity". He puts this concept more precisely when he calls "the modern world an autonomous, self-sufficient reality", in the face of which "Christianity must maintain an ancient truth". "Christianity and the churches face the task of founding their eternal truth anew in changed social structures which have become autonomous in this world."[14]

In Holland, P. Smits has characterized this formulation of Schelsky's as an attempt to give new life to the sociology of religion. According to Smits, Schelsky wants, in fact, to get rid of the theme of classical writers such as Weber, Troeltsch, and Sombart, by converting it and pushing into the foreground the "adaptation of religion or Christianity to modern society".[15] But the attentive reader of the formulations just quoted will see that conversion of the theme of classical sociology of religion is not the same as getting rid of it. It is more true to say that Schelsky re-emphasizes the classical formulation by contrasting modern society, on the one hand, and religion (or Christianity), on the other, as autonomous, which means basically separate, factors. The theme of classical sociology of religion has been put the other way round, but remains essentially the same.

[12] Goldschmidt, *op. cit.*, p. 57 and p. 143.

[13] F. Fürstenberg, Religionssoziologie. Article in: *Die Religion in Geschichte und Gegenwart (RGG)* (ed. by K. Galling), Band V, 3rd ed., Tübingen, 1961, p. 1031.

[14] Schelsky, *op. cit.*, pp. 154 ff.

[15] P. Smits, Schelsky's poging tot vernieuwing der godsdienst-sociologie. In: *Mens en Maat.* **36**, 1961, No. 3, p. 152.

Many contemporary presentations of the subject matter of the sociology of religion support Wach's general formulation. Bernhard Häring holds that the subject matter of the sociology of religion is "the interaction between religion and social relationships, taking special account of the distinctive, community aspects of religion".[16] Norbert Greinacher, quoting many authors who hold similar views, considers that Wach's formulations can be taken over unchanged.[17] In his *Introduction to Sociology* Pieter J. Bouman assigns to the sociology of religion the task of examining the role of faith, and its social avowal, in social life. In addition, it should study the extent to which faith, and church organization, influence professional life in general and the individual's social orientation in particular. This introduces another problem, namely the extent to which community life and social changes affect religious experience and can make religious organizations develop on defined lines.[18] Milton Yinger concludes that "the sociology of religion is broadly speaking the scientific study of the ways in which society, culture and personality influence religion —influence its origin, its doctrines, its practices, the types of groups which express it, the kinds of leadership, etc. And, oppositely, it is the study of the ways in which religion affects society, culture and personality—the processes of social conservation and social change, the structure of normative systems, the satisfaction or frustration of personality needs, etc. One must keep continuously in mind the interactive nature of these various elements."[19]

In all these formulations Wach's definition of the problem can clearly be discerned. The words have changed, but not the

[16] B. Haering, *Macht und Ohnmacht der Religion. Religionssoziologie als Anruf*, Salzburg, 1956, p. 18.

[17] N. Greinacher, *Soziologie der Pfarrei, Wege zur Untersuchung*, Colmar–Freiburg, 1955, pp. 6, 8.

[18] P. J. Bouman, *Begrippen en problemen*, 7th ed., Antwerp–Amsterdam, 1958, p. 145.

[19] J. M. Yinger, *Religion, Society and the Individual. An Introduction to the Sociology of Religion*, New York, 1957, p. 20 f.

problem. There is, however, one difference, that—at least in non-Catholic writers—religion, while still regarded as an independent, distinctive phenomenon, is no longer one that is immune from questioning. Bouman asks how far society and changes in social structure affect religious experience. Goldschmidt includes in his formulation of the sociology of religion not only religious behaviour, but also religious content. He asks: "What is the immutable core, the Kerygma, of the Christian message when one relates it socially not only to the form and content of religion but also to Christian beliefs, church ways and church-dominated modes of behaviour?"[20] Schelsky inquires into the "institutional or social and tactical adaptations required, in this changed modern world, not only in religious life but also in the content of the Christian doctrine itself". Similarly, he includes in the subject matter of sociology of religion "the changes in forms of faith which can be regarded as changes in belief and in the form of man's inner life".[21] Thomas Luckmann combines these definitions in his concept of "the social impress of forms of faith" and considers this to be a justifiable reformulation of the problem.[22]

Fürstenberg draws attention to the secularization hypothesis, already formulated by Weber, which has given to the sociology of religion at the moment "its most sustained impetus". At the heart of the problem lies "the progressive turning away of the people from the church and their indifference to religious questions".[23] It has, however, become increasingly clear that this theme is interwoven with that of the relationship between religion and the modern world. Schelsky moved in explicitly to the foreground with his "adaptation hypothesis". The narrowing of the theme to current adaptation problems is only apparent: in fact the sociology

[20] Goldschmidt, op. cit., p. 57 and p. 143.

[21] Schelsky, op. cit., p. 157 f.

[22] T. Luckmann, Neuere Schriften zur Religionssoziologie. In: K. Z. f. S. S., 1960, 12, No. 2, p. 321.

[23] Fürstenberg, op. cit., p. 1027 f.

of religion still includes human society in its subject matter. This breadth of theme can be discerned even more clearly in the above quotations. Religion finds expression in a distinctive social system, which touches on society as a whole. The sociology of religion must therefore rank as "one of the central areas of sociology".[24] Its treatment as an independent sub-discipline of sociology still lies beyond a distant thematic horizon.

We must deduce from all this that the themes dealt with currently in the sociology of religion are little more than variations of the themes of the older, classical school, transparently disguised. It is true that the central theme has been converted but it still has not been conquered. The general theoretical implications of the problems encountered have not been made clear. Luckman goes so far as to say that current sociology of religion still lacks an adequate conceptualization. "The chief problem in the sociology of religion today (is) its insufficient anchorage in general sociological theory." Its investigations are carried out in a theoretical vacuum, in the hope that complete systematic understanding will come to light of its own accord.[25]

On the whole sociology of religion today is based on a dichotomy of religion and society. Schelsky points the argument decisively. The most important task is, then, to define more closely religion and religious phenomena. The central question is undeniable: how does the sociologist of religion, as a sociologist, define religion (or Christianity) and its influence on or adaptation to human behaviour and society (or vice versa)? He can do this only by assuming that religion has an original, specific character: otherwise he can hardly say which influence or which adaptation process is confirmed: he can say even less how he defines such influences and adaptations, and why and how far he qualifies them as influences or adaptations of religion. He can thus scarcely do without a closer definition of religion.

[24] Yinger, *op. cit.*, p. 18.

[25] Luckmann, *op. cit.*, p. 316.

III. SOCIOLOGICAL DEFINITIONS OF RELIGION

In reaction against the "isms" of their predecessors and contemporaries, psychologists and sociologists alike, the classical
writers adopted the view that the essence of religion should not be
questioned but should be left outside consideration. In analysing
their reasons for this, we shall confine ourselves here to the
writings of Weber and of Wach. Wach's thought is easy to follow
and his deductions can more easily be reviewed. With Weber this
is more difficult. Moreover, their standpoints differ in several
respects. We will therefore leave Weber's concepts aside for the
moment and begin by analysing the ideas of Wach.

Wach says in several places that analysis of the sociological
implications of religion can in no way disclose "the nature and
essence of religion itself".[26] If it assumed otherwise, the sociology
of religion would fall back on Marxism or "Durkheimism". The
sociology of religion must therefore be regarded as a descriptive
science, auxiliary to the true science of religion, able to round it
off but never to replace it. No theological or philosophical
principles can be deduced from a descriptive analysis. "Principles
must rest on different grounds."[27] This does not mean that the
theological, philosophical and metaphysical problems that arise
in sociological analysis must remain unsolved. But it is not the
task of the sociology of religion to achieve their solution.[28] Wach
therefore considers himself exempt from this task. His final conclusions about religion can be regarded as more or less an
appendix: it is nowhere made clear what these conclusions have
to do with his investigations or vice versa.

The reason for this divorce may well be that for Wach religion
is a strictly *personal* matter, a relationship between God and the
individual man. The true essence of religion must be sought in the
inner religious experience. "The ultimate source and the meaning
of an expression or form valid in the realm of religion is its origin

[26] Wach, *Sociology of Religion*, p. 4 f.

[27] *Ibid.*, pp. 6, 384.

[28] *Ibid.*, p. 384.

from and testimony to a significant religious experience. Wherever such expressions are genuine, they are meant not to serve external —that is social, political, economic, aesthetic—or personal aims and purposes, but to formulate and perpetuate man's deepest experience, his communion with God." Man needs "communication with the Infinite". Therefore religion cannot be identified with finite concepts, rites or institutions. Religion is "that profoundest source from which all human existence is nourished and upon which it depends in all its aspects: man's communion with God".[29]

It must now be asked how, from the peculiar nature of religious experience, its sociological expression can be deduced and understood. Wach here expresses himself equally plainly. "Although communion with God necessarily implies detachment from finite things and may, at least occasionally, lead to temporary isolation, producing a profound feeling of loneliness, there can be no doubt that the examination of one and every genuinely religious attitude reveals the intrinsically social quality and character of religion. In the very beginning of this study we attempted to show that inherent in all religious experience is an *imperative* urging the believer to *act*, to act according to the will of the deity or the nature of the universe as revealed to him. This is, in a broad sense of the term, the moral and social implication in all true religious experience."[30] The possibility and necessity of *social* action is here deduced from *individual* experience and conduct. Wach warns emphatically against mixing these two dimensions. "Fundamentally and ultimately religion makes for social integration, though it should definitely not be identified with its effect. We have tried to show that social integration is not the 'aim' or 'purpose' of religion. Religion is sound and true to its nature only as long as it has no aim or purpose except the worship of God."[31] It is religious experience which brings man to this

[29] *Ibid.*, pp. 385 ff., 393.

[30] *Ibid.*, p. 388.

[31] *Ibid.*, p. 391.

interaction and allows him to form specific groups. Personal, inner religious experience is primary and transcendent: its sociological expression can be regarded only as a worldly, external consequence. The social form of religion is derived, not original.

This brings us to the central question, namely, how can Wach, as a sociologist, be sure that specific sociological forms of expression are those of *religion*. Wach recognized this question clearly. "Where in all the various expressions of religious experience is this spirit still present, and where is it not? Which are the criteria by which we can identify so-called 'genuine' religious experience?"[32] At the end of his book he puts a last question: "Why should religion be credited with so decisive a role as we attribute to it in defining it as the paramount force of social integration? Are there not other means to achieve this end? Why should a secular society not find ways and means to integrate effectively and lastingly?"[33] In Wach's view, the recognition "that perfect integration of a society never has been or can be achieved without a religious basis", could provide the answer to these questions. The demand for criteria which would define the specific religious nature of this social integration and of religious groupings remains, however, unsatisfied. Because Wach leaves the essence of religion as an individual experience outside consideration he must as a sociologist—in spite of his warnings—identify religion even more closely with its social effects. It is in the circle thus created that Wach leaves the reader at the end of his work. His conclusions have, as already said, no real meaning in relation to his exposition of the sociology of religion.

We have already mentioned that the sociology of religion as defined by Weber "has nothing to do with the 'essence' of religion". As a sociologist he is concerned with "understanding social behaviour", in which he includes religious behaviour. He calls such behaviour religious when and in so far as it postulates

[32] *Ibid.*, p. 385.

[33] *Ibid.*, p. 393.

something "behind" or "beyond" the external appearance of specific events, objects and persons. They mean something: they point to a power (or powers) experienced as supernatural and sacred. Weber regards this supernatural, transcendental character of religion as linked to the sense endowment of man and therefore to human existence as such. In other words, religion is given, according to Weber, with human existence as such. In introducing his sociology of religion (in *Economy and Society*) it is therefore noteworthy that he uses the remarkable title "The Rise of Religions" and begins his exposition by pointing out "that a definition of what religion is is impossible at the beginning but should be possible at the end of a work such as the present".[34] This definition therefore remains "this-worldly" and has nothing to do with the "essence" of religion. How this is possible, Weber does not discuss.

It has been said that Weber could not help in many ways giving an anthropologically orientated meaning to religion. This reproach is—according to Max zu Solms—irrelevant and unjust, because Weber leaves the "essence" of religion completely outside his theme. The sociological analysis of religion and its effects must be kept strictly separate from the "essential definition" of religion. Solms also notes, in reference to A. Dempf, "that Max Weber's approach to religion, and his limitation of it to the 'here below', can be practical and fruitful even for those who are conscious of the fundamental 'other-worldliness' of religion".[35] With this remark he seeks to absolve Weber from the reproach of concealed psychological or sociological bias. But he evades the deeper issue implicit in this reproach. Max Weber had already implicitly asked the basic question: how *can* man be conscious of the other-worldliness of religion? He already recognized that *any* more precise definition of religion and religious phenomena was essentially a *human* matter. His sparing reference to the "essence"

[34] M. Weber, *op. cit.*, p. 227.

[35] M. E. Graf zu Solms, *Max Weber, aus den Schriften zur Religionssoziologie, Auswahl, Einleitung und Bemerkungen*, Frankfurt a. M., 1948. Introduction, pp. 26, 33.

of religion point in this direction. They refer to a religious, mystical experience, which in its highest forms defines all reproduction.[36] For this reason, perhaps, he leaves it out of account. This experience, however, remains an item of human knowledge and is not, in principle, beyond human perception. For Max Weber religion, even in its "essence", is not the *introitus* of a transcendental autonomous power, but an act of human perception.

Max Weber deduces religion as a social phenomenon from individual behaviour. Socio-religious behaviour is, it is true, related to other behaviour, but its trend is individually determined. Therefore "the conditions and effects of a specific kind of *social behaviour* can be discovered only by studying the subjective experiences, ideas and aims of the *individual*, only by reference to the individual's "sense". For Weber, as for Wach, the social form of religion is not primary in character but deduced. Weber is no longer concerned with the qualification of this form as an expression of religion. For him religion is not a specific effect of a supernatural autonomous power, but humanly motivated behaviour which can be understood and classified as such. It is at this point that the decisive difference between Wach and Weber becomes apparent. Wach sees religion in the last resort as an autonomous, transcendental power: its relationship to society is one of mutual interaction, and its influence is specific. His studies can therefore be regarded as functionally orientated. For Weber, on the other hand, the central object of attention is religion as a human phenomenon. He is not concerned with analysing a specific effect or function but with understanding a human sense. Wach's standpoint was that he disregarded the essence of religion and had to do so. The similarity between his formulation and Weber's should be regarded rather as a consequence of certain philosophical hypotheses. Weber implicitly questions religiousness and therefore humanity as such. But he does not draw as clear conclusions as one would wish. His concept of religion—and

[36] Cf. M. Weber, *Gesammelte Aufsätze zur Religionssoziologie*, 1st ed., Tübingen 1920–1, 4th ed. (photo-reproduction), Tübingen, 1947; Band 1, p. 112.

his concept of human existence—like those of Wach, still bear the individual, idealistic stamp. It is from this philosophical and anthropological standpoint that the theme of the so-called classical sociology of religion can best be understood, and appraised. It should be clear from this that any attempt to revive the classical concepts will also mean a reconsideration of this approach. We shall revert to this later (in Section IV).

In general, recent workers in the sociology of religion continue to abstain from inquiry into the essence of religion. This applies particularly to Catholic authors and is in keeping with Catholic theology and anthropology. In non-Catholic authors, too, one constantly comes up against the same restraint. According to Bouman, this branch of sociology is not concerned with the essence of faith but with the role of faith and of its public avowal in social life.[37] According to Otto Heinrich von der Gablentz, the content of religion, the relation of man to the powers experienced as holy, falls outside sociological consideration.[38] Milton Yinger renounces definitions of what religion really is, or should be, and confines himself, as does von der Gablentz, to a functional definition.[39] Schelsky's statement "that religious life as an inner act of faith (cf. Wach's 'religious experience') is not of socio-logical concern", points in the same direction.[40] Goldschmidt, in the passage quoted, expresses himself less clearly but immediately goes on to say that he naturally does not wish to return to the naïve thinking of Marxist or other Enlightenment writers. Schelsky, as already quoted, inquires into "adaptations not only in the form but also in the content of Christian doctrine" and into "changes in the form of faith, which can be regarded as changes in belief and in the form of man's inner life". This seems to imply that the content of religion, or of Christianity, should also be

[37] Bouman, *op. cit.*, p. 147.

[38] O. H. v.d. Gablentz, Religion. Article in: *Wörterbuch der Soziologie* (eds. W. Bernsdorf and F. Bülow), Stuttgart, 1955, p. 414.

[39] Yinger, *op. cit.*, p. 9.

[40] Schelsky, *op. cit.*, p. 156. See also Schelsky, Religionssoziologie und Theologie. In: *Zeitschrift f. evangelische Ethik*, 1959, No. 3, p. 135.

subjected to sociological analysis. Schelsky leaves it in no doubt, however, that he is concerned with adaptations of doctrine and the *form* of faith. One is left with the impression that he would like the real essential content of religion to be excluded from consideration.

If religion by its very being is regarded as an encounter with a supernatural power,[41] the sociology of religion as a human science can hardly do otherwise than concern itself with those aspects which can be perceived in this world, with the consequences of such an encounter. This line of thought leads to sociological-functional definitions of religion, of which the best known is Milton Yinger's. He says that religion is "a system of beliefs and practices by means of which a group of people struggle with these ultimate problems of human life": knowledge of death and of suffering, and generally of the powers which threaten human life and happiness. Yinger further characterizes religion as "an organised effort to make virtue of our ultimate necessities".[42] Talcott Parsons similarly sees religious ideas as "answers to the problems of meaning. On the one hand they concern the cognitive definition of the situation for action as a whole, on the other hand, however, they must include the problems of meaning in the larger philosophical sense, of the meaning of the objects of empirical cognition, of nature, human nature, society, the vicissitudes of human life, etc."[43] T. F. Hoult defines religion as "the belief in, and the attempt to relate favorably to values thought to have some transcendental importance, and/or ultimate power or powers thought responsible for all, or some significant aspect of the fundamental order of the universe".[44] In the last definition,

[41] G. Mensching recently reformulated this definition in classical terms, in reference to R. Otto: "Religion is the experience of encountering the Divine, and the consequent behaviour of man determined by the Divine." (G. Mensching, *Die Religion-Erscheinungsformen, Strukturtypen und Lebensgesetze*, Stuttgart, 1959, p. 18.)

[42] Yinger, *op. cit.*, pp. 9, 12.

[43] T. Parsons, *The Social System*, London, 1952, p. 367.

[44] T. F. Hoult, *The Sociology of Religion*, New York, 1958, p. 9.

Yinger's terms take on cosmic dimensions, not confined to a certain view of life (why after all must death and suffering be regarded as the ultimate problems of human life?). But basically Yinger's definition is retained.

These and other functionally orientated definitions can be taken together, since in them religion appears as the sense of the incomprehensible in earthly life, through which man's preservation is assured. "Religion is an attempt to explain what cannot otherwise be explained, a citadel of hope built on the edge of despair" (Reinhold Niebuhr).[45] Religion is the (an?) answer to the conflict of human existence, the acknowledgement of human insufficiency, which seeks fulfilment in a higher power. Fürstenberg incorporated such definitions of religion in his concept of "compensation".[46]

It is clear that religion, according to the above concept, is basically an individual matter. It now has to be asked, how this kind of definition can be at all relevant to a sociological–functional approach. According to Parsons the meaning he has in mind is partly in the nature of a "moral obligation" which exercises an integrating effect on personal and social life.[47] H. M. Johnson maintains that "the system of beliefs and practices concerning a supernatural order of beings has for its adherents implications for their behaviour and welfare, implications that the adherents in varying degrees and ways take seriously in their private and collective life".[48] Parsons and Johnson do not give reasons for thus mentioning personal and social life in the same breath. Hoult points out that religion can remain limited to "a purely personal philosophy".[49] How or when it merges or makes the transition to social institutions likewise remains obscure. Yinger

[45] Yinger, *op. cit.*, p. 10.

[46] Fürstenberg, *op. cit.*, p. 1027.

[47] Parsons, *op. cit.*, p. 368.

[48] H. M. Johnson, *Sociology: A Systematic Introduction*, London, 1960, p. 392.

[49] Hoult, *op. cit.*, p. 9.

holds that the individual aspect of religion attains perfection through its social aspect. "A complete religion is a social phenomenon; it is shared; it takes on many of its most significant aspects only in the interaction of the group. Both the feelings from which it springs and the 'solutions' it offers are social, they arise from the fact that man is a group-living animal. The 'ultimate questions' which we have identified as the center of the religious quest are ultimate because of their impact on human association. Even death is not fundamentally an individual crisis, but a group crisis, threatening to tear the fabric of family and community."[50]

It will be seen from the above that Yinger includes in his definition of religion "a group of people" and "an organised effort". This does not solve, however, the problem of the social character of religion and the relationship between its individual and its social aspects. One might perhaps say that religion is the human sense of the incomprehensible in life: this sense, however, can be different. When a man's attitude agrees more or less with that of others, he conforms with the rest. His attitude is also formed and influenced by others. The result is a communion and a grouping of like-minded religious adherents (cf. von der Gablentz, p. 24). But it is still uncertain whether and how far this grouping arises from similarity of attitudes and feelings or from the character of man as a group-living animal, or from both. Yinger, like the other authors quoted, takes this problem into his definition. Strictly speaking, religion and religious phenomena are defined as problems, and some fundamental questions are left open.

In the definitions of religion quoted, the personal individual meaning and attitude are put logically and phenomenologically in the foreground, and from them religion as a social phenomenon is deduced. The sociologically relevant functions of religion are thus derivative in nature. Several authors, however, see in religion a social phenomenon *per se*: for some this proposition is

[50] Yinger, *op. cit.*, p. 12.

self-evident, for others it is governed by theological premisses.[51] This, however, still does not clarify the primary social character of religion and still leaves obscure the nature of these functions of religion that are sociologically relevant.

In general, the integrating effect of religion is regarded, both by the classical and by the newer schools, as its most important and sociologically most relevant function. The works of several sociologists of religion can thus best be understood as an analysis of this function. Fürstenberg speaks of the "integration hypothesis" as the second basic hypothesis of the sociology of religion, the first being that of "compensation".[52] Charles Y. Glock has shown that social integration cannot be accounted for primarily in terms of religion (or religions) but that many other factors are involved.[53] The urgent question is, again, whether and how far it can be confirmed that integration is a *religious* function. von der Gablentz merges religion and social integration one into the other. "Society, in striving for salvation, becomes integrated in the pursuit of the meaning of salvation. Integration is the function of religion. Or conversely, when this function of integration is truly fulfilled, the sociologist must speak of religion, even in the case of secular ideologies and rites."[54] In this formulation religion is defined directly in terms of its function and not the reverse, as might perhaps be expected. The question is now whether the integrating effect is to be defined in terms of religion, or religion in terms of the integrating effect. If the latter, it is difficult to

---

[51] Of the many examples that might be given, the following represent an earlier and a more recent point of view: E. Troeltsch, *Die Soziallehren der christlichen Kirchen und Gruppen*, Tübingen, 1912; 3rd ed., Tübingen, 1923. Translation: *The Social Teaching of the Christian Churches*, New York, 1960, p. 5. And J. M. Jammes, La Sociologie et le phénomène religieux. In: *Sociologie et religion. Recherches et débats de Centre Catholique des Intellectuels Francais*. Nouvelle série, No. 25, Paris, 1958, p. 32.

[52] Fürstenberg, *op. cit.*, p. 1027.

[53] C. Y. Glock, Religion and the Integration of Society. In: *Review Rel. Res.* 1960, No. 4, pp. 49–62.

[54] von der Gablentz, Die anthropologischen Voraussetzungen soziologischer Grundbegriffe. In: *Festgabe für Fr. Bülow*, Berlin, 1960, p. 117.

define at all precisely the boundaries of religious phenomena. von der Gablentz is prepared to include in religion secular ideologies and rites. As a sociologist he rejects "the difference between religion and pseudo-religion".[55] "Are non-theistic systems of belief to be called religion?",[56] asks Yinger. The formulation of this question implies that it expects an affirmative answer. Yinger maintains that "non-theistic systems of belief", such as nationalism and communism, show religious characteristics. The boundary between religion and non-religion is clearly difficult to draw, all the more so when religion is identified with personal and/or collective sense giving meaning as such. This extension of the concept of religion is already implicit in the definitions of Yinger and Parsons.

von der Gablentz explicitly pursues this question. According to him "the sociological concept of religion embraces all experiences and beliefs that have social consequences".[57] Religion is thus a feature of social (and personal) life as such. It is difficult to recognize why and in what cases one can and must speak of religion as a *specific* experience. von der Gablentz sees this clearly. Therefore he wishes to claim for religion a specific (really fulfilled, *loc. cit.*, p. 23) integrating effect. This leads to a fourth basic category or social life (along with community, society, *Gemeinschaft, Gesellschaft, Bund*) which is incorporated in the concept of congregation (*Gemeinde*). The congregation consists of men who through the same inner experience have come to hold the same view of life, and it is therefore marked by personal but objective and stable relationships.[58] von der Gablentz thus takes

[55] Such was Schelsky's formulation in *Religionssoziologie und Theologie*, p. 136.

[56] Yinger, *op. cit.*, p. 13 f.

[57] von der Gablentz, Religion. Article in: *Wörterbuch der Soziologie*, p. 415.

[58] von der Gablentz, The anthropological hypotheses . . . (Anm. 55), p. 111. According to E. Rosenstock-Huessy (*Soziologie I*, Stuttgart 1956, p. 264), H. Schmalenbach mentioned a fourth form of pure religion, which, however, he did not name. P. Joachimsen used the word "congregation" to designate this fourth form. Like von der Gablentz, he defined a congregation as a gathering of men who through the same inner experience have arrived at the same view of the world (Joachimsen, Zur Psychologie des deutschen Staatsgedenkens. In: *Die Dioskuren*, Band I, Munich, 1922, p. 118).

the personal, inner experience to be the cause and origin of the collective view of life. The congregation, too, has therefore a derivative, not a primary, social character. We will not enter here more closely into the positive implications of such a concept. The chief question is once more how this inner experience and this view of life are to be recognized and acknowledged as religious, i.e. as resting on—or springing from—religion. By the specific structure and the special kind of social relationship in the congregation? If this question is answered in the negative, the previous question is unanswerable. If in the affirmative, we are yet again caught in the vicious circle which has already been pointed out several times.

In the end we must conclude that there is a striking agreement between the classical and the newer sociology of religion in regard to the definition of religion. The new approach does not solve the problem of the classical one, but only conceals it; because the general theoretical point of departure is still the relationship between religion and society. Even attempts at a fresh approach, such as Schelsky's, are enmeshed in this *schema*. With religion regarded more or less separately as a transcendental, autonomous fact, even a metaphysical dichotomy arises. According to Parsons, "this distinction between the order of nature and the supernatural in Western thought is a kind of methodological prototype of the relationship, an analytical order".[59]

This view goes hand in hand with the functionalism that is now everywhere being revived. The essential aspects of religion lie outside sociology, which can only concern itself with the effects of religion as social phenomena. There is not much inclination today to study the effects of religion in all areas of society. Sociologists prefer to confine themselves to structural and functional analysis of the specific forms in which the effects of religion are seen in religious communities and institutions. This limitation of study to the perceptible, "this-worldly" effects of religion leads us back inevitably into a vicious circle so far as

[59] Parsons, *op. cit.*, p. 369.

interpretation is concerned. M. Weber is the only one who escapes from this circle, by circumventing the interrelationships of religion and society as a general theme and starting with religion as a *human phenomenon*. We must therefore devote further attention to him. Finally, we would show that the sociology of religion cannot break out of this hermeneutical circle by its own strength. To do so it needs the support and collaboration of other sciences, particularly theology and philosophical anthropology. The following section therefore deals with the theological analysis of religion and religious phenomena. At the same time it will be shown how far the sociology of religion has already, imperceptibly and perhaps unconsciously, turned to these sciences.

IV. THE THEOLOGICAL ANALYSIS OF RELIGION

It used to be said that religion was, in sociological terms, generally defined as the meaning or acknowledgement of man's insufficiency, the "something" or "someone" that is postulated to support or explain the world. The definitions of the so-called classical school emphasized the transcendental aspects of religion, while those of the newer schools put more stress on its human, "this-worldly" aspects.

Human limitations are interpreted in various ways in theology. Roman Catholic theology sees them as signs of the natural acknowledgement of God. God and man, natural and supernatural, are factually, but not basically, separate. The Church is the *introitus* and institute of the supernatural. It is the earthly form of religion. In Roman Catholic circles, the sociology of religion therefore puts special emphasis on the Church and can almost be equated with the sociology of the Church, or with analysis of the group life of Christians.

The relationship between religion and society is closely allied to this theological concept of natural and supernatural. It is therefore not surprising that the interaction between religion and society is a theme that has been mentioned particularly by the Roman Catholic sociologists of religion. This theme, and the functionalism that goes with it, is not so much a sociological problem as a theological one; it is even a declaration of faith.

In his "adaptation hypothesis" Schelsky contrasts the modern world and religion (or Christianity) as two autonomous realms. Christianity and the Church face the task of finding a new form in this world. Underlying this concept is the Lutheran doctrine of the "Two Kingdoms". This christological, eschatologically directed doctrine has in time become a static dualism, a dichotomy of two autonomous dimensions: "Laws for this world, Church for eternal truth and salvation of the soul."[60] Schelsky seems to be also orientated to this concept.

For him, as for Wach, the personal inner life is the hall-mark of religion. This is in keeping with the concept of religion found in so-called natural theology, as developed in the 19th century. Schelsky therefore seems to equate religion with Christianity, or at least he always mentions them together. There is a direct connection between natural religion and this dichotomy of an earthly, temporal order and a divine, supernatural one. Here again we can trace the origins of Schelsky's contrast between the modern world and religion. Schelsky's concept, like that of Roman Catholic authors, has theological implications which are decisive in shaping its formulation.

Karl Barth has expressly rejected natural religion. His polemic with Emil Brunner about the *analogia entis* as the so-called point of contact between God and man is generally well known. His dialectical theology drew an absolute distinction between man and God, rejecting any similarity between them. Christianity as a religion or revelation was thus unmeasurably different from the human "natural" religion. "The student who, as Karl Barth does in his dialectical theology, starts from an orthodox claim of the absoluteness of Christianity, will not count Christianity among religions, which will be defined as human attempts and vain strivings to gain religious values not given in Christianity."[61]

[60] H. D. Wendland, Die Weltherrschaft Christi und die zwei Reiche. In: *Botschaft an die soziale Welt*, Hamburg, 1959, p. 87.

[61] Mensching, *op. cit.*, p. 18.

A. Köberle has shown that interest in the psychology and
sociology of religion has long been hampered by this separation,
because among theologians the problem of the theological point
of contact has been too strongly identified with the pastoral and
educational one. These sciences are considered irrelevant to
pastoral practice, condemned to psychologism and sociologism.[62]
In Barth's later writings, especially in Dogmatics, the emphasis in
regard to point of contact is placed on analogy. This change does
not mean a return to *analogia entis,* but an accentuation of
analogia fidei, rising out of the revelation of God in Christ. Only
in and through the faith granted to him can man discover something of God and the Divine. Religion, however, still remains a
human phenomenon and it is as such that it must be esteemed.[63]

Bonhoeffer opposes this Barthian revelationary positivism, in
which man and the world are left too extensively to their own
resources.[64] He puts the emphasis on man and on human life. He
maintains the distinction between religion and evangelical faith,
he even accentuates it. Religion is not "religious *a priori*", not a
"condition of faith".[65] It is no longer possible to regard God as an
assumption made by man to "fill in the gap in our incomplete
knowledge".[66] Man no longer needs this "*deus ex machina*". He
sees through this God as an obsolete, irrelevant illusion.[67] He has
come of age, and lives without religion. Bonhoeffer is concerned

[62] A. Köberle, Allen bin ich alles geworden. Zum Problem der Anknüpfung
in der Theologie der Gegenwart. In: *Sammlung und Sendung Festgabe für
H. Rendtorff,* Berlin, 1958.

[63] Cf. E. Wolf, Glaube und Erkenntnis. Ueber die Einheitlichkeit im Denken
K. Barths. In: *Evangelische Theologie,* May 1961.

[64] Bonhoeffer, *Widerstand und Ergebung,* Munich, 1955, p. 184 f. Cf. also
G. Ebeling, Die nicht-religiöse Interpretation biblischer Begriffe. In: *Die
mündige Welt,* Band II, Munich, 1956, p. 13. And R. Prenter, Dietrich Bonhoeffer und Karl Barths Offenbarungspositivism. In: *Die mundige Welt,* Band
III, Munich, 1960.

[65] *Ibid.,* pp. 178, 221.

[66] *Ibid.,* p. 210 f.

[67] M. Fischer, Zum Problem der religionslosen Verkündigung. In: *Sammlung
und Sendung,* Berlin, 1958, p. 180.

with earthly life without religion, and asks whether and how man, in and through his life as man, can meet God.

Bonhoeffer thus achieves a *radical anthropologization of religion and of faith*. Religion is a human sense endowment, a "cipher for transcendence" (Jaspers), an extension of the world.[68] "The basis of religion is the achievement of complete reality through God."[69] This God has nothing to do with God as revealed in Christ. Religion must therefore be to Christendom and to the Church an obsolete and dangerous misunderstanding.[70] Christian faith must free itself from religion. The central question is: how can man believe and live without religion—*etsi deus non daretur*?[71] "How can man come to terms with reality without God?" This is the culmination of Bonhoeffer's analysis of modern, non-religious man.[72] Our relationship to God is not a religious relationship to an all-high, all-powerful, superlative being—this is not a true transcendence—but a new life in "living for others", in participation in the being of Jesus. The transcendental is not the unending, unattainable tasks, but the, at any time given, reachable neighbour. It is not at the utmost limit of our possibilities that God should be recognized, but in the middle of our lives, just beyond us.[73] Man must act on the fact that he is given only the world and his own existence. It is in this that he must seek and realize his faith. "The basis of faith is therefore to stand out or to bear reality before God."[74] Faith means existing as a man, existing for others. Man can serve God in and through his existence, can give a meaning to his existence (cf. the Dutch word for religion, *godsdienst*, service of God). This meaning which he gives has not as its goal a defined attitude to God and to the Divine, but man's

[68] O. Hammelsbeck, *Die veränderte Weltsituation des modernen Menschen als religiöses Problem*, Munich, 1955, p. 35.

[69] Ebeling, *op. cit.*, p. 60.

[70] Hammelsbeck, *op. cit.*, p. 48.

[71] Bonhoeffer, *op. cit.*, p. 241.

[72] Ebeling, *op. cit.*, p. 62 f.

[73] Bonhoeffer, *op. cit.*, pp. 182, 211, 259 ff.

[74] Ebeling, *op. cit.*, p. 72.

mode of existence. The Christian does not believe in God but lives his life *in reference to God*. He does not incorporate God into human life but recognizes and honours God's inscrutability and divinity as *true* transcendence. Christian faith is therefore "the antithesis of religion".[75] Faith is manifest in true humanity, in "service of God".

Barth and Bonhoeffer both seek to establish the incontrovertible truth that God is God and man is man. In doing this Barth emphasizes the former, Bonhoeffer the latter element. Both reject natural religion and its assumption or transcendence. "Epistemological transcendence has nothing to do with the transcendence of God."[76] "True religion is immanent, this-worldly transcendence, it is a religion of this world."[77] In living with others man can serve God. The world and his fellow men are essential components of his faith. Bonhoeffer thus reveals religion as a *primarily social phenomenon* (particularly in his dissertation *Sanctorum Communio*). True religion (true service of God) is not a personal, inner experience, but one shared with other men, it is worldly service.[78] Therefore "brotherhood is the Christian existence on earth".[79] The historical nature of religion as a human phenomenon is here clearly seen. Religion is subjected to mutation, in content as well as in form. While once it may have been natural religion, today it is a question of a non-religious, worldly Christianity.[80] This concept is basically different from that of an external, timeless truth, which is only occasionally moulded into new forms, adapted anew. Every era has its own truth and its own religion.

In this concept the ontological, metaphysical dichotomy of this world and the other world—what Bonhoeffer called "thinking in

[75] Ebeling, *op. cit.*, p. 47.

[76] Bonhoeffer, *op. cit.*, p. 182.

[77] G. Meuss, Arkandisziplin und Weltlichkeit bei D. Bonhoeffer. In: *Die mündige Welt*, Band III, p. 107. Cf., also, R. G. Smith, Diesseitige Transzendenz. In: *Die mündige Welt*, Band II.

[78] Bonhoeffer, *op. cit.*, pp. 233, 235.

[79] W. Dirks, *Die Antwort der Mönche*, Frankfurt a. M., 1952, p. 47.

[80] Bonhoeffer, *op. cit.*, p. 178 f.

two spheres"—is finally overcome. Religion and faith are, in man, reduced to one denominator and based theologically in *the man*, Jesus Christ.[81] "Thinking in two spheres means viewing the dichotomics or worldly–Christian, natural–supernatural, profane–sacred, reason–revelation, as ultimate static antitheses which denote certain mutually exclusive data. It fails to recognize the primary unity of these dichotomies in the Christian reality, and substitutes for this the deduced unity of a system, sacred or profane, embracing the antitheses."[82] This is how Bonhoeffer overcomes the dichotomies that are also familiar in the sociology of religion. In doing so he calls in question the main theme of the sociology of religion with which they are so closely allied. Its premises can no longer be left out of the discussion or handed over without further ado to theology and/or philosophy. That is not to say that the sociology of religion has to unravel and examine these premises itself. It means that it must be aware of them and take note of what follows from them. How much theology can help in this task should now be clarified.

V. SUMMARY: THE THEME AND DEFINITION OF THE SOCIOLOGY OF RELIGION

The concept of religion applicable in the reconsidered sociology of religion is clearly still allied to so-called natural religion. In the light of history, this alliance is easily understandable. The sociology of religion developed as a science by analysing historical and primitive societies in which natural religion was of central significance. Its hypotheses and its conceptual tools are therefore basically orientated towards the position occupied by religion and by the church in such conditions and it is only natural that the shattering of that position has given to the sociology of religion its "most sustained impetus" (Fürstenberg). The sociology of religion is still much occupied with the remnants of natural religion that survive in and outside the church, and it is therefore

[81] Meuss, *op. cit.*, pp. 94, 111.

[82] Bonhoeffer, *Ethik*, Munich, 1961, p. 62 f.

E

understandable that Yinger and von der Gablentz are ready to include in religion "non-theistic systems of belief" and secular ideologies and rites, even "all experiences and beliefs which have social consequences". The real question is, of course, why in that case it is still necessary to speak of "*non-theistic* systems of belief", and of "*secular* ideologies and rites". Equally obscure is the converse: how can a phenomenon be defined as *specifically religious*? The sociology of religion runs the risk of approaching the modern, non-religious world with irrelevant concepts and occupying itself with areas that are inaccessible to it. Luckmann is therefore right when he says that current sociology of religion must give up the theme of secularization and its accompanying complex of ideas. "The sociologist must ask himself instead what is the concept underlying the symbolic reality that is now valid or is becoming valid, how has it been created, and how far is it a continuation of the Christian theme?"[83] This statement of the problem embraces also the comprehensive and difficult task of arriving at a *new* concept of religion which will be relevant to our era.

The sociology of religion is still tied to natural religion, with its associated dichotomy of natural and supernatural.[84] In theme and concept it has still hardly digested secularization, or rather the fact that the modern world has come of age. It still seems unable to recognize and adequately grasp the signs of lack of religion and of a non-religious worldly Christianity.

As has already been said, the sociology of religion, in trying to improve this state of affairs, needs the help of other sciences. In this connection Edvard Vogt speaks above all of the philosophy of values and the philosophy of religion: "There alone will we find the ultimate criteria of significance which can be applied to religious phenomena."[85] In my view, however, the accent should be rather on theology and philosophical anthropology. There still

---

[83] Luckmann, *op. cit.*, p. 326.

[84] This point is made frequently by Bonhoeffer (cf. Ebeling, *op. cit.*, pp. 45, 60).

[85] E. Vogt, Religion et idéologie, faussent-elles la sociologie des religions? In: *Archives Soc. Relig.* **6**, 1961, No. 12, p. 80.

remains the problem of recognizing the true religion that is appropriate to our times, and its expression in man and in society. A new concept of the church must also be evolved and here all kinds of new forms are already evident. A search is being made for the specifically Christian community, brotherhood, *koinonia*. This is not a "congregation" of men who have arrived at the same view of life by way of the same inner experience (von der Gablentz) but a flexible group turned towards others and open to others. "The church is a church only if it is there for others."[86] The emphasis in these small flexible groups is therefore on worldly service, and the static, institutional form of the church is challenged. The culmination of true religion is not inner possession of faith and the formation of a closed group, but participation, a stake, in the life of others.

Collaboration between theology and the sociology of religion does not mean that the latter should hand over to theology all responsibility for closer definition of religion and of the church: on the contrary, this work must be shared. Theology has no eternally valid concepts and external truths which must only be adapted to the circumstances of time and place. Like sociology, it is a human science, conducted by men and bound by their humanity. Both sciences face equally the task of seeking concepts of religion and church which will be valid *now*. The sociologist of religion will decide how far these concepts are applicable in his analyses. In this connection there are clear-cut differences between Roman Catholic and Protestant sociologists,[87] even if, as Vogt says, certain "ecumenical perspectives have now become evident".[88]

The central problem will be: how is religion—which occurs in specific *human* and social relationships—to be defined (as religious or as non-religious faith), and how can this religion be regarded

---

[86] Bonhoeffer, *Widerstand und Ergebung*, p. 261.

[87] The same view is found in N. de Volder, De actuele problematick van de godsdienstsociologie. In: *Tidschrift voor Philosophie*, No. 3, September 1954, pp. 477, 486.

[88] Vogt, *op. cit.*, p. 78.

as a primarily social phenomenon? This does not represent a
return to the hermeneutic circle: it seeks an answer to the
question which Weber had already implicitly asked: how can
man, as man, be religious, or non-religious? Gerhard Ebeling is
right when he points out the absolute necessity for "an existential
interpretation of religion and lack of religion"; in other words,
"what is the relationship of religion or lack of religion to the
humanity of man?" "This would call for study of the ground that
is common to religion and to lack of religion, study of the extent
to which they are identical, even in their antithesis. And
Christianity (which once wore the garb of religion but has now
exchanged this for the garb of non-religion) is patently concerned
with these two identical things and with the common ground in
which they are both rooted, rather than primarily with religion
or non-religion."[89] Ebeling is here considering the anthropological
conditions both of a worldly and of an other-worldly religion. It is
to this question above all that the sociology of religion, theology
and philosophical anthropology have to apply themselves
jointly.[90]

It can also be formulated as an inquiry into the philosophical
and anthropological background of the sociology of religion,
particularly the anthropological basis of socio-religious behaviour.
Weber, as has been said, concerned himself with the significance
of socio-religious behaviour and made this the subject of his
analyses. He regarded such behaviour as based on individual
behaviour, and comprehensible from this. "Only by studying the
meaning of individual conduct does social science gain access to
the meaning of those social relations and patterns which occur in
the transactions of individual actors on the social scene."[91]
Alfred Schuetz asks in detail, and his question is basic to Weber's
concept, how it is possible to have a science that studies subjective

[89] Ebeling, *op. cit.*, p. 49 f.

[90] Cf. W. Schweitzer, Die menschliche Wirklichkeit in soziologischer und
sozialethisch-theologischer Sicht. In: *Zeitschrift f. evangelische Ethik* 1959, 4,
p. 209.

[91] A. Schuetz, *Der sinnhafte Aufbau der sozialen Welt*, Vienna, 1932, p. 3.

meaning.[92] In his analysis of Weber's theory of social behaviour he points out that interpretation of individual action presupposes this possibility. He thus shows that the intersubjectivity of human existence is assumed as a primary, non-deducible datum of sociology and of the social sciences in general. Man as such is a social being, connected with others. In other words, the social nature of man must be regarded as an inherent part of his humanity. Man does not exist independently, in an enclosed individuality, but through his relationship with others. Human existence can thus be understood basically as *social* and *historical*. This is the anthropological basis of social behaviour and of its meaning. It cannot be derived from individual behaviour, but, conversely, individual behaviour must be understood in terms of social behaviour. Social behaviour is primary, individual behaviour is deduced from it.

Underlying this is the concept of *intentionality*, emphasized and developed by Edmund Husserl. This takes the fundamental division between man and the external world (a division that has been evident in European thought since Descartes) and traces it back to a relative division, a bipolar relationship. Husserl reverts to the human "Life world" (*Lebenswelt*) which he seeks to understand and explain in its self-evidency. Science, however, sets out unaware from this self-evidency since it is still too firmly imprisoned in the "natural order". This applies also to the sociology of religion and to its theme. It was for this reason that we drew attention, in the review of subject matter and aims in part I, to the more or less conscious common opinion that obtains among sociologists of religion. The basic assumption that religion and society interact as two separate, independent factors, adapting to each other, seems in sociology of religion to be taken for granted as more or less self-evident. Vogt points out the idealistic, nominalistic background of the problem of this interrelationship, and of the functionalism that is associated with it.[93] This construction, however, may not supply a decisive definition

[92] *Ibid.*, p. 255.
[93] Vogt, *op. cit.*, p. 79.

of the theme of sociology of religion and of the social sciences in general. The central theme must be socio-religious behaviour as such: and functionalism must be considered as the grasping of its meaning.[94] Functionalism is thus not aiming at a sociologically relevant effect, but at the understanding of social behaviour in human group life.[95]

Weber's thesis cannot be regarded as abandoned or out of date. It is still of central significance in the sociology of religion. Weber could regard socio-religious behaviour as giving meaning to the supernatural. Today it is a question of giving meaning to religion centred on this world. How can man's socio-religious behaviour be understood *today* as religious (or as stemming from faith)? What is the meaning of the symbolic reality which is valid *now* or which is becoming valid, and how far is it a continuation of the Christian theme? How is this "religion" formed and "shared" in the institutions of modern society? (Luckmann).

This will be the central problem which the sociology of religion must tackle in the coming years. Its solution is not yet in sight and much work lies ahead. The question in our title, "What is the sociology of religion?", thus remains unanswered for the time being. Perhaps this article could show in what direction the answer should be sought.

[94] Cf. Schuetz, Concept and Theory Formation in the Social Sciences. In: *J. Philosophy*, April 1954, p. 269.

[95] This is in contrast to the definition given by R. K. Merton of the concept of "social function", in which he relates this concept to the "observable objective consequences and *not* to subjective dispositions (aims, motives, purposes)" (R. K. Merton, *Social Theory and Social Structure*, Glencoe, Ill., 1957, p. 24).

The Sociology of Religion in England

J. A. BANKS

ALTHOUGH complete courses on the subject are provided at four English universities,[1] and although it forms part of the sociology curriculum elsewhere, it cannot be claimed that the sociology of religion is a striking feature of British sociology. There are, for example, no university departments which organize team research into its problems, as is the case with industrial sociology, and there is no widespread interest in it among individual scholars up and down the country, as is the case with the sociology of education. As a subject in its own right it simply does not fire the imagination of English sociologists; and while it may be claimed that this is probably true of the sociology of religion in most countries,[2] it is all the more remarkable in the English case by reason of the impressive tradition of the subject in this country in the past. A very large part of the "data of sociology" in Spencer's *Principles of Sociology* was composed of religious phenomena of one kind or another; Tyler's *Primitive Culture* was, similarly, largely concerned with religious and quasi-religious ideas; and from these pioneers it is possible to trace a continuous line of development through to the evolutionary theories of religion held by Hobhouse and Westermarck, on the one hand, and to the detailed comparison of religion and science in the erudite volumes of Fraser, on the other. Perhaps, indeed, it is the case that this type

[1] The universities of the South-West (Exeter), Leeds, London and Sheffield.

[2] See the Trend Report on work published since 1940, prepared by Le Bras and published in *Current Sociology* 5, 1956.

of analysis was taken as far as it would go in such works as *The Golden Bough, Totemism and Exogamy, The Belief in Immortality and the Worship of the Dead*, and *The Worship of Nature*—the very titles are redolent of a past age, but, for all that, the explanation for the current lack of interest in the sociology of religion does not lie at Fraser's door, for there are other traditions of the subject which were flourishing as late as the 1930's, and these too are languishing today.

Spencer's work, as is well known, was also taken up and modified out of all recognition by Durkheim, from whom it returned to England to be developed further by Malinowski into the methodology of studying the function of religious beliefs and practices as "always the core of civilization and the mainspring of moral values . . . closely associated with every form of organization at lower and at higher levels".[3] Detailed studies, inspired by this point of view, have been carried out by such social anthropologists as Evans-Pritchard and Firth, but the lessons which might be drawn from such works for the study of complex, industrialized societies have largely been ignored by sociologists, especially as the gap between social anthropology and sociology has broadened since 1939. At the same time, a completely different tradition, finding its origins in the work of Max Weber and passed on into British social history by R. H. Tawney and his students, Grubb, Warner and Bebb, has also been almost completely ignored by sociologists, otherwise influenced by Weber himself. Hence, while social anthropologists continue to maintain *their* tradition, and while social historians continue to maintain *theirs*, seeking, for example, to trace the origins of the trade union movement and of the Labour Party in the methodism and nonconformism of the nineteenth century, sociologists have tended on the whole to turn their back on a tradition which might equally be claimed to be theirs, and look instead for their source of inspiration to the

---

[3] B. Malinowski: Sir James George Fraser, in *A Scientific Theory of Culture and Other Essays*, University of North Carolina Press, 1944, pp. 200–1. In Malinowski's view Fraser "never became aware of the social factor in folklore and mythology", *ibid.*, p. 188.

revival of interest in the subject which has occurred in America and, especially, France in recent times.[4]

Foreign observers of contemporary British sociology might be tempted, it is true, to regard this Continental and American basis for enthusiasm to be typical of the subject generally. After all, British industrial sociology owes more to Roethlisberger and Dixon, to Mayo, and to Moore than it does to the native work of Sargent Florence and the few empirically minded British economists of the 1930's. Even the sociology of education gets some of its energy from America, although in this instance the emphasis on social stratification probably owes more to the work of the statisticians and demographers of the 1920's and 1930's. What is, in fact, particularly noticeable is the difference in the type of mind which is attracted to sociology today as compared with the past. From domination of the subject by men of primarily philosophical bent, such as Hobhouse and his successor Ginsberg, post-war sociology has attracted a growing number of empirically based investigators, whose interests are set in the framework of scientific rather than philosophical speculation. It should be emphasized that this distinction is methodological and epistemological but not normative. There is nothing to choose between the generation in terms of their views on the relationship between sociological theory and social policy. What has changed, and in such a fashion as to appear as a sharp break with the past, is the approach to the problem of how to obtain valid information which may be used for the sociological analysis of human behaviour.

Broad evolutionary and comparative studies have given way to more precise and narrowly confined investigations into relatively limited fields. Breadth of scope, based often on meagre evidence, has been sacrificed for greater precision in the data, and although

[4] For details see N. Birnbaum: La Sociologie de la religion en Grande-Bretagne, *Archives de Sociologie des Religions*, Vol. 1, No. 2, 1956, and N. Birnbaum: Sociologie der Kirchengemeinde in Grossbritannien, in D. Goldschmidt, F. Greiner and H. Schelsky, *Sociologie der Kirchengemeinde*, Stuttgart, 1960.

the contemporary sociologist certainly does not eschew sociological theory, as did some of the earlier social empiricists such as
Charles Booth, he is much more ready to subordinate it to the
painstaking collection and assessment of relevant fact than was
his pre-war predecessor. It is also noteworthy that the empirical
content of post-war sociology has resulted in a great deal of head
counting, with an according interest in social structure, as con-
trasted with the pre-war interest not in individuals but in mass
movements of ideas. This is true of sociology generally, but it has
a special relevance for the sociology of religion.

An extreme example of the present fashion in the English
approach to the sociology of religion will perhaps make the
contrast clearer. In his study of the priests and parishioners of a
Catholic parish in Liverpool, Dr. Conor Ward was interested in
the opinions of the people he interviewed but only in so far as they
provided information on their willingness to participate in parish
societies and parish activities, and only in so far as these could
provide information on what he chose to regard as the extent of
parish unity and group consciousness. He was not interested, as a
sociologist, in his respondents' acceptance of what he referred to
as "the ultimate values and norms of the Catholic Church".[5]
Indeed, by omitting from his terms of reference every baptized
Catholic in the area who has severed all connections with the
Catholic Church, he was able to concentrate on common values
and norms "inherent in the parish system" at the expense of the
ideology of Catholicism as such. Apart, therefore, from certain
concepts based on the terms "Mass" and "Priest", which indicate
that it really was a Catholic parish which he was studying, there
is very little in his account which would help to distinguish his
group of people from any other territorially organized body,
religious or secular. Durkheim's conception of the sacred—"things
set apart and forbidden"—which he regarded as the very essence
of the distinction between religious and other social—"profane"
—phenomena plays no part in such a framework of analysis, and

[5] C. K. Ward, *Priests and People, A Study in the Sociology of Religion*, Liverpool,
University Press, 1961, p. 108.

as a result Ward made no attempt to consider the extent to which the relationship between priests and people was influenced by the very special nature of Catholic dogma, Catholic eschatology and Catholic social ethics.

The contrast between this type of inquiry and the attitude of mind displayed by Fraser, the social anthropologists and the social historians when concerned with religious beliefs and religious ritual should be quite plain. For the latter the central issue is the human predicament of mortality and how human beings cope with the uncertainty of existence, including the translation of cosmic principles into moral inspirations. They have little concern for the minutiae of organization. This does not mean that Ward's study is valueless. It does provide an interesting study of role performance as seen in the context of the formal structure of the parish system of the Catholic Church, on the one hand, and as interpreted in terms of the "ideal of a parish unit" derived from interviews with parishioners, on the other. Indeed, his analysis of participation is directly comparable with those usually carried out under the rubric of "community studies" and with those made of participation in trade unions, political parties, and in industry generally; and in this sense it may be said that *Priests and People* is as much a contribution to the sociology of organization as it is to the sociology of religion. In this sense also it is perhaps illustrative of another facet of contemporary British sociology, namely that the traditional division of the subject into various "specialisms" such as industrial sociology, the sociology of education and the sociology of religion are becoming more obviously matters of administrative convenience than matters of sociological content. Perhaps the actual divisions of the subject which are just emerging might be better described as the sociology of social persistence and social change, the sociology of organizations, and the sociology of ideology.

Another contemporary example, looked at from the point of view of the sociology of religion, offers ample confirmation of this claim. In 1954 Brennan and his colleagues published a study of South-West Wales which was concerned with the changes in the general pattern of "associational life", that is, with changes in the extent of interest shown by the inhabitants of that area in trade unionism, religion, politics, social and recreational clubs, and organizations catering for hobbies. But its concern with religion was not confined to documenting the extent of the decline in the church and chapel membership. It set out to explain the decline "in terms of the nature of the churches' constitutions, the social composition of their leadership or the taking over of some of their functions by organized political groups, especially the Labour Party".[6] What the authors show is that over time leadership of religious organizations in South Wales has become shared between the middle and the working classes, and that in consequence class conflicts over political issues which otherwise might have disturbed religious unity have been avoided in their organizations by the simple expedient of avoiding involvement in such issues. Superficially, at any rate, it would appear from this study that Wales also rejected the Dutch solution of this problem —*verzuiling*—at the expense of a loss of mass membership. The rank-and-file members of religious bodies have turned away from them towards the purely secular Labour Party. Thus, Brennan and his colleagues account for the decline in religious adherence not in terms of a decline in belief in the Christian apocalyptic, in Christian eschatology, in Christian dogma, and in religious ideology generally—although this may also have occurred. They explain it in terms of the failure of organized religion in this country to come to grips with the social realities of the lives of its membership. Participation in religious organizations, that is to say, is seen as one type only of participation in group life for the realization of certain values, and the function of religion in this respect may, apparently, be performed equally well by a political party.

At this point this study of social change in South-West Wales may be said to provide data which closely approximates those which are relevant for the explanation of contemporary religious

[6] T. Brennan, E. W. Cooney and H. Pollins: *Social Change in South-West Wales*, London, 1954, p. 138.

behaviour in non-religious terms. A secular society, Norman Birnbaum has asserted, *"ist eine Gesellschaft, in der private und oeffentliche Entscheidungen ohne Berücksichtigung obernatuerlicher Imperative oder Sanktionen getroffen werden"*. But this is not all; in a secular society even religious decisions, apparently deriving from supernatural convictions, are *"Reaktionen auf Impulse, die von sichtbaren sozialen Prozessen ausgehen"*.[7] In so far as this is true, and in so far as England, like Wales, has tended increasingly since the turn of the century to make private and public decisions without reference to Christian dogma, it would also help to account for the current lack of interest shown by sociologists in religious phenomena. They have other and more important issues to concern themselves with. As the functions performed by religious associations become transferred to other social institutions, the focus of attention becomes directed away from religious to secular ideology, and from the church to other social institutions.

The one exception to this supports, nevertheless, Birnbaum's contention. Purely religious organizations might be studied by sociologists but not as phenomena in themselves so much as for the information they provide and the extent to which they exemplify the assertion that they are the products of observable social processes. The recently published study by Bryan Wilson of the religious ideologies, the social ethics and the social composition of three minority groups, the Elim Foursquare Gospel Church, Christian Science, and the Christadelphians, falls clearly into this category. He concludes that such bodies serve as "deviant" reference groups "in which the individual may seek status and prestige and in terms of whose standards he may measure his own talents and accomplishments in more favourable terms than are generally available in the wider society".[8] Christian apocalyptic,

[7] N. Birnbaum, Saekularisation, zur Sociologie der Religion in der heutige Gesellschaft des Westens, in *Monatschrift für Pastoral-Theologie*, Vol. 48, No. 3, 1959, p. 68.

[8] B. R. Wilson, *Sects and Society, a Sociological Study of Three Religious Groups in Britain*, London, 1961, p. 354.

Christian eschatology and Christian dogma may thus be said still to have a function but not in its official form. Only by modifying the official doctrine into a new system of belief is a sect able to maintain an identity, and it is able to do this only because its adherents are in effect deviant individuals in the social structure. The sociology of religion in this kind of study, that is to say, is indistinguishable from the sociology of deviation generally, and Wilson's study might easily have been comprised of the Anarcho-Syndicalists, the Socialist Party of Great Britain and the Revolutionary Communist Party—three deviant political groups in this country—for he makes little systematic attempt to analyse the "teachings" of these three sects in terms of the Paretonian scheme of residues and derivations or in terms of some other satisfactory sociological method of studying ideology.

This does not mean that *Sects and Society*, any more than *Priests and People*, is not sociology. What it does mean is that the kind of sociological analysis it employs, largely a deviative of the Weberian exegesis of the routinization of charisma, demonstrates once again the radical departure of contemporary English sociology of religion from the tradition of its founders. In many respects, of course, this is an excellent thing. All sociologists are conscious of Whitehead's aphorism on the danger of hesitating to forget the past, which stands at the head of Merton's *Social Theory and Social Structure*. But there is equally something to be said for the opposite point of view in the present instance. Might it not be that a greater awareness of the achievements of the *Golden Bough* would revive amongst English sociologists an interest in those divergent, yet complementary, belief systems, science, magic and religion, which are still important today? The general trend may well be from the older divisions of the subject to new specialisms in sociology, in which the church is being cared for along with the other organizations of our secular society, but it is also important that its doctrine should be studied along with the other belief systems of our time.

PART III

Religion and Sociological Theory

The Theoretical Development of the Sociology of Religion

A Chapter in the History of Modern Social Science[1]

T. PARSONS

THE present paper will attempt to present in broad outline what seems to the writer one of the most significant chapters in the recent history of sociological theory, that dealing with the broader structure of the conceptual scheme for the analysis of religious phenomena as part of a social system. Its principal significance would seem to lie on two levels. In the first place, the development to be outlined represents a notable advance in the adequacy of our theoretical equipment to deal with a critically important range of scientific problems. Secondly, however, it is at the same time a particularly good illustration of the kind of process by which major theoretical developments in the field of social theory can be expected to take place.

Every important tradition of scientific thought involves a broad framework of theoretical propositions at any given stage of its development. Generally speaking, differences will be found only in the degree to which this framework is logically integrated and to which it is explicitly and self-consciously acknowledged and analyzed. About the middle of the last century or shortly thereafter, it is perhaps fair to say, generalized thinking about the

[1] This paper was presented to the Conference on Methods in Philosophy and the Sciences at the New School for Social Research, New York, November 29, 1942.

F

significance of religion to human life tended to fall into one of two main categories. The first is the body of thought anchored in the doctrinal positions of one or another specific religious group, predominantly of course the various Christian denominations. For understandable reasons, the main tenor of such thought tended to be normative rather than empirical and analytical, to assert its own religious position and to expose the errors of opponents. It is difficult to see that in any direct sense important contributions to the sociology of religion as an empirical science could come from this source.[2] The other main category may be broadly referred to as that of positivistic thinking. In the phases which culminated in the various branches of utilitarianism, this great stream of thought had, of course, long been much concerned with some of the problems of religion. In its concern with contemporary society, however, the strong tendency had been to minimize the importance of religion, to treat it as a matter of "superstition" which had no place in the enlightened thinking of modern civilized man. The result of this tendency was, in the search for the important forces activating human behavior, to direct attention to other fields, such as the economic and the political. In certain phases the same tendency may be observed in the trend of positivistic thought toward emphasis on biology and psychology, which gathered force in the latter part of the nineteenth century and has continued well into our own.

Perhaps the first important change in this definition of problems, which was highly unfavorable to a serious scientific interest in the phenomena of religion, came with the application of the idea of evolution to human society. Once evidence from non-literate societies, not to speak of many others, was at all carefully studied, the observation was inescapable that the life of these so-called "primitive" men was to an enormous degree dominated by beliefs and practices which would ordinarily be classified according to the common-sense thinking of our time as magical and religious. Contemporary non-literate peoples, however, were in

---

[2] It was far less unfavorable to historical contributions than to those affecting the analytical framework of the subject.

that generation predominantly interpreted as the living proto-types of our own prehistorical ancestors, and hence it was only natural that these striking phenomena should have been treated as "primitive" in a strictly evolutionary sense, as belonging to the early stages of the process of social development. This is the broad situation of the first really serious treatment of comparative religion in a sociological context, especially in the work of the founder of modern social-anthropology, Tylor,[3] and of Spencer,[4] perhaps the most penetrating theorist of this movement of thought. Though there was here a basis for a serious scientific interest, the positivistic scheme of thought imposed severe limitations on the kind of significance which could be attributed to the observed phenomena. Within the positivistic *schema*, the most obvious directions of theoretical interpretation were two. On the one hand, religious phenomena could be treated as the manifestations of underlying biological or psychological factors beyond the reach of rational control, or interpretations in terms of subjective categories. Most generally this pattern led to some version of the instinct theory, which has suffered, however, some very serious scientific handicaps in that it has never proved possible to relate the detailed variations in the behavioral phenomena to any corresponding variations in the structure of instinctual drives. The whole scheme has on the level of social theory never successfully avoided the pitfalls of reasoning in a circle.

The other principal alternative was what may be called the "rationalistic" variation of positivism,[5] the tendency to treat the actor as if he were a rational, scientific investigator, acting "reasonably" in the light of the knowledge available to him. This was the path taken by Tylor and Spencer with the general thesis that primitive magical and religious ideas were ideas which in the situation of primitive men, considering the lack of accumulated

[3] *Primitive Culture.*

[4] Esp. *Principles of Sociology*, Vol. 1.

[5] See the author's *Structure of Social Action*, Chaps. II and III.

knowledge and the limitations of the technique and opportunities of observation, it would reasonably be expected they would arrive at. With beliefs like that in a soul separable from the body, ritual practices in turn are held to be readily understandable. It is, however, a basic assumption of this pattern of thinking that the only critical standards to which religious ideas can be referred are those of empirical validity. It almost goes without saying that no enlightened modern could entertain such beliefs, that hence what we think of as distinctively religious and magical beliefs, and hence also the accompanying practices, will naturally disappear as an automatic consequence of the advance in scientific knowledge.

Inadequate as it is in the light of modern knowledge, this *schema* has proved to be the fruitful starting-point for the development of the field, for it makes possible the analysis of action in terms of the subjective point of view of the actor in his orientation to specific features of the situation in which he acts. Broadly speaking, to attempt to deal with the empirical inadequacies of this view by jumping directly, through the medium of anti-intellectualistic psychology, to the more fundamental forces activating human behavior has not proved fruitful. The fruitful path has rather been the introduction of specific refinements and distinctions within the basic structural scheme with which "rationalistic positivism" started. The body of this paper will be concerned with a review of several of the most important of these steps in analytical refinement, showing how, taken together, they have led up to a far more comprehensive analytical scheme. This can perhaps most conveniently be done in terms of the contributions of four important theorists, Pareto, Malinowski, Durkheim, and Max Weber, none of whom had any important direct influence on any of the others.

It is of primary significance that Pareto's[6] analytical scheme for the treatment of a social system started precisely with this

[6] *The Mind and Society.* See, also, the author's *Structure of Social Action*, Chaps. V–VII; and Pareto's Central Analytical Scheme, *Journal of Social Philosophy* 1, 244–62 (1935).

fundamental frame of reference. Like the earlier positivists, he took as his starting-point the cognitive patterns in terms of which the actor is oriented to his situation of action. Again like them, he based his classification on the relation of these patterns to the standards of empirical scientific validity—in his terms, to "logico-experimental" standards. At this point, however, he broke decisively with the main positivistic tradition. He found it necessary, on grounds which in view of Pareto's general intellectual character most certainly were primarily empirical rather than philosophical, to distinguish two modes of deviance from conformity with logico-experimental standards. There were, on the one hand, the modes of deviance familiar to the older positivists, namely the failure to attain a logico-experimental solution of problems intrinsically capable of such solution. This may be attributable either to ignorance, the sheer absence of logically necessary knowledge of fact, or possibly of inference, or to error, to allegations of fact which observation can disprove or to logical fallacy in inference. In so far as cognitive patterns were deviant in this respect, Pareto summed them up as "pseudo-scientific" theories. Failure to conform with logico-experimental standards was not, however, confined to this mode of deviance, but included another, "the theories which surpass experience". These involved propositions, especially major premises, which are intrinsically incapable of being tested by scientific procedures. The attributes of God, for instance, are not entities capable of empirical observation; hence propositions involving them can by logico-experimental methods neither be proved nor disproved. In this connection, Pareto's primary service lay in the clarity with which the distinction was worked out and applied, and his demonstration of the essentially prominent rôle in systems of human action of the latter class of cognitive elements. It is precisely in the field of religious ideas and of theological and metaphysical doctrines that its prominence has been greatest.

Pareto, however, did not stop there. From the very first, he treated the cognitive aspects of action in terms of their functional interdependence with the other elements of the social system, notably with what he called the "sentiments". He thereby broke through the "rationalistic bias" of earlier positivism and demonstrated by an immense weight of evidence that it was not possible to deal adequately with the significance of religious and magical ideas solely on the hypothesis that men entertaining them as beliefs drew the logical conclusions and acted accordingly. In this connection, Pareto's position has been widely interpreted as essentially a psychological one, as a reduction of non-logical ideas to the status of mere manifestations of instinct. Critical analysis of his work[7] shows, however, that this interpretation is not justified, but that he left the question of the more ultimate nature of non-cognitive factors open. It can be shown that the way in which he treated the sentiments is incompatible in certain critical respects with the hypothesis that they are biologically inherited instinctual drives alone. This would involve a determinacy irrespective of cultural variation which he explicitly repudiated.

It is perhaps best to state that, as Pareto left the subject, there were factors particularly prominent in the field of religious behavior which involved the expression of sentiments or attitudes other than those important to action in a rationally utilitarian context. He did not, however, go far in analyzing the nature of these factors. It should, however, be clear that with the introduction, as a functionally necessary category, of the non-empirical effective elements which cannot be fitted into the pattern of rational techniques, Pareto brought about a fundamental break in the neatly closed system of positivistic interpretation of the phenomena of religion. He enormously broadened the analytical perspective which needed to be taken into account before a new theoretical integration could be achieved.

The earlier positivistic theory started with the attempt to analyze the relation of the actor to particular types of situations common to all human social life, such as death and the experience of dreams. This starting-point was undoubtedly sound. The difficulty lay in interpreting such situations and the actor's relations to them too narrowly, essentially as a matter of the

[7] Cf. *Structure of Social Action,* pp. 200 ff., 241 ff.

solution of empirical problems, of the actor's resorting to a "reasonable" course of action in the light of beliefs which he took for granted. Pareto provided much evidence that this exclusively cognitive approach was not adequate, but it remained for Malinowski[8] to return to detailed analysis of action in relation to particular situations in a broader perspective. Malinowski maintained continuity with the "classical" approach in that he took men's adaptation to practical situations by rational knowledge and technique as his initial point of reference. Instead of attempting to fit all the obvious facts positively into this framework, however, he showed a variety of reasons why in many circumstances rational knowledge and technique could not provide adequate mechanisms of adjustment to the total situation.

This approach threw into high relief a fundamental empirical observation, namely that instead of there being one single set of ideas and practices involved, for instance in gardening, canoe-building, or deep-sea fishing in the Trobriand Islands, there were in fact two distinct systems. On the one hand, the native was clearly possessed of an impressive amount of sound empirical knowledge of the proper uses of the soil and the processes of plant growth. He acted quite rationally in terms of his knowledge and above all was quite clear about the connection between intelligent and energetic work and a favorable outcome. There is no tendency to excuse failure on supernatural grounds when it could be clearly attributed to failure to attain adequate current standards of technical procedure. Side by side with this system of rational knowledge and technique, however, and specifically not confused with it, was a system of magical beliefs and practices. These beliefs concerned the possible intervention in the situation of forces and entities which are "supernatural" in the sense that they are not from our point of view objects of empirical observation and experience, but rather what Pareto would call "imaginary" entities, and, on the other hand, entities with a specifically sacred character. Correspondingly, the practices were not rational

[8] See especially Magic, Science, and Religion, in *Science, Religion, and Reality*, J. Needham, ed., and *The Foundations of Faith and Morals*.

techniques but rituals involving specific orientation to this world of supernatural forces and entities. It is true that the Trobriander believes that a proper performance of magic is indispensable to a successful outcome of the enterprise; but it is one of Malinowski's most important insights that this attribution applies only to the range of uncertainty in the outcome of rational technique, to those factors in the situation which are beyond rational understanding and control on the part of the actor.

This approach to the analysis of primitive magic enabled Malinowski clearly to refute both the view of Lévy-Bruhl,[9] that primitive man confuses the realm of the supernatural and the sacred with the utilitarian and the rational, and also the view which had been classically put forward by Frazer[10] that magic was essentially primitive science, serving the same fundamental functions.

Malinowski, however, went beyond this in attempting to understand the functional necessity for such mechanisms as magic. In this connection, he laid stress on the importance of the emotional interests involved in the successful outcome of such enterprises. The combination of a strong emotional interest with important factors of uncertainty, which on the given technical level are inherent in the situation, produces a state of tension and exposes the actor to frustration. This, it should be noted, exists not only in cases where uncontrollable factors, such as bad weather or insect pests in gardening, result in "undeserved" failure, but also in cases where success is out of proportion to reasonable expectations of the results of intelligence and effort. Unless there were mechanisms which had the psychological function of mitigating the sense of frustration, the consequences would be unfavorable to maintaining a high level of confidence or effort, and it is in this connection that magic may be seen to perform important positive functions. It should be clear that this is a very different level of interpretation from that which attributes it only to the primitive level of knowledge. It would follow that wherever such uncer-

[9] *Primitive Mentality.*
[10] *The Golden Bough.*

tainty elements enter into the pursuit of emotionally important goals, if not magic at least functionally equivalent phenomena could be expected to appear.[11]

In the case of magic, orientation to supernatural entities enters into action which is directed to the achievement of practical, empirical goals, such as a good crop or a large catch of fish. Malinowski, however, calls attention to the fact that there are situations which are analogous in other respects but in which no practical goal can be pursued. The type case of this is death. From the practical point of view, the Trobrianders, like any one else, are surely aware that "nothing can be done about it". No ritual observances will bring the deceased back to life. But precisely for this reason, the problem of emotional adjustment is all the greater in importance. The significance both practically and emotionally of a human individual is of such a magnitude that his death involves a major process of readjustment for the survivors. Malinowski shows that the death of another involves exposure to sharply conflicting emotional reactions, some of which, if given free range, would lead to action and attitudes detrimental to the social group. There is great need for patterns of action which provide occasion for the regulated expression of strong emotions, and which in such a situation of emotional conflict reinforce those reactions which are most favorable to the continued solidarity and functioning of the social group. One may suggest that in no society is action on the occasion of death confined to the utilitarian aspects of the disposal of the corpse and other practical adjustments. There is always specifically ritual observance of some kind which, as Malinowski shows, cannot adequately be interpreted as merely acting out the bizarre ideas

[11] For example, the field of health is, in spite of the achievements of modern medicine, even in our own society a classical example of this type of situation. Careful examination of our own treatment of health even through medical practice reveals that though magic in a strict sense is not prominent, there is an unstable succession of beliefs which overemphasize the therapeutic possibilities of certain diagnostic ideas and therapeutic practices. The effect is to create an optimistic bias in favor of successful treatment of disease which apparently has considerable functional significance.

which primitive man in his ignorance develops about the nature of death.

Malinowski shows quite clearly that neither ritual practices, magical or religious, nor the beliefs about supernatural forces and entities integrated with them can be treated simply as a primitive and inadequate form of rational techniques or scientific knowledge; they are qualitatively distinct and have quite different functional significance in the system of action. Durkheim,[12] however, went farther than Malinowski in working out the specific character of this difference, as well as in bringing out certain further aspects of the functional problem. Whereas Malinowski tended to focus attention on functions in relation to action in a situation, Durkheim became particularly interested in the problem of the specific attitudes exhibited toward supernatural entities and ritual objects and actions. The results of this study he summed up in the fundamental distinction between the sacred and the profane. Directly contrasting the attitudes appropriate in a ritual context with those toward objects of utilitarian significance and their use in fields of rational technique, he found one fundamental feature of the sacred to be its radical dissociation from any utilitarian context. The sacred is to be treated with a certain specific attitude of respect, which Durkheim identified with the appropriate attitude toward moral obligations and authority. If the effect of the prominence which Durkheim gives to the conception of the sacred is strongly to reinforce the significance of Malinowski's observation that the two systems are not confused but are in fact treated as essentially separate, it also brings out even more sharply than did Malinowski the inadequacy of the older approach to this range of problems which treated them entirely as the outcome of intellectual processes in ways indistinguishable from the solution of empirical problems. Such treatment could not but obscure the fundamental distinction upon which Durkheim insisted.

The central significance of the sacred in religion, however,

[12] *The Elementary Forms of the Religious Life*. See, also, *Structure of Social Action*, Chap. XI.

served to raise in a peculiarly acute form the question of the source of the attitude of respect. Spencer, for instance, had derived it from the fact that the souls of the dead reappeared to the living, and from ideas about the probable dangers of association with them. Max Müller, on the other hand, and the naturalist school had attempted to derive all sacred things in the last analysis from personification of certain phenomena of nature which were respected and feared because of their intrinsically imposing or terrifying character. Durkheim opened up an entirely new line of thought by suggesting that it was hopeless to look for a solution of the problem on this level at all. There was in fact no common intrinsic quality of things treated as sacred which could account for the attitude of respect. In fact, almost everything from the sublime to the ridiculous has in some society been treated as sacred. Hence the source of sacredness is not intrinsic; the problem is of a different character. Sacred objects and entities are symbols. The problem then becomes one of identifying the referents of such symbols. It is that which is symbolized and not the intrinsic quality of the symbol which becomes crucial.

At this point Durkheim became aware of the fundamental significance of his previous insight that the attitude of respect for sacred things was essentially identical with the attitude of respect for moral authority. If sacred things are symbols, the essential quality of that which they symbolize is that it is an entity which would command moral respect. It was by this path that Durkheim arrived at the famous proposition that society is always the real object of religious veneration. In this form the proposition is certainly unacceptable, but there is no doubt of the fundamental importance of Durkheim's insight into the exceedingly close integration of the system of religious symbols of a society and the patterns sanctioned by the common moral sentiments of the members of the community. In his earlier work,[13] Durkheim had progressed far in understanding the functional significance of an integrated system of morally sanctioned norms. Against this

[13] Especially *De la division du travail* and *Le Suicide*. See also *Structure of Social Action*, Chaps. VIII, X.

background the integration he demonstrated suggested a most important aspect of the functional significance of religion. For the problem arises, if moral norms and the sentiments supporting them are of such primary importance, what are the mechanisms by which they are maintained other than external processes of enforcement? It was Durkheim's view that religious ritual was of primary significance as a mechanism for expressing and reinforcing the sentiments most essential to the institutional integration of the society. It can readily be seen that this is closely linked to Malinowski's view of the significance of funeral ceremonies as a mechanism for reasserting the solidarity of the group on the occasion of severe emotional strain. Thus Durkheim worked out certain aspects of the specific relations between religion and social structure more sharply than did Malinowski, and in addition put the problem in a different functional perspective in that he applied it to the society as a whole in abstraction from particular situations of tension and strain for the individual.

One of the most notable features of the development under consideration lay in the fact that the cognitive patterns associated with religion were no longer, as in the older positivism, treated as essentially given points of reference, but were rather brought into functional relationship with a variety of other elements of social systems of action. Pareto in rather general terms showed their interdependence with the sentiments. Malinowski contributed the exceedingly important relation to particular types of human situation, such as those of uncertainty and death. He in no way contradicted the emphasis placed by Pareto on emotional factors or sentiments. These, however, acquire their significance for specifically structured patterns of action only through their relation to specific situations. Malinowski was well aware in turn of the relation of both these factors to the solidarity of the social group, but this aspect formed the center of Durkheim's analytical attention. Clearly, religious ideas could only be treated sociologically in terms of their interdependence with all four types of factor.

There were, however, still certain serious problems left unsolved. In particular, neither Malinowski nor Durkheim raised the problem of the relation of these factors to the variability of social structure from one society to another. Both were primarily concerned with analysis of the functioning of a given social system without either comparative or dynamic references. Furthermore, Durkheim's important insight into the rôle of symbolism in religious ideas might, without further analysis, suggest that the specific patterns, hence their variations, were of only secondary importance. Indeed, there is clearly discernible in Durkheim's thinking in this field a tendency to circular reasoning in that he tends to treat religious patterns as a symbolic manifestation of "society", but at the same time to define the most fundamental aspect of society as a set of patterns of moral and religious sentiment.

Max Weber approached the whole field in very different terms. In his study of the relation between Protestantism and capitalism,[14] his primary concern was with those features of the institutional system of modern western society which were most distinctive in differentiating it from the other great civilizations. Having established what he felt to be an adequate relation of congruence between the cognitive patterns of Calvinism and some of the principal institutionalized attitudes towards secular rôles of our own society, he set about systematically to place this material in the broadest possible comparative perspective through studying especially the religion and social structure of China, India, and ancient Judea.[15] As a generalized result of these studies, he found it was not possible to reduce the striking variations of pattern on the level of religious ideas in these cases to any features of an independently existent social structure or economic situation, though he continually insisted on the very great importance of situational factors in a number of different connections.[16] These

[14] *The Protestant Ethic and the Spirit of Capitalism.*

[15] *Gesammelte Aufsätze zur Religionssoziologie.* See also *Structure of Social Action*, Chaps. XIV, XV, and XVII.

[16] See especially his treatment of the rôle of the balance of social power in the establishment of the ascendancy of the Brahmans in India, and of the international position of the people of Israel in the definition of religious problems for the prophetic movement.

factors, however, served only to pose the problems with which great movements of religious thought have been concerned. But the distinctive cognitive patterns were only understandable as a result of a cumulative tradition of intellectual effort in grappling with the problems thus presented and formulated.

For present purposes, even more important than Weber's views about the independent causal significance of religious ideas is his clarification of their functional relation to the system of action. Following up the same general line of analysis which provides one of the major themes of Pareto's and Malinowski's work, Weber made clear above all that there is a fundamental distinction between the significance for human action of problems of empirical causation and what, on the other hand, he called the "problem of meaning". In such cases as premature death through accident, the problem of *how* it happened in the sense of an adequate explanation of empirical causes can readily be solved to the satisfaction of most minds and yet leave a sense not merely of emotional but of cognitive frustration with respect to the problem of *why* such things must happen. Correlative with the functional need for emotional adjustment to such experiences as death is a cognitive need for understanding, for trying to have it "make sense". Weber attempted to show that problems of this nature, concerning the discrepancy between normal human interests and expectations in any situation or society and what actually happens, are inherent in the nature of human existence. They always pose problems of the order which on the most generalized line have come to be known as the problem of evil, of the meaning of suffering, and the like. In terms of his comparative material, however, Weber shows there are different directions of definition of human situations in which rationally integrated solutions of these problems may be sought. It is differentiation with respect to the treatment of precisely such problems which constitutes the primary modes of variation between the great systems of religious thought.

Such differences as, for instance, that between the Hindu philosophy of Karma and transmigration and the Christian doctrine of Grace with their philosophical backgrounds are not of merely speculative significance. Weber is able to show, in ways which correlate directly with the work of Malinowski and Durkheim, how intimately such differences in doctrine are bound up with practical attitudes towards the most various aspects of everyday life. For if we can speak of a need to understand ultimate frustrations in order for them to "make sense", it is equally urgent that the values and goals of everyday life should also "make sense". A tendency to integration of these two levels seems to be inherent in human action. Perhaps the most striking feature of Weber's analysis is the demonstration of the extent to which precisely the variations in socially sanctioned values and goals in secular life correspond to the variations in the dominant religious philosophy of the great civilizations.

It can be shown with little difficulty that these results of Weber's comparative and dynamic study integrate directly with the conceptual scheme developed as a result of the work of the other writers. Thus Weber's theory of the positive significance of religious ideas is in no way to be confused with the earlier naïvely rationalistic positivism. The influence of religious doctrine is not exerted through the actor's coming to a conviction and then acting upon it in a rational sense. It is rather, on the individual level, a matter of introducing a determinate structure at certain points in the system of action where, in relation to the situations men have to face, other elements, such as their emotional needs, do not suffice to determine specific orientations of behavior. In the theories of Malinowski and Durkheim, certain kinds of sentiments and emotional reactions were shown to be essential to a functioning social system. These cannot stand alone, however, but are necessarily integrated with cognitive patterns; for without them there could be no coordination of action in a coherently structured social system. This is because functional analysis of the structure of action shows that situations must be subjectively defined, and the goals and values to which action is oriented must be congruent with these definitions—must, that is, have "meaning".

It is, of course, never safe to say a scientific conceptual scheme has reached a definitive completion of its development. Continual change is in the nature of science. There are, however, relative degrees of conceptual integration, and it seems safe to say that the cumulative results of the work just reviewed constitute in broad outline a relatively well-integrated analytical scheme which covers most of the more important broader aspects of the rôle of religion in social systems. It is unlikely that in the near future this analytical scheme will give way to a radical structural change, though notable refinement and revision are to be expected. It is perhaps safe to say that it places the sociology of religion for the first time on a footing where it is possible to combine empirical study and theoretical analysis on a large scale on a level in conformity with the best current standards of social science and psychology.

When we look back, the schemes of Tylor and Spencer seem hopelessly naïve and inadequate to the modern sociologist, anthropologist, or psychologist. It is, however, notable that the development sketched did not take place by repudiating their work and attempting to appeal directly to the facts without benefit of theory. The process was quite different. It consisted in raising problems which were inherent in the earlier scheme and modifying the scheme as a result of the empirical observation suggested by these problems. Thus Malinowski did not abandon all attempt to relate magic to rational technique. Not being satisfied with its identification with primitive science and technology, he looked for specific modes of difference from and relation to them, retaining the established interpretation of the nature and functions of rational technique as his initial point of reference. It is notable, again, that in this process the newer developments of psychological theory in relation to the rôle of emotional factors have played an essential part. The most fruitful results have not, however, resulted from substituting a psychological "theory of religion" for another type, but rather from incorporating the results of psychological investigation into a wider scheme.

In order for this development to take place, it was essential that certain elements of philosophical dogmatism in the older positivism should be overcome. One reason for the limitations of Spencer's insight lay in the presumption that if a cognitive pattern was significant to human action, it must be assimilable to the pattern of science. Pareto, however, showed clearly that the "pseudo-scientific" did not exhaust significant patterns which deviated from scientific standards. Malinowski went further in showing the functional relation of certain non-scientific ideas to elements of uncertainty and frustration which were inherent in the situation of action. Durkheim called attention to the importance of the relation of symbolism as distinguished from that of intrinsic causality in cognitive patterns. Finally, Weber integrated the various aspects of the rôle of non-empirical cognitive patterns in social action in terms of his theory of the significance of the problems of meaning and the corresponding cognitive structures, in a way which precluded, for analytical purposes, their being assimilated to the patterns of science.[17] All of these distinctions by virtue of which the cognitive patterns of religion are treated separately from those of science have positive significance for empirical understanding of religious phenomena. Like any such scientific categories, they are to the scientist sanctioned by the fact that they can be shown to work. Failure to make these distinctions does not in the present state of knowledge and in terms of the relevant frame of reference[18] help us to understand certain

[17] See the writer's paper, The Rôle of Ideas in Social Action, *American Sociological Review* **3**, 1938, for a general analytical discussion of the problem.

[18] Every treatment of questions of fact and every empirical investigation is "in terms of a conceptual scheme". Scientifically, the sole sanction of such a conceptual scheme is its "utility", the degree to which it "works" in facilitating the attainment of the goals of scientific investigation. Hence the conceptual structure of any system of scientific theory is subject to the same kind of relativity with "arbitrariness". It is subject to the disciplining constraint both of verification in all questions of particular empirical fact, and of logical precision and consistency among the many different parts of a highly complex conceptual structure. The "theory of social action" is by now a theoretical structure so highly developed and with so many ramifications in both these respects that elements structurally essential to it cannot be lightly dismissed as expressing only "one point of view".

critically important facts of human life. What the philosophica
significance of this situation may be is not as such the task of the
social scientist to determine. Only one safe prediction on this leve
can be made. Any new philosophical synthesis will need positively
to take account of these distinctions rather than to attempt to
reinstate for the scientific level the older positivistic conception o
the homogeneity of all human thought and its problems. If these
distinctions are to be transcended it cannot well be in the form o
"reducing" religious ideas to those of science—both in the sense o
Western intellectual history—or vice versa. The proved scientific
utility of the distinctions is sufficient basis on which to eliminate
this as a serious possibility.

Weber's Sociological Theory, and the Modern Dilemma of Value and Belief in the Social Sciences

Lord Simey

THE world of social science and social philosophy is at present greatly preoccupied by the discussion of the problem of the logical status of the social sciences. A split has occurred between the theories that are oriented towards facts, or the scientific universe of what is, and the beliefs which relate to what ought to be, or the meaning and purpose of human existence; the latter comprise the universe of values. The result is that the man who studies human affairs from the "arts" viewpoint tends to see the world very differently from the man who studies them as the data of a "science", and the two are tending to drift apart from each other. Sir Charles Snow has, in the course of the last four years, repeatedly drawn attention to the critical importance of the growth of "two cultures" in the modern society, which has, he thinks, made it increasingly difficult for those whose lives are lived within the one culture to communicate with those who have identified themselves with the other, and this, he argues, is undermining the foundations of modern civilization.[1] The consequences are not restricted to the dangers which arise when scientists are allowed to run wild, as it were, and even encouraged to produce the tools which, if misused, will destroy human life altogether; the collision between the two cultures disrupts modern

[1] *The Two Cultures and A Second Look*, Cambridge University Press, 1964.

thought itself, and prevents the growth of a synthesis of fact and value, or of theory or principle and evidence or practice, which will make it possible for man to shape his social world anew, and learn to live with science in the enjoyment of some degree of purpose and security. Intellectual and moral disintegration, it seems, go hand in hand.

At the same time, Sir Charles Snow believes that, though it is too early to speak of a third culture as already in existence which can unite the world of science with that of the humanities, he is convinced that it is coming to birth. Notwithstanding any evidence to the contrary, he believes that a bridge will be built between them, and in the building of it the social sciences, particularly sociology, will play a leading part. But there is also a split within the social sciences themselves, which runs along much the same line as the main split referred to above, and prevents the disease from producing its own remedy. It is significant, therefore, that social scientists are rapidly becoming more and more aware, in their own way, of the existence of the intellectual troubles which beset them, and that a large amount of the work that they have done since the last war has related in one way or another to the problems that Sir Charles Snow has brought to light. They have gradually aroused themselves from their dogmatic slumbers as positivists, and some of them at least are now very wide awake indeed. Over and over again, for instance, we encounter the discussion of the philosophical and scientific status of values. Are they merely matters of personal preference, or do they possess any degree of validity in their own right? Are we really condemned to live in two intellectual worlds of "is" and "ought" that are becoming increasingly estranged from each other? And what of religion? Can this only be an integral part of the way of life of one of these worlds, and merely regarded as an object of scientific examination by the other? If so, what of purpose? By what standards is man to live? Is his life to have any meaning for him, or is he to devote it entirely to the service of one kind of technology or another?

Simple as they may seem, these issues are coming more and more to the fore in the social sciences. Political scientists are split between two camps; the one, with links with philosophy and theology, opposes the other, to which the "naturalists" and positivists belong. From the psychological point of view, "behaviouralists are likely to regard political theorists as pedantic, moralistic, uninterested in and a hindrance to the development of science; political theorists are likely to regard the behaviouralists as philistine".[2] There are many signs that the dichotomy between these opposing attitudes of mind has caused so much concern that a reappraisal of the fundamental assumptions on which they rest has been forced upon many of us. It is in the sociology of religion that the need for this reappraisal is most urgent. If there is to be any sociology of religion at all, otherwise than the merely positivistic interpretations that deny any reality *per se* to religious experiences, it is necessary to deal with the problem of the kind of validity which these experiences have. The same problem arises as in the case of values, but in a much more direct form.

It is true that it was still possible to adopt a somewhat naïvely positivistic epistemology as late as 1959, when Professor Duverger published his *Introduction to the Social Sciences*,[3] but it is perhaps significant that in this case the author found it necessary to introduce substantial qualifications and limitations into his argument. The social sciences may still appear to him, as they have appeared to many others from the eighteenth century onwards, to be based on the resolution of "the primitive confusion which persisted for centuries, of the objective scientific with the moral and metaphysical", and on the notion that "social phenomena have a regular character, and are therefore subject to natural laws more or less analogous to those which govern the physical universe". Nevertheless, he also had to recognize that "values give social phenomena their essential meaning", and that

---

[2] Dwight Waldo, *Political Science in the United States of America*, Unesco, 1956, pp. 35–6.

[3] Maurice Duverger, *Méthodes des sciences sociales*, Presses Universitaires de France; George Allen & Unwin, 1964.

as the social sciences can "assist human emancipation", they have thus a revolutionary character. Although, therefore, systems of values might be, in his opinion, merely "beliefs without objective foundation", he found it necessary to temper the raw positivism which has been so prevalent amongst so many social scientists in the recent past with an awareness that as a matter of fact the world can have no meaning for us without values, and that social realities are changed by the process of understanding them. Facts and values cannot therefore be as sharply separated as the positivists have demanded.[4]

Changes in the direction of thinking in the social sciences, especially in America, have often manifested themselves of late years in a reappraisal of the work of Max Weber. This reappraisal has been easy enough to set in motion, because his ideas have been badly misunderstood; it is high time for some of the more egregious errors concerning them to be put right. For instance, Weber has been thought to be a positivist; his famous assertion that "it can never be the task of an empirical science to provide binding norms and ideals from which directives for immediate practical activity can be derived", and his "insistence on the rigorous distinctions between empirical knowledge and value-judgments" have led some (who have read no further) to suppose that he restricted his definition of "knowledge" to what could be obtained inductively from the study of the phenomena of external reality.[5] "Ever since Max Weber," it has been said, "the dominant

[4] Doubts and difficulties concerning the attempts to reconcile scientific positivism with philosophic humanism have occasioned much discussion in recent years. The dilemma of our times is well expressed in David Easton's *The Political System* (Knopf, 1959), Eric Voegelin's *The New Science of Politics* (University of Chicago Press, 1952), John H. Hallowell's *The Moral Foundation of Democracy* (University of Chicago Press, 1954), Leo Strauss' *Natural Right and History* (University of Chicago Press, 1953), and W. G. Runciman's *Social Science and Political Theory* (Cambridge University Press, 1963). From the psychological point of view, there is much of interest in Gordon W. Allport's *Becoming* (Yale University Press, 1955); a more general examination of the problem from a rather narrow angle is contained in K. R. Popper's *The Poverty of Historicism* (Routledge, 1957).

[5] *Max Weber on the Methodology of the Social Sciences*, E. A. Shils and H. A. Finch, The Free Press, 1949, pp. 49, 52.

position in the social sciences, at least *de jure*, has been *Wertfreiheit*: that science itself must not make value judgements, but confine itself to judgements of fact, since ultimate ends can be only sheer personal preference not subject to rational argument."[6] In other words, there has been a gradual shift away from the position adopted by such social scientists as Charles Booth and Sidney and Beatrice Webb when they sought, as responsible citizens, to achieve an intelligent understanding of individual societies and their specific problems, in order to make it possible to promote the social action in regard to them that their researches justified. The alternative is one which has gradually and imperceptibly come to bind many of their more modern and perhaps less logical successors to "facts" and "facts" alone, and has required them to attempt to formulate general "laws" of human association based on observable data. This is sometimes done by way of invoking Weber's name, but, as will be seen, however, it is more correct to describe it as a move away from Weber's position, rather than an attempt to follow in his footsteps.

In Weber's work, we find not only that the problem of the scientific status of values is posed with the greatest directness, but also that there is a similar directness of approach to the related question of the logical status of the general ideas (especially his "ideal types") which explain the course of events within societies. Weber accepts the common practice to call sociological generalizations "scientific laws", but only in the sense that they are "typical probabilities confirmed by observation . . . that under certain conditions an expected course of social action will occur, which is understandable in terms of the typical motives and

---

[6] Murray N. Rothbard, *The Mantle of Science*, in Shoeck and Wiggins' (ed.) *Scientism and Values*, Van Nostrand, 1950, p. 173. "Most well trained sociologists", writes William L. Kolb, "have transformed Weber's neutrality in science into the positivist position that values are expressions of personal and social preference, and have no ontic status that can be apprehended by reason and intuition. . . . Positivism transforms Weber's attitude of humility before values into one of arrogance." Values, Positivism and Functional Theory, in J. Milton Yinger, *Religion, Society and the Individual*, Macmillan, 1957, pp. 601, 603.

typical subjective intuitions" of those concerned.[7] Although his
appeal to "observation" introduces a positivist element into the
argument, it is "motives" and "subjective intuitions" which are
for him the characteristic data of sociology; on the other hand, the
forging of concepts to make it possible to understand the behaviour
to which they give rise, which is the outcome of sociological
analysis, gave his work a strongly idealist flavour. Fundamentally,
therefore, Weber was neither a positivist nor an idealist, but he
was also each of them in turn, in accordance with the demands of
the social problems he was endeavouring to deal with from time
to time. His basic position, however, required that theory should
take second place to fact, and it was this which dictated his
attitude towards values.[8] Professor Talcott Parsons remarked in
1944 that Weber's sociology, embodying as it did his theory of the
significance of the problems of meaning, could not be "assimilated
to the pattern of science".[9] This conclusion was, of course, an
extrusion of the argument contained in the former's earlier work,
The Structure of Social Action, first published in 1937,[10] and it has
led the way to a consideration of the logical problem which has

[7] *The Theory of Social and Economic Organization*, translated by A. R. Henderson and Talcott Parsons, Wm. Hodge & Co., 1947, p. 98.

[8] It must not be forgotten that the famous editorial policy statements,
published in the *Archiv für Sozialwissenschaften und Sozialpolitik* in 1904 (to which
Weber subscribed with his colleagues), stated that the "express purpose" of the
journal had been "the education of judgment about practical social problems,
and . . . the criticism of practical social policy". No doubt there had been
allegations that the journal had taken an *ex parte* line from time to time, and it
was in this context that it was asserted that "the *Archiv* has firmly adhered . . .
to its intention to be an exclusively scientific journal, and to proceed only with
the methods of scientific research". This made it necessary to discuss whether
the scientific attitude was compatible with an interest in practical social
problems, and this, in turn, led to a more fundamental discussion of the
relationship of values to scientific research. Max Weber on the Methodology of
the Social Sciences, p. 50.

[9] In his paper on The Theoretical Development of the Sociology of Religion,
Journal of the History of Ideas, Vol. V, republished in *Essays in Sociological Theory,
Pure and Applied*, p. 65, and in this volume.

[10] The Free Press. See the argument in the second edition, 1949, especially at
p. 712.

arisen when attempts have been made to widen the scope of the social sciences to include as part of its data the kind of human behaviour which is motivated by either intelligence or conscience. But this attempt has been based on the distinction Weber made between strictly scientific study of human behaviour and other kinds of study, and many sociologists, particularly in the U.S.A., have misinterpreted his purpose; they have treated him as denying the validity of the values influencing social action rather than as affirming it, which is the opposite of what can only be regarded as his fundamental position.

It would be too kind to the authors who have attacked Weber as a positivist to say that they have not read his works with sufficient care. Some of these attacks are so extreme as to lead one to believe that those responsible for them have not read him at all. So far as Weber is concerned, one cannot but agree with Professor Voegelin when he says that "in the work of Max Weber positivism has come to an end", but only in the sense that it was Weber who gave it the *coup de grâce*. It is also true to say that Weber "knew what he wanted, but somehow could not break through to it. He saw the promised land, but was not permitted to enter it".[11] There is a sense, of course, in which Weber's position was very close to positivism, as, for instance, when he defined "sociology" as "a science which attempts the interpretive understanding of social action in order thereby to arrive as a *causal* explanation of its course and effects".[12] But over and over again he reached out towards a means of understanding social phenomena which took into account the fact that the phenomena of social experience are not "given things" as the data of the natural sciences are, but are given their form and content by man's ideas and motives:

[11] *Op. cit.*, p. 22.

[12] *The Theory of Social and Economic Organization*, translated by A. R. Henderson and Talcott Parsons, Wm. Hodge & Co., 1947, p. 80. Author's italics. Weber's attempt to clarify German methodology so far as the impact on it of Kantian idealism was concerned led to a widespread belief in Germany that he was a positivist. Talcott Parsons, *The Structure of Social Action*, p. 591.

"The historical influence of ideas in the development of social life has been and still is so great [he wrote, that it cannot be ignored in any] ordering of empirical reality. . . . The fate of an epoch which has eaten of the tree of knowledge is that it must know that we cannot learn the *meaning* of the world from the results of its analysis, be it ever so perfect; it must rather be in a position to create the meaning itself. It must recognize that general views of life and the universe can never be the result of increasing empirical knowledge, and that the highest ideals, which move us most forcefully, are always formed only in the struggle with other ideals which are just as sacred to others as ours are to us."[13]

Weber's work on the sociology of religion was, indeed, based on the assumption that religion (and the values embodied in any specific religion) was, in itself, an operative cause of social change.[14] This is, in fact, the main underlying theme of *The Protestant Ethic and the Spirit of Capitalism*, which, in itself, established him as having adopted a philosophical position that was far removed from positivism. Weber must therefore be regarded as having begun to open up a path which led towards a much fuller understanding of man's true nature as an intelligent and responsible being. For him, as William L. Kolb has pointed out, "science is only one possible mode of cognition and it is extremely limited in the type of problems that it can solve. . . . Weber's claim that science must be value-free forced a new humility upon those who grasped his argument."[15] This is to approach Weber's work from an entirely different angle from that of the neo-positivist, and may be regarded as establishing a Copernican revolution in its appraisal. It may be agreed that science, narrowly defined, must and can be value-free, but that can be interpreted in at least two ways. In the first place, science is seen as the only way to knowledge; this leads to the positivist position. Secondly, it is possible (and much easier and more logical) to accept

[13] *Methodology*, pp. 54, 57. He "also pointed out that as yet he had done nothing to assess the impact of social and economic conditions on the Reformation", adding "in a whimsical aside, . . . that once he did so his critics would probably accuse him of materialism, as they now accused him of idealism." Reinhard Bendix, *Max Weber, An Intellectual Portrait*, Heinemann, 1960, p. 90.

[14] Cf. Talcott Parsons, Religion as a Source of Creative Innovation, in Yinger, *op. cit.*, pp. 558 ff.

[15] *Loc. cit.*, p. 600.

Weber's position as thus recognizing "that the sphere of science is limited", and that "beyond that sphere there are other modes of knowledge and responsibility. . . . The sociologist can use his reason, intuition, ethical inclinations, and conscience in renouncing the (positivist) position that makes human existence meaningless."[16]

As Weber left the argument, he imposed on the social scientist an obligation to develop a means of understanding our social affairs which would accept a primary responsibility to take individual motivations, values, and purposes into account in our explanations of human conduct. This means that our understanding of human nature will differ from that of the natural order of things. There were, he appears to have thought, two bodies of knowledge, and though there may be no logical distinction between them, the understanding we derive from the one (*Verstehen*) differs from that which we get from the other (*Begreifen*).[17] In order to have any valid sociology at all, we have to start with the "value-free" study of facts, "for their own sake", to use the hackneyed phrase. But we only become sociologists rather than collectors of information about societies when we examine the facts of social behaviour from the point of view of responsibility and purpose. As Dr. Runciman has pointed out, "we must try to behave as though we could be positivists, but . . . this is on condition that we realize that positivistic procedures must be supplemented (or preceded) by a further procedure which is different in kind".[18] A valid sociological generalization can, it is plain, only be made if there is some kind of proof that its subject matter does in fact exist; even more important than this, it must also be shown that it makes sense in terms of its intrinsic meaning. It must embody a statement which is not only true in

[16] *Ibid.*, p. 608.

[17] "In German, *Verstehen* has come to be applied to the situation where a subjective motivational or symbolic reference is involved, while *Begreifen* is employed for the 'external' grasp of uniformities where no such additional evidence is available." Talcott Parsons, *The Structure of Social Action*, p. 584.

[18] *Op. cit.*, p. 13.

terms of fact, but it must also afford an explanation of a state of
affairs or course of events which makes it more comprehensible as
a matter of human concern. It is not what exists that is important,
so much as how it has come to be, and what its human significance
is both for the present and the future.

Weber, therefore, found the essential truth of a sociological
generalization, as such, to arise not so much out of its accordance
with an existent reality as out of its contribution to the understanding of social relations and social purposes. For Professor
Talcott Parsons, however, this is an inadequate analysis of the
problem. For him, "science" is the integration of "bits of knowledge . . . with reference to fairly clear-cut theoretical systems",
the truth or falsehood of which is determined pragmatically by
the test of time.[19] That might make it possible to integrate
Verstehen and *Begreifen* into a single body of knowledge. Though he
only claims for Weber that he had come "near to completely
overcoming the predominant idealist empiricism that then
flourished in Germany", he added that Weber had "definitely
succeeded in vindicating the logical necessity of general concepts
for valid empirical knowledge", thus establishing a *via media*
between positivism and idealism.[20] His argument is, however, open
to the objection that in it truth, as well as value judgements,
become relative; relative, that is, to systems of explanation. It is
impossible not to conclude if that is so that Weber's position is no
less vulnerable than idealism from the positivist point of view.

The problem of the *via media* was encountered by Professor
Parsons, significantly enough, when he sought to bring to a
conclusion his discussion of the contributions of Pareto, Malinowski, Durkheim and Weber to the sociology of religion. His discussion was penetrating, but it seems to have ended in a blind alley.

[19] "It is at least unlikely that such a system should play an important part in
canalizing the thought of a considerable number of intelligent men over a
period of time, if it were not that the propositions of the system involved
empirical references to the phenomena which were real and, within the framework of the conceptual system, on the whole correctly observed", *op. cit.*, p. 16.

[20] *Ibid.*, p. 638.

He thought that any new philosophical synthesis of empirical and non-empirical modes of thought which might be developed to replace "naïvely rationalistic positivism" would have to take account of the distinctions between them, rather than "attempt to reinstate for the scientific level the older positivistic conception of the homogeneity of all human thought and its problems"; if this were done, religion would be explained away rather than understood. "If these distinctions are to be transcended," he went on, "it cannot well be in the form of 'reducing' religious ideas to those of science . . . or vice versa. The broad scientific utility of the distinction is sufficient basis on which to eliminate this as a serious possibility."[21] But, if this is so, and there were nothing more to be said, we have come to the end of the road, logically speaking. Whatever science is or is not in this system of analysis, science and religion embody, after all, different modes of thought, and we are still left asking ourselves how precisely they exist apart from each other, and what supportive contacts can be established between them. This argument seeks to show, however, that religion as well as science exists in its own right for both Professor Parsons and Weber, and that represents an immense stride forward in the twentieth century from the naïve positivism of the nineteenth. It also embodies a revolution of ideas in so far as it asserts that there are very close affinities between the logic of the sciences and of processes of evaluation and judgement.

But it must be asked whether, in advancing from the positivist position, we should abandon it altogether. In doing so, we may find that we have emptied the baby out with the bath water. Positivism has, perhaps, been too lightly discarded by Professor Parsons, though not, it seems, by Weber. The reconciliation between positivism and religion might be established by a retreat on the positivist front, but it must be remembered that positivism itself represented a dramatic advance in human thought. Gordon Allport, for instance, has called attention to the fact that, when psychologists:

[21] Talcott Parsons, *Essays in Sociological Theory, Pure and Applied*, The Free Press, 1949, pp. 63–5.

adopted the methods of the laboratory and clinic and turned their backs upon the altars of religion . . . forsaking the philosopher's armchair . . . their reward came quickly in the accumulation of verifiable facts and in a growing area of agreement with fellow scientists. If the agreement was not perfect it at least surpassed by far the agreements previously reached by religionists and by philosophers. Since the progress and the prestige of psychology depend upon its preserving a strictly scientific orientation, there is no prospect—unless an authoritarian darkness should engulf the world— that the historical separation of inductive psychology from deductive ideology, whether philosophical, political or religious, will end.[22]

The examination of human relationships in accordance with the categories of the natural sciences has undoubtedly introduced an element of objectivity into the discussion of individual and social affairs which it lacked before. It may create the logical problems of the status of the value-systems which are not an integral part of the subject matter of science, but solution must be attempted by way of the advancement of knowledge, not retreat from the line established by Weber, which we should now hold. "To renounce positivism," it has been said, "is not fully to solve the problem. Ethical scepticism, rationalism, pragmatism, and finally positivism were in a large measure the intellectual result of a revolt against authoritarianism in religion and ethics. To agree that their final implication is to deny human freedom is not to deny that in their inception they were designed to make men free." If we were to attempt to resolve our dilemma by asserting the belief that "our own system of value ideas represents an exact perception of the objective value structure of the universe" would be "to return to authoritarian realism and to lose all that the intellectual revolt has gained".[23]

[22] Gordon W. Allport, *The Individual and His Religion*, Constable, 1951, pp. vii–viii.

[23] Kolb, *loc. cit.*, pp. 608–9. The word "free" is, of course, used in two senses in this quotation. The freedom that is denied is freedom from social conditioning; the freedom that is asserted is freedom from political and social domination. The idea of freedom was, moreover, viewed from a third point of view by the "progressive thinkers" of the eighteenth century, such as Condorcet, "the advance of natural knowledge being seen (by them) as freedom from servitude to ignorance, and increasing moral awareness". Charles Vereker, *The Development of Political Theory*, Hutchinson University Library, 1957, p. 186. It was

This has been seen very clearly in recent years in Poland, where there has been strong resistance to the domination of thought by a philosophy that is both doctrinaire and materialist. The issue has been fought out, to some extent at least, in a battle between "socialist realism" and what may be termed sociological realism. The communist government of Poland has attempted to govern the country in accordance with a tightly organized system of preconceived ideas, and has been prepared to use both intimidation and cajolery to attain its ends. It therefore sees things as it wishes to see them, rather than as they are. Sociology has become, in effect, part of a resistance movement, in so far as Marxist–Leninist "totalists" have had "to engage not only Catholic philosophy but also empirical sociology".[24] Since the upheaval of 1956, an important development has been the revival of the great tradition of Polish sociological research, and this, again, has brought to the fore outstanding sociologists such as Professor Stanislaw Ossowski, who has played a leading part in this movement.[25]

Whatever its practical value, however, the claims of so many positivists that scientific study is the only "objective" means of adding to human knowledge cannot be accepted. It is not that such people leave values and religion out of their range of interests; if this were so, the *modus vivendi* of co-existence with those who acknowledge wider responsibilities and possess deeper sympathies might be possible. But the positivists have adopted an aggressive attitude towards their intellectual opponents; their

Condorcet who relied on the analogy of the natural sciences to support his argument that man's intellectual and moral faculties develop according to necessary and constant laws, thus establishing the logical conflict between ideas of necessity and freedom which "remains one of the most challenging questions in social theory" (*ibid.*, p. 159). It is this question that lies at the root of the logical problems discussed in this paper.

[24] *New Society*, 9 April 1964, p. 3.

[25] Professor Ossowski, lately deceased, has stated that the planning activities of the Gomulka government have suffered "from the lack of a serious knowledge of the social reality subject to planning. This last factor has become . . . particularly significant in the countries where sociological surveys are considered useless, and has been replaced by the images suggested by wishful thinking." *Transactions of the Fourth World Congress of Sociology*, p. 202.

theories are combative, and demand a reply. The battle ground has come to be in the field of religion rather than in that of values. It has been said, for instance, that "in modern societies, the sociology of religion was originally developed by opponents of religion. Auguste Comte, Durkheim and their disciples sought more or less to establish that religion is a survival of a primitive mentality".[26] "In its concern with contemporary society," writes Professor Talcott Parsons, there has been a "strong tendency . . . to minimize the importance of religion, to treat it as a matter of 'superstition' which had no place in the enlightened thinking of modern civilized man".[27]

It is only too easy to enlarge on this. "The unseen world," it has been said by a sociologist who shares the positivist point of view, "is of course fictitious. . . . The sharpest conflict between religion and science comes when religion itself is subjected to scientific analysis. Dependent as it is upon subjective faith, religion withers like a leaf before a flame when the scientific attitude is brought to bear on it."[28] It has also been claimed, at the end of an empirical study of a number of religious sects, that "religious adherence generally can be fully understood only in terms of psychological and sociological analysis—by reference to actual psychic, social, and cultural circumstances—and in terms of the functions which religious belief, application, and activity actually fulfil. It is only such a focus—not the mystical quality called 'faith' which theologians tend to invoke—which can help to explain specific allegiance to the diverse movements which may be broadly labelled 'Christian'."[29]

[26] Duverger, *op. cit.*, p. 52. "Social Science has, in the main, avoided the issue (of the social status of religion) by turning its back upon the whole matter on the ground that prevailing religions and their churches are anachronisms." Robert S. Lynd, *Knowledge for What?*, Princeton University Press, 1940, p. 239.

[27] *Essays in Sociological Theory, Pure and Applied*, The Free Press, 1949, p. 53.

[28] Kingsley Davis, *Human Society*, Macmillan, Seventh Printing, 1955, pp. 527, 536.

[29] Bryan R. Wilson, *Sects and Society*, Heinemann, 1961, pp. 353–4. For a valuable discussion of the functionalist attitude to religion, see Kolb, *loc. cit.*, pp. 603–6.

In general, pseudo-scientific "explanations" are often designed to "explain away religion as understood by those who practise it". "While valuable information about religious behaviour and organization can be acquired by sociologists who confine their research to the use of the natural sciences . . . such information will be considered complete only by those who accept psychological behaviourism and a pragmatic philosophy which implies extreme nominalism".[30] To those to whom the practice of religion is a vitally important part of their lives, endeavours of this kind amount to "a manoeuvre to destroy in men's minds the sense of the spiritual, the consciousness of human liberty, and the transcendence of religion".[31] The sociology of religion has, of course, derived much useful material from the use of positivist methods, and this is evident in the work of Professor Le Bras and his followers, though they have not, of course, been exclusively relied on by them.[32] But such work is narrowly limited to the study of religion as a special form of social behaviour, and no attempt is made in it to link together the social and the religious elements in human experience. As has recently been pointed out, it is "when we try to isolate (social) factors or reveal their mode of operation (that) we begin to sense the inadequacy of all sociological 'explanation' of phenomena that in their very nature transcend the sociological". It is, indeed, an empirical fact of which all of us have direct knowledge and experience that men behave morally; every social scientist, whatever his professional views on this matter may be, still pays respect (at least in his personal relations with students, colleagues, and other persons he meets in his academic and private life) to basic values such as individual freedom, truth, honesty and moral responsibility generally.[33]

[30] Fr. Conor K. Ward, *Priests and People*, Liverpool University Press, 1961, pp. 25–6.

[31] A. Lemonnier, quoted, Ward, *op. cit.*, p. 3.

[32] "The behavioural method has had the advantage of introducing objectivity and precision. In this field, the works of Gabriel Le Bras have had a great influence." Duverger, *op. cit.*, p. 52.

[33] See Kolb, *op. cit.*, p. 603.

H

"That a person holds values," writes David Easton, "and that these have consequences for action, are social facts in the same sense as any other part of his activity or convictions."[34] So much the more for sociological explanations which refuse to admit that experience transcends the social.

It is, indeed, difficult to see how the positivist, who (with Durkheim) treats values as "social facts" as arising solely out of the system of organization of any given society, can account for the facts of changes in systems of values. In Professor G. D. H. Cole's view, "what this attitude seems . . . to leave out of account is that changes in value patterns, if they occur, must occur from somewhere, and cannot be derived from the structure of expectations as it exists in the prevailing value pattern". The basic attitude of the positivist is that he endeavours to study social behaviour as if it were something outside the control of the human mind, existing, as it were, outside the range of responsibilities and intentions, controlling people's lives, rather than the subject of control by their understanding. Professor Cole's argument continued as follows:

> I am well aware that one must know the actual in order to know how best to change that in it which needs changing. But I am quite unable to see how there can be any derivation of values from facts alone, or from actual values regarded simply as facts. I want certain things because I believe them to be worth wanting, not because they are actually wanted. I agree that it is vain and utopian to set out in search of imagined goals which no one actually wants or can be induced to want. If I came to believe that all men's actions were simply the outcome of fundamentally irrational drives quite beyond the reach of education or persuasion of any sort I would simply cease to be interested in Sociology or indeed any branch of social study. My interest in these studies rests on a belief that there is in man a rational element which can be extended and improved by proper cultivation, or impaired and debilitated or perverted by means of education, propaganda, or social coercion.[35]

[34] *Op. cit.*, p. 321. "No statement", he adds, "can ever refer exclusively to facts, values, or theories. . . . Every (political) theory is consciously oriented to values", *ibid.*, pp. 310–11.

[35] Sociology and Social Policy, *The British Journal of Sociology*, 1957, pp. 163, 167.

The argument is simple, straightforward, and compelling. The only difficulty in it arises out of man's almost incorrigible desire to achieve omniscience. If one's desire is to understand the nature of the world so as to enable oneself to have one's way with it, *rerum cognoscere causas* would be a good maxim, with the accent on the last word. But this means that the individual who adopts it is arrogating to himself not only omniscience but also omnipotence. It is one of the easiest paths to mental illness to regard oneself as possessing powers of this kind, for one has to separate oneself off from the rest of mankind when one does so. It is only possible, humanly speaking, to seek to understand the lot of one's fellows and to improve upon it if one establishes strict limitations on one's task; it is also wise to refrain from the enjoyment of both the power and the glory which a successful endeavour of this kind might be deemed to entitle one to possess.

It is perhaps because it has not yet proved possible to establish these limitations that social scientists have flinched from the assumption of social responsibility, and in doing so have sought to justify themselves by asserting that they have to maintain a strict neutrality in regard to values; thus, it has been suggested, taking Weber's dictum out of its context and misinterpreting it in the process. In venturing into the field of social policy, therefore, they have sought to find a way of avoiding the assessment of the validity of individual values, *per se*. Professor Harold Lasswell, for instance, has sought to establish the truth of some values, and the falsehood of others, by demonstrating that they are (or are not) the outcome of psychological processes common to humanity at large, though the psychoanalytic processes involved in this inquiry seem to depend on the exercise of judgement and intuition rather than to be akin to more truly scientific analysis and demonstration.[36] David Easton has pointed out in this connection that the extension of political science to include the problems of policy-making has involved the resurrection of an older form of positivism. This is because it is impossible to

[36] The State as a Manifold of Events, in *The Political Writings of Harold D. Lasswell*, The Free Press, 1951, pp. 265–7.

formulate policy otherwise than in terms of values, and the political scientist is inadequately equipped, philosophically, to give an adequate account of their logical status. The best he can do is to try to derive the "ought" from the "is" of personal preference or whim, and to build a model of man on this foundation. "In essence," he writes, "this attempt to remarry science and philosophy through the bond of human nature is symptomatic of the pressure to which social scientists are subjected today to solve the crucial problem of the relation of values. By training, social scientists have refused to pass beyond relativism; by necessity they are seeking to do so."[37] But social scientists do not appear to be making much headway in their approaches to problems of values, even when they seek to do so in an attempt to "understand" them, as Weber or Dilthey would have put it,[38] let alone explain them in accordance with the canons of positivism. They are still prone to try to follow the latter path, despite its logical pitfalls, because they find themselves compelled to reject any alternative way by which objective knowledge can be obtained, directly or indirectly, of values. This, we must accept, involves us in a problem which it is exceedingly hard to solve.[39]

Some light may be thrown upon it, however, if we examine it from the point of view of first principles. It is not Weber but Kant, and behind him Hume, who established in the first instance the logical distinction between statements of fact and statements of

[37] Quoted, Waldo, *op. cit.*, p. 32. "It is clear", David Easton adds, "that in Lasswell there is a recurrence of a historic tendency towards a closed scientific system in which the prospect is held out that all the issues vital to man can be tentatively entertained and, as the occasion permits, answered within the scope of science. The claim is broad and perhaps arrogant and premature, but it has a history in the last three centuries that cannot be ignored." Harold Lasswell, Policy Scientist, in *The Journal of Politics* **12** (1950), 476–7.

[38] Dilthey's version of understanding (or *Verstehen*) was more a matter of empathy or insight, rather than of explanation or analysis. See H. A. Hodges, *Wilhelm Dilthey: an Introduction*, Kegan Paul, 1944, especially pp. 15, 49.

[39] "I must confess that I have not read any major work, or written any myself, which fully satisfies me as really meeting the demands of how properly to deal with facts and valuations in social science." Gunnar Myrdal, Social Theory and Social Policy, *The British Journal of Sociology*, 1953, p. 241.

value. The making of this distinction has since become an ideal that sociologists in general, following their eighteenth-century predecessors, have put before themselves. But the validity of the distinction itself has now been questioned. It has recently been remarked that: "Its insufficiency is generally recognized today; if one severs the factual content of a phenomenon from the values it embodies, one also severs it from reality".[40] It is true that Weber said that: "Verification of subjective interpretation by comparison with the concrete course of events, is, as in the case of all hypotheses, indispensable." But this is more difficult to achieve than the bare assertion implies. "Unfortunately," Weber adds, "this type of verification is feasible with relative accuracy only in the very few special cases susceptible of psychological experimentation. The approach to a satisfactory degree of accuracy is exceedingly various, even in the limited number of cases of mass phenomena which can be statistically described and unambiguously interpreted." For the rest, there remained for Weber the methods of comparative sociology, an instance of their application having been given by him in Gresham's Law. (*The Theory of Economics and Social Organization,* p. 88.)

The truth appears to be that Weber's attempt to find a *via media* which was neither positivist nor idealist was unsuccessful, even if it was highly significant for logical analysis, and a most important event in the history of sociology. This supports the conclusion that a realistic answer to the problem of objectivity in sociology and the social sciences demands that due importance be attached both to the empirical existence and the logical validity of values.

In everyday human experience, fact and value are inseparable if the natural sciences are developed in a watertight compartment, only made for the purpose of explaining something of the nature of inanimate non-human nature, and are regarded as the only "real" or "objective" study of man's social conduct, other studies

<hr>

[40] Professor Edvard Vogt, Über das Problem der Objectivät in der Religionssoziologischen Forschung, in *Probleme der Religionssoziologie,* Westdeutscher Verlag, 1962, p. 215.

being regarded as "illusory" or "irrelevant"; this is against common sense. How far, we have to ask, can the categories of scientific explanation be used to explain phenomena which, because they are human, are certainly not inanimate? It is no good arguing that it is possible to treat them as if this were so, because if one does so they lose their characteristic meaning. To quote David Easton again, "no statement can refer exclusively to facts, values, or theories". In political science, "inquiry into moral theory cannot be assigned to a separate compartment for research. It invariably requires knowledge about the facts of political life."[41]

This argument is all pre-Weber, logically if not chronologically. Let us now try to build on his work rather than retreat from it. To regard man's conduct, the object which the social sciences study, as being conditioned solely by his social environment is to ignore its real nature. It is *also* conditioned by man's intelligence, his understanding of the situations in which he is placed, and his endeavours to transform them by acting within them in accordance with the dictates of his own conscience, or, in other words, in accordance with the moral ideas which his intelligence accepts and transforms into purposive action. We find ourselves, therefore, balancing on a tight-rope intellectually. On the one side, we are prone to fall to destruction into the abyss of materialism, when we endeavour to apply the notion of social determinism to our conduct as a sufficient means of understanding what we do. On the other, we have to beware lest we fall into the other abyss of philosophical idealism, by allowing ourselves to believe that, given sufficient knowledge and determination, we are able to escape social influences entirely, and to shape our lives as we will. Both extremes must be rejected. Human experience is shaped out of a complex system of interaction; on the one hand, between creative activities of the mind exerting their influences upon the material it encounters in the world around it, on the other, the mind is receptive to the influence of this environment which is part and parcel of the individual's life and consciousness. What is

[41] *Op. cit.*, pp. 311, 314.

done to us and how we behave as members of a society, I suggest, can, even in the narrow sense of the term, be examined scientifically; what we do in relation to it is the essence of the study of human action, which is as yet only in its infancy.

This interplay between the positive and negative aspects of social life and behaviour can also be studied in terms of institutions as well as individuals. This is clearly apparent in the sociology of religion. There can be no doubt that churches are influenced by social pressures. They also exert influences themselves. As Joachim Wach has put it:

> Scholars tend to forget that, however far-reaching the influence of social motives on religion has undoubtedly been, the influences emanating from religion and reacting on the social structure have been equally great. A thorough examination of the effects of religion on the social life of mankind and of the influence of religion on the cohesion of groups, on the development and differentiation of social attitudes and patterns, and on the growth and decline of social institutions is likely to yield results of the utmost importance.[42]

When one endeavours to apply this argument to the religious life which one finds in the world around one, one encounters surprisingly few difficulties in doing so. It is obvious that religion, as a social phenomenon, has to be examined from two angles; on the one hand, as a series of social institutions that are part of the complex that constitutes a society; on the other, as a source of ideas and concepts that have an important influence on the structure of the society and on the rate and direction of social change in it. The most recent discussion of religion from the point of view of its nature in itself and in its social aspects is contained in Fr. Ward's *Priests and People*: "An individual", he argues, "is influenced simultaneously by religious and other values, and by social factors. The interaction of these two influences might be said to be of the nature of a dialogue rather than of a dichotomy."

---

[42] *Sociology of Religion*, Kegan Paul, 1947, p. 13. The same author quotes appreciatively A. N. Whitehead's definition of religion (the "art and theory of the internal life of man"), adding Whitehead's comment that he considered this to be "the direct negation of the theory that religion is primarily a social fact", *ibid.*, p. 34.

"Little is known", he continues, "of (this) living dialogue of religious values and influences and social and sociological factors. Some of the knowledge which is lacking on these and other related subjects might be provided by detailed systematic empirical study. The possibility of achieving it in any other way does not appear to be great."[43] The churches must thus be regarded as social institutions which are meeting-places of the empirical and the transcendental; this being so, their nature cannot be fully understood by either sociologist or philosopher alone. It is to the "living dialogue", to use Fr. Ward's phrase, to which we need to turn our attention today if we wish to understand the realities of their lives and problems. Moreover, if we obtain a measure of clarity on this issue, we can also achieve a much better understanding of the nature and value of the contribution the social sciences can make to the comprehending of social realities in general.

"The crucial question", it has been said, "is how far the meaningfulness of social action makes a social science impossible."[44] That is exactly the question that Weber tried to answer when he drew his distinction between *Verstehen* and *Begreifen*. But it seems plain from the foregoing discussion of the sociology of religion that it can be answered in much simpler terms than has been supposed hitherto. This is only so, however, if it can be agreed that there are various kinds of interpretation of human activities that are open to the social scientist, and that the difficulties with which we are confronted do not arise out of the nature of these interpretations, so much as from the establishing of precise limitations that should be set to the use of each of them. As remarked above, Professor Le Bras and many others have shown beyond question that the positivist or sociographic approach to religion is valuable and, indeed, indispensable to the understanding of the place the churches occupy in the social structure. That has, indeed, been fully evident from the time of the publication of the great survey carried out by Charles Booth into religious influences in London,

43 *Ibid.*, pp. 124, 129.

44 Runciman, *op. cit.*, p. 11.

in 1902-3, in which he showed how deep an impression had been made on religious institutions by the structure, particularly the class structure, of the society which contained them.[45] But it is very important to observe that a positivist study of this kind should be regarded only as one type of study, and, as it has no bearing on value judgements, it must be considered to be only a relatively superficial (even if very useful) form of social inquiry.

More important, there is the kind of sociological inquiry that is designed to examine the way in which ideas influence the course of social history, and play a part in the shaping of social institutions. Values are an inseparable part of it. Much attention has been paid to this question under the heading of the sociology of knowledge, and few theoretical problems thus arise in connection with it which remain unexplored. But the study is still in its infancy, and has been allowed to remain there for a very long time. A most impressive beginning was made by Weber, followed by Tawney, in the examination of the impact of Puritan teaching on English economic life, but it has not been developed to anything like the extent which the present state of affairs in sociology demands, and the sociology of religion, in particular, shows signs of becoming engulfed in a rising tide of positivism. Much work needs to be done from the sociological point of view in the amplification of Weber's theories. In writing a brief appreciation of them, Tawney called attention to the fact that Weber's concern was not with the "conduct of Puritan capitalists, but with the doctrines of Puritan divines", and it was to this that he turned his own attention. A consolidation of Tawney's work with that of Weber, together with an extension of the general line of their researches, is therefore called for.[46] It has, for instance,

---

[45] See T. S. and M. B. Simey, *Charles Booth: Social Scientist*, Oxford University Press, 1960, Chapters 7 and 11, and Conclusion.

[46] Max Weber, *The Protestant Ethic and the Spirit of Capitalism*, translated by Talcott Parsons (General Introduction by R. H. Tawney), Allen & Unwin, Sixth Impression, 1962 (first published 1930), p. 10. R. H. Tawney's very important works were closely connected with this, especially *The Acquisitive Society* (first published 1921), *Equality* (first published 1931), and *Religion and the Rise of Capitalism* (first published 1926). The last book, it is of great significance

recently been pointed out by Professor Asa Briggs that nineteenth-century religious developments in England led to strong resistance by the churches against the early excesses of capitalist development. His conclusion is that "Nonconformity, which according to Tawney and Weber had moulded capitalism, became an agency for its destruction. And it was not only at the working-class level, where class and religion were directly related to each other, that subversion began. Nineteenth-century Christian socialism . . . was in frontal opposition to the values . . . of economic individualism,"[47] and here again extensions of earlier work, this time in a new field, are urgently called for.[48]

to note, was based on the Holland Memorial Lectures which Tawney gave in 1922. The terms of the Trust required that the subject of the lectures to be given under it should be "the religion of the Incarnation in its bearing on the social and economic life of man". Tawney was a personal friend of both Archbishop Temple and Bishop Gore, the founder of the Religion and Life Movement.

[47] *The Listener*, 27 February 1964, p. 341. It should be remembered that Professor Halévy, in his *Histoire du Peuple Anglais*, attached the greatest importance to the part which the Methodist movement played in promoting stability and order in England during the Industrial Revolution. See the concluding sentences, pp. 563–4 of Vol. 1, *L'Angleterre in 1815*, Hachette, 1924: "Les hommes qui détiennent le pouvoir politique . . . savent que la constitution politique du pays ne leur donne pas l'autorité nécessaire pour réprimer une insurrection générale. Ils savent que les progrès de la civilisation industrielle aggravent l'instabilité sociale et multiplie les crises. Ils songent à la Révolution française, à la Révolution d'Amérique, et redoutent le 'méthodisme' presque à l'égal du jacobinisme. Plus éclairés, ils sauraient que le méthodisme est le véritable antidote du jacobinisme, et que l'organisation libre des églises est, dans le pays qu'ils gouvernent, le véritable principe d'ordre. 'L'Angleterre est un pays libre': cela veut dire, si l'on va jusqu'au fond des choses, que l'Angleterre est le pays de l'obéissance volontaire, de l'organisation spontanée."

[48] Mention must also be made, in extension of this example, of recent researches carried out in the fields both of the sociology of religion and of the sociology of education by Dr. Joan Brothers. In her recent work, *Church and School* (Liverpool University Press, 1964), she has examined the effect of educational changes on the social and religious life of the pupils concerned, and on the structure of the parish as a social institution. She demonstrates the need to restructure both the parochial and the inter-parochial institutions of the Roman Catholic Church so as to keep them in harmony with changes in the wider society. Her work also shows that, given the necessary institutional support, the religious life of individuals can assume new meaning and content, and that Christian values can play as effective a part in the social life of the present as they have in that of the past.

It is therefore apparent that sociology must accept within its field of investigation, not only those aspects of man's conduct which are socially influenced or determined, but also the converse phenomenon, whereby his theories, values, and beliefs influence the social world in which he lives. The phenomena of social behaviour are of these two kinds, but they are basically homogeneous. It is not in their fundamental nature that they differ, but in the way in which they are understood, and in the degree of certainty that results from the processes that are relied on to understand them.

Social science is not to be regarded as producing results that are entirely true or entirely false. To the extent that man is conditioned by his social environment in varying degree, his conduct can be made the subject of scientific inquiry, the validity of which can be very high at times, but much more low at others. It is only in a relatively small area of human experience that the social scientist can discount the freedom which the exercise of the human understanding and the human will brings with it, in particular because the results of his researches may change conduct in ways which he cannot forecast, when they are brought to the notice of the persons concerned. It is only in matters such as those of demography, over which we as human beings have only relatively small control, that we can speak with any high degree of certainty. And even here those who have sought to predict the movements of population have often gone very badly wrong. There are, therefore, areas within which the development of the social sciences may proceed with the accent on "science". In others, the accent may be on the qualifying adjective "social". The more the situation that is studied is under the influence of the human intelligence, in which I include voluntary purposes and decisions, the less it is possible to arrive at an understanding of it by subjecting it to scientific analysis. To expect that the social sciences will establish hard and fast laws of social interaction and development is to misunderstand their nature. Their purpose is not to predict the inevitable; their task is rather to understand so as to make it possible to control, to avoid the repetition of past errors, to clarify and reshape man's purposes, to create anew something that is more akin to them than what has gone before. "Though all sciences are sciences," it has recently been said, "some will always remain more scientific than others."[49] This is obviously true, and far from rejecting this idea, it is to be welcomed as providing some relief from the pessimistic notion, so prevalent amongst sociologists today, that the spirit of man itself, and the spark of the divine in him, has no part in the shaping of human destiny, and that, the more complex our societies become, the more limited in depth and range will be the individual's freedom to choose what to do with his own life. On the contrary, man must, if he is not to perish, now assume a growing part of the responsibility to master his fate as a social being, and to use to this end the intelligence and the capabilities with which he has been endowed. The social sciences should serve him as guides and as aids when he sets out on his pilgrimage in this direction. His reward will be, not the fruits of his struggle, but the awareness that the struggle itself accords with the ultimate nature of his being.

The Charter of Liberties for the sociologist who wishes to live to some purpose as such in the world of today may therefore be said to have been written by Weber, whose closest affiliation is with those of us who accept responsibility for the identification of the true nature of the problems which endanger our civilization, and for the discovery of the methods that are best suited for understanding, if not also solving, them. We remember, today, the slogan which gave the *Archiv* its objective: the "education of judgment about practical affairs". Weber's triumph was to show how this could be done in accordance with the requirements of relationship, and thus to establish the sociologist's social role in his own society. The sociologist of our own times need do no more than consolidate the position that has already been won for him, but it is even easier to lose what he has got than to preserve it, and there is thus a practical reason why we should pause in the middle of the century and re-examine the heritage Weber has given us.

[49] Runciman, *op. cit.*, p. 21.

Objectivity in Research in the Sociology of Religion[1]

EDVARD VOGT

SCEPTICISM exists in varying degrees. Like Kant, one may doubt the possibility of empirical contact with *das Ding an sich*, the thing in itself, and reduce to mental categories all science which is based on empirical research. Neglecting such subtle questions, others may accept the standard of objectivity achieved by natural sciences as sufficient, and on this basis they may still be sceptical about the objectivity of sociological findings. When the sociologists themselves advance a claim of objectivity for their own science, they may rejoin to these sceptics that standards of objectivity must necessarily vary with the degree of determinism in the subject matter of the science. A sociologist cannot doubt that "social phenomena" represent a specific realm of reality. His science is objective in so far as it mirrors this specificity.

What about religious phenomena? Are they beyond the border line between the realms of reality and the subjective states of mind? Are they beyond the reach of empirical research? Does the information contained in religious statistics relate merely to remote concomitant circumstances and not to realities that have a real, causal relationship to the religious phenomena, themselves— not to mention the religious *noumena*—to religion as such?

However this may be, sociologists of religion express their belief that the interrelationship of religious and social phenomena

[1] A development of a paper presented at the International Colloquium on Sociology of Religion in Oxford (Nuffield College), 24 to 26 March 1961; cf. also a version in French in *Archives* (328), and in the *Kölner Zeitschrift für Soziologie*, Sonderheft 6, 1962.

can be studied objectively in practice, and that some degree of empirical contact may be established with causal determinants of this interrelationship. Frequently this view may derive more from "existential" decisions than from a philosophical solution to the problems raised above. However, the problem will always return whenever the sociologist of religion is confronted with divergent theories put forward by other sociologists of religion. He can never for long escape the fact that the sociologist's method of thinking and his subjective background throw up grave problems affecting the deepest realms of reality and human consciousness.

"VALUE-FREE" SOCIOLOGY

The classical solution to the problem of bias in sociology is the proclamation of the ideal of a *Wertfreie* sociology. Before progress can be made in the search for objective knowledge it is essential that we distinguish between the value content of the phenomena under observation and their factual existence. The former is thought to be imposed on the facts by the sociologist's own ideology or religion.

The inadequacy of this ideal, which stems from Kant's philosophy and was formulated by Max Weber, is now generally recognized: to separate the factual content of a phenomenon from its value content is to separate it from reality. This is particularly true in the case of religious phenomena. By putting himself in a completely disinterested frame of mind with no standard of value to guide his thought and the direction of his research, the sociologist can do no more than record passively an endless series of trivial and insignificant data from the purely phenomenological world. To provide a realistic answer to the problem of objectivity in the sociology of religion we must first recognize the existence of and the need for values both as elements in the subject matter of the discipline and as factors in the activity of the sociologist. Let us consider the problems raised by this last aspect more closely.

DIVIDING FACTORS

The most important of the unchartered and therefore uncontrollable factors in the formation of socio-religious theories are probably the sociologist's mentality, and the elements of his existential situation that have contributed to the make-up of this mentality. It is the sociology of knowledge that studies these background variables of scientific thought. We shall confine ourselves here to considering which of such possible variables may cause differences in the thinking of sociologists and which may have a unifying effect.

To the first group belong the following:

1. The sociologist's personality structure (his temperament, inhibitions, interests, values, faith, morals, etc.), to some extent determined by his current circumstances, as well as by his personal history.

2. His social position (status and role in the family, the community, associations and national society, differences between the structure of his own groups and those of other sociologists).

3. His cultural and more particularly his academic environment, the sociological group to which he adheres (for example, positivist, organicist, psycho-analytical).

4. His socio-religious or socio-ideological position. For sociologists of religion this is the most important factor and it depends in its turn on a number of secular and cultural variables.

   Two fundamental possibilities may be distinguished:

   (a) The sociologist is not committed either directly or indirectly to any one religious or ideological social system. It may be doubted whether any sociologist of religion has ever remained so completely independent.

   (b) The sociologist is committed to a religious or ideological system. In this case there are three interesting alternatives, each with a number of sub-alternatives.

(i) The sociologist is committed to some militant anti-religious system.

(ii) He belongs to an expressly a-religious humanistic system.

(iii) He belongs to an expressly theistic religious system. The differences between the various systems are in their turn important.

Not only the commitment of the sociologist to an ideological system, but also his status within that system will influence his conception of the nature of religion and of the sociology of religion. For example, his approach to sociological questions will differ according to whether he is an appointed official, an ordinary member or a marginal member of the system.

5. An important element in the creation of a particular sociology of religion is the actual motivation context or operational context in which it is set. Where several sociologists have common background variables and even accept the same definition of religion, they will still translate this definition differently in their research and theorizing according to whether they concentrate on the purely theoretical implications of a phenomenon (academic context), the integrating effects of religion (social action context), the spread of religion among those religiously deprived (pastoral context), or the effective organization of religious life (bureaucratic–ecclesiastical context).

Realizing the importance of these variables in their influence on the sociologist of religion, one might easily conclude that this science is wholly immersed in relativism, which would spell its end as a serious science. Instead we should ask ourselves what available means have we with which to surmount these difficulties.

UNIFYING FACTORS

It should be remembered that sociologists of religion do not work in neatly separated, watertight compartments of different sets of values and suppositions. Those personal, social and cultural factors which influence them individually constantly interact. They may cancel each other out and they may to a certain extent be common to all of them. They all have their roots in a common cultural heritage and, likewise, in common basic requirements and experiences. The sociologists are all moulded in the scholastic and scientific traditions and organizations of the West. They all belong to the same international associations, study the same classical scientific works, write for the same public. Each one is raised in the confines of monogamous family life, as a member of similar kinds of social groups, under the same type of bureaucratic control and informed by the same types of mass media. Despite variations in the democratic nature of the political institutions under which they live, certain characteristics remain common to them all. The personal desires and ambitions of the common man (as well as of the sociologist) will probably differ little whether he be in Chicago, Leningrad or Tokyo: happy family life, good living conditions, a modern home, a livelihood, ability to work and appreciation for his efforts.

The importance of these common elements may vary with personality structure and spiritual experience, but we have to recognize the existence of an extensive range of common values—if we have not armed ourselves against such a reorganization by an *a priori* metaphysical denial of any objective connection between the phenomena and their values.

Viewing the position of the sociologist of religion in this light the chances of establishing inter-subjective, if not quite objective, criteria in observation and evaluation appear more favourable. These latter aspects and factors might be called "ecumenical" and those listed earlier "sectarian". Their mutual relations and the possibility of giving greater scope to the ecumenical than to the sectarian aspects should be considered carefully. In other branches of sociology the ecumenical aspects may more easily become predominant.

Where the phenomena under examination are parts of more immediately ecumenical fields, such as law, industry, education, the question is to what extent the ideological and religious phenomena, forming the subject matter of the sociology of religion, are controlled by such ecumenical dimensions. The answer may differ from one phenomenon to another. Even accepting that the very concept of religion may be different when applied within different religions it may well be that some of the phenomena attributable to various kinds of religion have a common value and significance within all the types in question, just as others may change their significance according to their context. This opens up a whole range of possibilities for truly "ecumenical" co-operation between sociologists of varying "sectarian" backgrounds.

SAFEGUARD AGAINST BIAS AT THE LOWER LEVELS OF PROBLEMATICS

One further observation may improve the prospects of fruitful co-operation between sociologists committed to different religions and ideologies, even though the final questions, far from being solved, are not even formulated. The observation is this, that any sociological subject matter, regardless of its value content, can be studied on different planes and that on these different planes the ideological implications will vary widely. These different levels of operation may be described roughly as follows.

1. *Statistical Level*

Here only the quantitative aspects of socio-religious factors are considered. Where they can be identified they represent as it were a pre-sociological level of problematics.

It is just a question of basic material, but frequently this material is the necessary basis for subsequent sociological analysis, and in this way an "ecumenical" co-operation in the "counting-of-heads" points towards subsequent possibilities of co-operation.

Inter-subjective agreement at statistical level becomes always less probable as the facts counted become more interesting sociologically and depend in their identification on the solution of sociological problems, like typologies and significances. So long, however, as even the most elementary bureaucratic "counting-of-heads" remains as rudimentary and fragmentary as it is today, in the field of religious phenomena, there will be a wide range of possibilities for non-problematic "ecumenical" co-operation on the statistical level.

2. *Descriptive Level*

At this level quantitative aspects are dominated by qualitative typological and phenomenological aspects. The descriptive techniques evolved in our scientific tradition are based on common standards of objectivity and verifiability and they should also normally ensure a high degree of inter-subjectivity in the difficult field of sociology of religion. It would be a definite advantage were these standards to be elucidated to a greater degree than is customary in our somewhat naïve monographs. It would be useful if a codification of our standards of descriptive objectivity were reached, which, by extending the common scientific rules, would also meet the greater demands of socio-religious study.

3. *Level of Interrelations*

Here we turn from the phenomenological aspects to the "middle range" theoretical ones. It is, namely, here not just a question of establishing the existence of parallel or interlinked movements of two types of phenomena, but rather of establishing the causal correlation or meaning of such parallels—in other words, of comprehension and interpretation.

Some methods of attempting to solve these problems are objectively more satisfactory than others—for example, the modern multi-factorial analysis as compared with the classical uni-factorial approach. A better method can, however, fail to produce better results when used on the basis of unsound metaphysical suppositions. Generally we find the relationships that we look for, if we are not controlled by something more than general methodology.

For a time it seemed as though a superior method was available through functional analysis, but it is now clear that this approach too may easily become vitiated by sectarian and metaphysical suppositions. When it becomes from a method, an -ism, function-alism leads us back to nominalism and, more specifically, to Kant. Through the metaphysics behind it, certain types of phenomena are arbitrarily claimed as basic, whilst others, equally arbitrarily, are viewed as functionally related and dependent.

A salutary practice has developed in recent years of explaining at the beginning of a monograph its underlying interrelational "model". Such a model does not represent an hypothesis which the rest of the book will set out to prove, but represents the frame-work within which the study and its explanations are placed. Only an indirect verification of the model is possible through a global evaluation of its relevance, but this judgement of relevance will in the last resort depend on a person's philosophical assumptions. A dialectical process may, however, be started through the con-frontation of various models, that may in the end also bring these assumptions into the right focus and on the move towards common denominators.

4. *Systematic Level*

At this level we are concerned with general, long-range theories, with condensed synthesized suppositions, models, observations and theorems. This is the highest level of problematics and we cannot here expect much success with direct ecumenical contact or broad communication between the various schools of thought.

With regard to general theories put forward by researchers whose ideological backgrounds differ from our own, we tend to limit our interest to their methodological, system-building aspects, as well as to their statistical, descriptive and, to some extent, their interrelational results, in so far as these can be extracted from the hold of the alien system and "translated" into our own. Such general theories may also be of indirect significance if they make us aware of our own basic suppositions and challenge us to verify them on an inter-subjective basis.

RESERVATIONS ON THE BIAS-CHECKING EFFECT OF MAKING EXPLICIT OUR SUPPOSITIONS

On the basis of the foregoing consideration of the bias-checking significance of some of the background variables of sociologists themselves and of the varying importance of biases on different planes of sociological problematics, we should now be in a position to assess the utility of the methodological strategy frequently recommended as a solution to the problem of bias: namely, to make explicit the background variables of the sociologist.

A proclamation of an author's assumptions would no doubt serve as a warning against reaching conclusions too rashly, but the problem itself is not thereby solved. Some of the more crude cases of bias may certainly be censured, but these are the cases that would in any case be revealed by closer scientific examination. It is an elementary requirement of membership in the "guild" of sociologists of religion that the general academic standards of formal objectivity are observed. If the sociologist does not accept these standard requirements his own declarations of his ideological background will have limited, or even negative, value. Yet even if he does accept the standards of objectivity, his declarations will carry little weight with his reader, or worse still might tempt him to rash *a priori* acclamation or refusal of the content of the publication. Such self-definitions are superfluous to the practised reader, since he can ascertain the author's suppositions and preliminary conclusions from the type of sociological argument he adopts.

TYPOLOGY OF BASIC POSITIONS

One of the reasons our own self-definitions carry such little weight is that we lack the relevant categories in which to classify our positions. More thought should be given to the problem of typologizing the various basic positions as they affect the sociological work. A typology based on the definition of religion used by the sociologist would be inadequate since it would not be sufficiently etiological; whilst a typology based on the ideological affiliation of the sociologist would run the risk of grouping together sociologists that on other important points are very different. More interesting, though still not wholly satisfactory, would be a typology based on "membership", to the various academic schools of sociology—for example, a le-Play type, Durkheim type, M. Weber type, Le Bras type.

We leave the problem unsettled, in the hope that others will take it up. Only when we succeed in formulating a relevant typology of the many approaches to sociology will we be in a position to assess their significance and their possible convergences and reach a better understanding of the findings of research in the various fields.

Philosophia Ancilla Sociologiae

After raising a number of somewhat negative aspects of the problem of bias in the sociology of religion, our conclusion is that a final solution must be a philosophical one. We must search outside our own discipline for the Archimedean point from which to start bringing order to the present confusion. The fields of philosophy of immediate interest are the philosophy of values and, more particularly, the philosophy of religion. As sociologists of religion it is only here that we will find the ultimate criteria for the significance of religion generally and, in particular, of the various types of religious phenomena.

This view does not imply that the sociology of religion is not an independent scientific discipline. *All* empirical sciences have their sets of philosophical suppositions. The sociology of religion, the most difficult of disciplines, should least of all try to make do with a few elementary philosophical commonplaces in the way more technical disciplines can.

This does not mean that philosophical argument should or could be substituted for research. Scholastic philosophers have adopted a formula which we might well adapt for the sociology of religion. We should make philosophy the handmaid of our discipline, assigning to her certain basic preparatory tasks, so that we may become free to devote ourselves to our own task of empirical research.

PART IV

Types of Research

1. Religious Sociology
2. Institutional Analysis
3. Religion and Society

1. RELIGIOUS SOCIOLOGY

Religious Sociology and Science of Religions

G. Le Bras

Behind this Review,[1] of which this is the first issue, lies a brief history. Its publication offers an opportunity to repay some of the debts which the sociology of religion owes to science. When we recall the birth of this enterprise, the recent contributions from the disciplines sponsoring it and the service we hope to render in exchange, it seems that both the form and content of this preface, dedicated to all who are interested in sacred and secular matters and in their relationship, are laid down for us.

Ever since it was founded by the C.N.R.S.[2] in 1945, the Centre d'Études Sociologiques has incorporated a section for religious sociology, and without interruption the pick of young researchers has met in the various offices of the C.N.R.S. for courses and conferences,[3] until the directors of the Fondation Nationale des Sciences Politiques, with exemplary generosity, made available to us the accommodation which is essential for any form of regular activity.[4]

[1] *Archives de Sociologie des Religions.*

[2] *Centre Nationale de Recherche Scientifique.*

[3] Rue de Montpensier et Boulevard Arago. Despite the goodwill of the C.N.R.S. conditions in the early days were not very comfortable because of the housing crisis.

[4] Our group now occupies premises recently furnished by the Foundation at 30 rue Saint Guillaume, where we shall be pleased to welcome anyone interested in our Review and in our work.

The Sociology of Religions group, encouraged by Henri Desroches and François Isambert, set out to collect and classify the studies which over the years have become widely scattered or gone out of print. Two more volumes were thus added to the collection of books on contemporary sociology.[5]

Immediately afterwards a second project was begun in the preparation of one section of Current Sociology commissioned by U.N.E.S.C.O. For six months references were collected, sorted and classified, and out of a total of 4500 some 900 were selected for publication. None of the references dated back to before 1940, and in fact we had to make our selection from those of the last fifteen years. The results not only exceeded our expectations, but also the slender proportions of the section of the publication allotted to us.[6]

The work of the committee charged with preparing the material revealed three simple facts; firstly, the scattered and fragmentary state of the bibliography, its non-existence almost, since it is not to be found in any one periodical, but has to be extracted in bits and pieces from heterogeneous lists or critical reports.[7] *A fortiori*, there are no records; some idea of congresses, research projects and notices has been given by chance reading or by word of mouth. We are better acquainted with our own early days; the existence of reports, diploma dissertations and doctoral theses which have been unknown because they are only stencilled.[8]

---

[5] *Études de sociologie religieuse*; Vol. 1, *Sociologie de la pratique religieuse dans les compagnes françaises*; Vol. 2, *De la morphologie à la typologie*. Presses Universitaires, Paris, 1955 and 1956.

[6] It is being published at the same time as this issue under the title "Sociologie des Religions" in *La Sociologie contemporaine* 5 (1956) 1, 87 pp. (U.N.E.S.C.O.). It will be referred to throughout these notes as the *Bibliographie*.

[7] *La Bibliographie internationale de l'histoire des religions*, published in Leyden, is an exception. Mention is made in our Bibliographical Bulletin. It gives, with the necessary details, many of the references which appear here in more concise form.

[8] In France, dissertations for the diploma in higher studies in history (Arts Faculties), or history of law (Law Faculties); dissertations at the École Pratique

Our threefold aim is therefore justified—to print or abstract works of merit which the rigours of time have banished to obscurity; to stimulate research, mutual assistance and a mood of inquiry by providing detailed and well-annotated reports; and finally to prepare every session as complete as possible a summary of all newly published books and articles.

Our proposals met with immediate support and encouragement. The editorial board of the Centre d'Études Sociologiques received them kindly.[9] Promises of co-operation came in from England and America.[10] Lastly, the C.N.R.S., always sympathetic to well-timed initiative, agreed to publish this Review which will fulfil so many wishes.[11]

It was immediately apparent that, instead of encroaching on the territory of others, we were providing a useful complement to the established periodicals. *L'Année sociologique* and *Les Cahiers internationaux de sociologie*, which between them embrace all areas of sociology, are only able to devote a comparatively small number of pages to religion and their editors have never planned to adopt any of our three objectives.[12] Our team, however, proposes to continue and to extend its collaboration with these two publications which have made such an outstanding contribution to the development of thought.

des Hautes Études; doctoral theses (Law and Arts). They are almost exclusively concerned with Catholicism. See Emile Poulat's summary of Archives in this issue.

[9] G. Davy (President), G. Friedmann, G. Gurvitch, H. Lévy-Bruhl and myself.

[10] The first came from E. Hughes, editor of the *American Journal of Sociology*, and from J. L. Adams, editor of the *Journal of Religion* and Chairman of the Society for the Scientific Study of Religion.

[11] From the start the enthusiasm of M. Dupouy, director of the C.N.R.S., and M. Lejeune, co-director, matched our own.

[12] *L'Année sociologique*, established by Durkheim, in its section on religious sociology, for which happily we are responsible, publishes abstracts of a number of books. In addition it publishes articles on religious sociology. *Les Cahiers internationaux de sociologie* also devotes a fair amount of space to articles and conference proceedings on the subject. Our review will be merely adding to a literature that already is both rich and vigorous.

We are honoured to follow a tradition strongly maintained by France. The religious sciences are deeply rooted in our soil.[13] At the present time they form the entire programme of one department of the École Pratique des Hautes Études, which has made particularly valuable contributions to the field.[14] The number of publications and libraries continues to grow. Ten learned periodicals, several of which are only recently established, cater for all the disciplines.[15] The one we serve here with this Review has its own tradition, which several schools have whole-heartedly supported, the best known being that headed by Émile Durkheim. We are therefore entering a family and a lineage whose strength will support us.

A glance at other countries makes us better aware of both our dependence and our support. Germany and the United States count among their illustrious dead Max Weber and Ernst Troeltsch, W. Dilthey and Joachim Wach, to name only four.[16] We are glad of the opportunity to co-operate with so many colleagues and to add our Review to the many throughout the world which have set an example of soundly and calmly organized work.[17]

In these preliminary remarks we have hinted at the nature of our Review. It is worth while to offer some definition and

[13] This point is implicitly emphasized in *L'Étude comparée des religions* by P. Pinard de la Boullaye.

[14] The School was founded in 1886 and today has twenty-four directors of study lecturing on the histories and systems of the world's great religions, both living and dead. Their *Annual Calendar* contains an outline of the courses available. Published works of staff and diploma students are housed in the school's library.

[15] *Revue d'histoire des religions*; *Revue des sciences religieuses*; *Année théologique*; *Année canonique*; *Revue de droit canon*; *La Maison-Dieu*; *Revue d'histoire de l'Église de France*; *Revue d'histoire et de philosophie religieuse*; *Recherches de sciences religieuses*; etc.

[16] In *La Sociologie au XXᵉ siècle* (published under the direction of G. Gurvitch). J. Wach gave a rather general list.

[17] In particular *American Journal of Sociology*; *American Sociological Review*; *Archiv für Religionswissenschaft*; *British Journal of Sociology*; *Journal of Religion*; *Kölner Zeitschrift für Soziologie*; *Sociological Review*; etc.

comment in order to avoid the ambiguities which have shackled the human sciences and in particular the religious sciences.

Although most of the founders devoted their research to Catholicism, our aim is to embrace every religion, whether living or dead, ancient or modern. To help us make comparative studies we have sought and obtained assistance from scholars of Islam, of Buddhism and of polytheism.

In our view it is essential to get the co-operation of every science. We find demarcation disputes objectionable. We share much common ground with ethnologists, psychologists and even mathematicians, not only in their particular fields but as part of the panorama of scientific discovery. We do not intend to distinguish between believers and unbelievers. Our review will not serve any one doctrine, either confessional or non-confessional. It will accept responsible reports of any research and any theories, with the sole aim of serving science.

To suppose that sociologists engaged in the study of religions will ever fully agree as to the scope, the aims and the methods of their research would be to display either childish optimism or senile resignation. Modern science is noted for its expanding frontiers, the diversity of the hopes it raises and the constant revision of its methods. All it need do to justify this exuberance is to state an objective. This condition will be realized as soon as a definition can attract sufficient opinion to support it. There will no doubt be a measure of unanimity for a simple formula which states that the sociology of religion sets out to study the structure and way of life of organized groups who find their rule of conduct and their purpose in things sacred.[18] This short sentence reveals three worlds: the communal, with its gatherings of believers; the supernatural, which conceals the hidden powers; and the civic in

[18] It goes without saying that we are not making a radical distinction between life and structure and that we are not disregarding the connections between the sacred (in the sense it is being discussed) and the secular; but we are stressing the importance of measuring vitality. Such a programme is valid for any religion.

which companionship is found.[19] Sociology's main interest is to describe and attempt to explain the composition and unity of the first of these aspects, to measure its strength and weakness, to understand its relations with the other two and the image it forms of them and of itself.

The sociologist is not alone in his undertaking of exploring the mysteries of the supernatural and the earthly city. He works with theologians and liturgists, canonists and jurists to try to understand relationships, images and languages. His task is to distinguish the structures and to measure the vitality of human groups in the light of all the sciences. He does not re-do their work and, if he thinks it necessary, he turns over to them the study of individuals. Every collective and consistent manifestation of religious life is his concern (shared, of course) whether it is centred in an institution or directly expresses the strength (or weakness) of a group.

There is a tendency for philosophers, whose contribution to the birth and development of the sociology of religions has been so important, to form general theories based on an intelligent selection of observations. We for our part have always recommended (and it is fair to say with their full consent) a more precise approach, which may be compared with a pyramid, the base of which is built at the level of the parish or the tribe, of legends and magic. Our readers will forgive us for restating these elementary positions.[20]

Each of the religions must be studied, in time and space, from the Yirkalla groups right up to Christianity. Their overall development as well as local variations must be considered by enlisting the aid of ethnologists and psychologists, historians and geographers, theologians and canonists, and all qualified assistants. For it would be a question of a series of specialized and co-ordinated investigations into beliefs, rites and disciplines,

[19] This tripartition was justified in Vol. 1 (*Prolégomènes*) of *Histoire du droit et des institutions de l'église en occident*, Paris, 1955.

[20] Presented less concisely in *Année sociologique*, 1948–9 (ed. 1952), pp. 287–94.

making a careful distinction (without actually separating them) between structure and experience, in other words between the system and reality.[21]

The sociologist would move cautiously on, content with the humblest jobs—gathering in stories, talking to scholars, reading treatises, interpreting ceremonies; then making factual observations, lists of monuments and records, collecting maps and monographs, and making semeiological and psychological studies of a cross-section of believers.[22] By studying the secular group he would come to understand the position of the religious group within the village or town—its confusion in Islam; its intimacy in Christian countries; its dispersal amongst secularized peoples. The relationship between the two visible worlds and their attraction to the invisible one will lead the sociologist to form a typology, an etiology, a discreet nomology, which when perfected will represent the hypothetical point of our pyramid.

Sceptics will lose heart, the impatient will reject the idea of working to a plan, while the dogmatic will be surprised when their beliefs are upset; is there a single member of this dissonant group who has not encouraged our optimism by his contribution, more valuable than all our programming? Let us remind you of some of the significant advances in the science of religion and the various branches of secular sociology during the past ten years alone.[23]

The history of religions has several times taken stock of itself and this is an excellent opportunity for improvement.[24] Every

[21] A dualistic approach which progresses with civilization. Among ancient peoples myths and rites are actually experienced; among the intellectual élite of Christian peoples the distinction between thought and action, which true believers seek to co-ordinate, is accentuated.

[22] See our preface to the *Bibliographie*.

[23] We have merely selected a few examples and abbreviated the references to books and articles already known to our readers, or else easy to locate (table in the *Bibliographie*).

[24] Mortier-Gorce, coll. *Mana, Christus und die Religionen der Erde*, Brillant-Aigrain.

K

ancient religion and every living religion, whether primitive or
scholarly, tribal or universal, every restless sect, has revealed the
pattern of its development to searching minds,[25] its form of
worship,[26] and sometimes the mystery of its origin.[27] Theology,
liturgy, discipline, each field produces its own critical works,[28]
original chapters and interim reports on development.[29]

Comparison between the religions and between these different
fields is common, suggesting mutual borrowing or independent
and typical solutions of identical problems.[30] The way is therefore
opened up for the general sciences: phenomenology of the myth
or of all religious ceremony;[31] psychology of individuals and of
communities;[32] ethnology, which embraces group life as a whole,

[25] Transformation of devotion in Egypt, with the political regime (Drioton,
Devotion privée, 1949), development of Brahmanism (Renou, *L'Inde classique*,
1949), prehistory of Islam (Philey, *Background of Islam*, 1947; Ryckmans,
Religions arabes préislamiques, 1951), of the Greek religion (Roux, *Argonautes*,
1949), break between magic and religion (Webster, *Magic*, 1942), between the
orthodox and the different sects (Desroche, *Année sociologique*, 1952, ed. 1955).

[26] Schilling's thesis on *Vénus*, 1955.

[27] Dead Sea scrolls.

[28] Numerous suggestions in the *Pontifical romain et les ordines*, edited by
M. Andrieu.

[29] Over the last five years several histories of the liturgy (Righetti) and of
canon law (Feine, Plöchl, Le Bras) have been published or are about to be
published.

[30] Comparative theology: Gardet and Anawati on Islam (*Introduction à la
théologie musulmane*, 1948). A tendency for archeology and liturgy to converge
(Lassus, *Sanctuaires*, 1947).

[31] The dictionaries of Grimal and Lavedan facilitate this work. Studies by
van der Leeuw, Eliade (1951), Hirschmann (1952). Historical examination of
numerous myths (Séchan, *Prométhée*, 1951), which, going right back to the
ancient peoples, might reveal some metaphysical aspect (Griaule, *Dieu d'eau*,
1948). In the *Revue internationale des droits de l'antiquité*, 1955, pp. 39–106, Denise
Cocquerillat gives a remarkable example of concordant institutions: patri-
monial prebends in the temples during the First Babylonian Dynasty (equivalent to ecclesiastical livings). See the bibliography of beliefs and ceremonies
in the *Bibliographie* (pp. 509–27).

[32] M. Leenhardt, *Do Kamo*, 1947. G. Dieterlen, *La Religion Bambara*, 1951.

from personal relationships to hunting rites, from the witches' incantations to the Shaman's trances.[33]

Yet every branch of sociology is growing and sending out offshoots. Urban sociology is thriving on the birth, expansion and reconstruction of towns, whilst belatedly rural sociology is hastening to conduct surveys in the countryside as it becomes depopulated.[34] Work and leisure, language and arts, law and ethics, all that concerns the structure and life of societies is attracting the attention of investigators and theoreticians, often happily of scholars following both vocations.[35]

Let us take another look at the scheme of the three worlds co-ordinated by religion and in so doing point out the progress made in the conclusions drawn by religious sociology and in its research programmes during the past ten years.

Attention has been given to the autonomous structure and life of the largest as well as the smallest religious societies. The trials and undertakings of Christianity and of Islam have provided the basis of an analysis of two world-wide systems in their arrangement and co-ordination, activities and human potential, and elements of spiritual and temporal power.[36] And yet ancient

[33] These four points bring to mind the names of C. Lévi-Strauss, K. Young, J. Aymard and Evelyne Lot-Falck, Contenau, Wagner, Eliade and Griaule. Neither at the beginning nor at the end of these works is there any unanimity as to the meaning of religion, its connection with magic, or even the functions of each of the sciences engaged in studying it.

[34] *Villes et campagnes*, published under the editorship of G. Friedmann, after "Sociology Week 1954", summarizes the problems and their bearing on religion. The works listed in the *Bibliographie de sociologie religieuse*, Nos. 747–90, deal with these more fully.

[35] Need we stress the indirect contribution (knowledge of civilization) or the direct contribution (affiliation with religions) which sociologists working on secular projects have made. G. Dumézil is an example of what linguistics can bring to religious sociology, while the jurist-philosophers encountered the belief in the sacred very early on.

[36] A glance at the *Bibliographie* will confirm this outstanding progress. Judaism and the great Asian religions attract many sociologists, but we too would like the help of historians of living and dead religions. Progress has been made in the sociology of Catholicism in finding criteria of membership (idea of marginality), which should be extended to all religions.

peoples whose customs are being threatened and whose sects are increasing in number rapidly continue to attract countless investigators to their limited field.[37] Common phenomena lead to duplication of research; for example, on the reduction in the numbers of active worshippers; the crisis of authority; comment on the priesthood.[38]

Progress in the study of the relations between religious and lay societies is perhaps more readily apparent. This can be explained by the far more topical and practical nature of this aspect. The religious communities of peoples which have progressed rapidly from fetishism to a civilization ruled by the atom, or even of those who have discovered the atom, either suffer a fatal shock or readapt their systems and activities. Between revolution and reform there is room for every degree of contamination and cult adoption. When new dams cause whole villages to be flooded, when missionaries cross the lost savannahs, and when the sons of cannibals begin to devour Bergson, the animist societies of Islam or Christianity are so greatly shaken by the juxtaposition of factories and farms, of the Koran or the Gospels with Voodoo, of Sorbonne professors with village sorcerers, that it becomes the main object of science to observe these dramatic upheavals.[39]

[37] Those until recently known as primitives, from whom Durkheim and Lévy-Bruhl took their principal themes, continue to provoke observations and reflections which throw light on the relations between religion and magic, mysticism and empiricism. Sects, little churches and utopias provide the main study areas for the sociology of religion. In addition to the *Bibliographie*, see an article by H. D. (Desroche): Sectes, utopies et modes de co-opération in *Année sociologique*, 1952 (ed. 1955).

[38] A general recession recorded by Fr. Naïdendorff, and analysed by Fr. Desqueyrat, Lee and Müller. Theoretical reflections (Congar) and practical reflections (O'Brien) on the priesthood. The contemporary evolution of the concept of submission of the clergy and congregation in Christianity would require more than a single volume. Inner tensions: for Islam, Gibb, *Modern Trends*, 1949; Fernau, *Réveil*, 1953.

[39] Syncretisms have resulted in numerous examples of fruitful contact. See the observations made by R. Bastide in Brazil, Fernandes in Africa, Briggs among the Kmers, Escarpit in Mexico, Lévi-Strauss in a Moy village, and Métraux in the Marbial valley. They assume a union which is only temporarily active, whereas integration of a new culture can cause an insensitive elimination

Even then we have still only considered casual encounters, whereas the essential fact in our time is the variety of contacts between societies of different types and beliefs. Never have such masses of refugees been uprooted and then resettled in Europe and Asia;[40] never have there been so many political disturbances to rock the disciples of Christ, of Mohammed and of Buddha;[41] never have human institutions been subjected to such extensive and corrosive changes;[42] we cannot overemphasize the value of *scientific* research on the effect of migrations, revolutions and social environment.

A religion reaches a critical stage when, rather than inspire the actions of lay society, it submits to them. Yet in this reversal of roles religious society does not lose all its force, since it turns its efforts to reconquest and persuasion. The religious "factor" has been given a place, and quite often a primary place, in recent

of all old religious values. See the papers presented at the 29th International Congress of American Scholars, 1952. The restrained acceptance of the Hutterites is probably an exception. No region currently offers a more exciting field of observation than Black Africa; cf. Islam's encounter with fetishism and Christianity *(Bibliographie,* Nos. 257–64); also P. Alexandre: L'Afrique noire et l'expansion de l'Islam, in *Le Monde Non-Chrétien*, 1955, pp. 315–54; the impact of the oldest forms of civilization with the modern.

[40] Since 1940 the religious consequences of transporting whole populations have been apparent. First of all there was the call-up of all eligible men into the army, then the semi-voluntary departures, followed by compulsory evacuations. The German refugees inspired many pertinent studies, but they were not only too few, but they were too short and came too late. India's separation from Pakistan displaced 14 million people; 7 million Moslems left India for Pakistan, while 7 million non-Moslems left Pakistan for India; a movement of this kind with religion as its cause cannot fail to have religious consequences.

[41] Islam's encounter with Communism has been studied in the U.S.S.R. (Monteil, 1953, and Chambre, 1955) and in Iran (Miller, 1951); that of Catholicism on many occasions in East European countries and more summarily in India. There were several works on the fate of orthodoxy.

[42] Whether considering the family or the factory, the sociology of religion must look beyond the place of worship; its real limits are set by society as a whole. By making a complete study of the structures and life of a people, a town or a village, we can understand the forms and influence of religious societies. In return religions help us to understand the social morphology (castes, confraternities, etc.), which is the subject of many studies which form the core of our science.

studies on politics, on the family, on towns or on rural life;[43] not just in countries such as those of Islam, where the unbelief of some modern generations, the urbanization which is ruinous to religious practices, and the relaxing of discipline are still not sufficient to disrupt the politico-religious society, but even in Western democracies and in peoples' democracies.[44] The growing irreligious attitude, a phenomenon equally of *class* and culture, also attracts our attention; this may take the form of dogmas, cults or ethics, or become a religion of temporal salvation.[45]

All these actions are accompanied by ideals and ideologies which the sociologist analyses just as he does the opinion of a group on its aims. In Christian confessions there has been an increase in the number of programmes and institutions in which the élite express their conception of a society based on evangelical principles.[46] The history of these accounts, skilfully recorded over the past ten years, illustrates the hopes and desires of a religious society professing a doctrine for the way of life.

Less well advanced is the study of communication with the supernatural worlds, which is the objective of every religion. So much light has been thrown on the social nature of giganto-machy,[47] the obsession with supernatural contact in the ancient

---

[43] To consider France alone, the role of Catholics and Protestants (Schram, *Protestantism and Politics in France*, 1954), in our domestic policy forms the subject of numerous monographs and theses, in particular those of François Goguel.

Each state must reckon with its religious societies: Canada (S. D. Clark) as well as Israel (R. Bloch). There is a tendency to exaggerate rather than play down the fact that religious societies have some bearing on international opinions and preferences. Nationalism (Baron, *Modern Nationalism*, 1947) and international groups get some support from religions. And political doctrines are not unrelated to the aspirations of religious societies, whether they are preached by a sectarian party or some form of socialism.

[44] H. Desroche, *Signification du marxisme*, 1949.

[45] Need for a sociology of atheism, recently undertaken.

[46] On social Catholicism in France: Duroselle, Rollet, Hoog; doctrinal statement in M. J. Williams (1950) and J. Villain (1953–4). A variety of tendencies among Protestants.

[47] F. Vian, *La Guerre desgéants*, 1952.

religions of salvation,[48] the concern for unity, manifest in the naturism of "primitives",[49] the anguish of the élite sensitive to the *corpus hermeticum*,[50] the Areopagite's concordance[51] and the eternal torches of propheticism and messianism[52] that, if we could turn ourselves into Greeks or Romans or Bantus, the organization of the Beyond and its contacts with human societies would become fully intelligible to us.

Even the sacred sciences themselves are being investigated by sociologists at the instigation of their own scholars. The liturgy, canon law, ethics and theology, each gains some measure of clarification from the various aspects of a discipline about which until recently they were quite apprehensive.[53]

The myths, rites and practices of all ages offer countless subjects for meditation to those interested in the ideas and feelings and thoughts which obsess human communities of honouring, modifying and at times creating gods.

The permanence of progress in the sociology of religion and the faster pace at which it is being achieved are strengthened by corresponding advances in the methods of research and in subsidiary sciences.

In its early, wholly descriptive phase, while still nothing more than sociography, sociology benefits from improvements in statistics and cartography, in teaching and in ethnography; with a more precise knowledge of numbers, an overall view of distribution and grouping, details of environment and statistics on

[48] F. Cumont, *Lux Perpetua*, 1949.

[49] Observed by O'Reilly among the Polynesians; Leenhardt in Asia and Africa.

[50] Festugière, *Le Dieu cosmique*, 1949.

[51] Roque, *L'Univers dionysien*, 1954.

[52] Neher, *Essence*, 1955.

[53] Let me refer here to my own studies: Liturgie et sociologie (*Mélanges*, Andrieu, 1956); Sociologie religieuse et droit canon (*Année canonique*, 1952). Many of our references show the approximation of moral and dogmatic theology.

customs, it was possible to gain an insight into both religious and secular society. Morphology and psychology of religious communities demonstrate to us their originality at the same time as they appear in the lay world officially described and catalogued.[54]

In the second stage, when it fully deserves its name, sociology attempts to explain the facts which its research has brought to light. Recent contributions from history, ethnology and psychology help it in this direction.

Systems and their interpretation develop with time. Theologies, liturgies, practice and behaviour vary constantly. Studies on these variations do not promote sociology. But without history, how would the sociologist distinguish the essential from the transitory, or even the many ways of regarding the essential? The span from second-century Christianity to that of the twentieth century is too great for an Origenist sociologist to be able to find his bearings in the Christianity of the present day without an hour's bafflement. From the wealth of particular facts accumulated and interpreted by history (the reporter merely arranges them), the sociologist takes precise generalities. While history continues to provide him with well-cut material, he is improving his typology of authority or of sects, of religious and secular powers, of the scheme of their internal or external relationships, and of ceremonies and rites. Why did we refer back to Origen? Studies on Manichaeism and Jansenism by numerous scholars have revived interest in the sociology of dissenting groups.[55]

Over and above this organic view of society we can, through history, obtain an understanding of certain causes; not, that is to say, the causes of a particular event—leave that to the pure historian—but the causes of the appearance and continuance of a type and even more so of a succession of types. The hagiography of Buddhism, Islam or Christianity gradually improves our

[54] Public institutions such as I.N.E.D. and I.N.S.E.E. are not content merely to supply statistical information; they sponsor, and very effectively, surveys on the sociology of religion.

[55] Of my colleagues at the École Pratique des Hautes Études I need only mention Puech and Orcibal.

sociology of sanctity, just as the history of monasteries or, unfortunately too rarely, of lamaseries and zaouias, improves our sociology of the *cœnobium*;[56] and the history of confraternities and institutions improves our sociology of corporate bodies and the cities in which these substitutes for tutelary communities prosper.[57]

But does history satisfy our inner searchings? It discloses immediate causes, processes and events; it reveals that heresy strengthens authority; that excessive luxury leads to asceticism; that a lethargic group of worshippers favours an abundance of fraternities and chapels.[58] Why? The secret, part of which escapes us, lies in the total activities of a group and in their inner selves. Ethnologists must tell us what is no longer a mystery; detailed data, analyses of specific aspects and even glamorous tales of travel can all help him to throw light on an entire civilization;[59] whilst under various guises the psychologists cross the thresholds of the conscious mind, suggesting collective as well as individual opinions and interpretations which are at least suggestive.[60]

A sociology of Roman religion which the abundance of new publications has rendered both possible and desirable would illustrate our purpose, which is to bring all the sciences together (on an equal footing) for the greater benefit of the sociology of

[56] Massignon and Dermenghem for Islam and Festugière and Lavelle for Catholicism reveal the social condition and particularly the criteria of perfection. Essay on the typology of religious orders by K. Francis.

[57] The annual congress of the Society for the History of Ancient Law, at our request, devoted all its meetings in 1954 and 1955 to foundations. In 1954 we had the honour of summing up the papers in the final session and we propose shortly to give our sociological findings. Eberhard F. Brück has already put forward the most obvious in *Über römisches Recht im Rahmen der Kulturgeschichte*, Berlin, 1954.

[58] These are social facts which are recorded gratefully by the sociologist who must then perfect an explanation, formulate a typology and establish constants.

[59] If it is at all possible, may we continue to have more books like *Tristes Tropiques*.

[60] L. Gernet, *Histoire des religions and psychologie*, 1954; Kardiner, etc., *Psychological Frontiers*, 1945; Balandier, *Convergences*, 1948; Mauss, *Sociologie et anthropologie*, 1950.

religion.[61] Doubtless the first centuries would see bloody combats again between Latin brothers, but there would be agreement about the nature of the worship—civic and family, official and authoritative, temporal and formal. Personalism, liberalism and a degree of soteriology are brought to light in funerary epigraphy at the end of the Republic. And so the threefold system of relationships—communal, civic and supernatural—has completely changed. History shows this whilst offering plausible explanations, such as social revolutions and foreign contacts. The signs of change will be classified by archeologists, ethnologists and linguists, while psychology, psychopathy and psychoanalysis will help us to understand the declines, the substitutions and the syncretisms which history adroitly reveals. Structural changes, fluctuations in vitality, find expression in the temples, the religious ornaments, the décor and the customs which express a mode and a level of common existence, and the learned and everyday vocabulary. The sentiment which holds up the whole system and which in turn is fostered by the system also suffers the shock of collective distress, of new images of the world, of the censures or temptations brought into the very heart of the city by Hellenic, oriental or African societies.[62]

Sociology of religions could graciously repay its debts if general sociology and the science of religions were to accept some of the fruits of its labour. By proposing its specific solutions to general problems, it is not urging generalization and extrapolation, but suggesting methods and probabilities.

Already scholars engaged in the study of religions have shown their confidence in it. "Society can provide a complete definition and explanation of the religious factor only through sociology

[61] I am summarizing here a discussion at the École Française in Rome in 1954 on the evolution of religious sentiment in Rome, based on legal authorities.

[62] I stress the lessons to be learned from a psychology of collective anguish in the study of society as a whole. How would our generation, tortured by fears, look on the invasions and massacres of the past as mere subjects from literature? Fromm (1951) and Jones (1951) have given some indications.

which in its turn relies on the data provided by the comparative science of religions; similarly the science of religions can be integrated into the social sciences as a whole only through sociology."[63] This declaration by two of the most highly qualified historians of religious science has been subscribed to by numerous scholars, who, in handing over the results of their research on a particular belief or liturgy, invite the sociologist to continue their fruitful work.[64]

In effect, many of these historians are themselves sociologists whose knowledge of collective behaviour and drives, of the entire life of human groups, of the system of organic, affective relations has enabled them to solve so many apparent enigmas of beliefs, cults and disciplines.

Sociologists of all categories find in our investigations partial answers to their long list of questions. Where better than in the religions can we see the sacrificial uniting of the individual and society for the attainment of personal salvation; the differentiation of status and the specialization of duties for the sake of unity; the constitution of legal or voluntary groups? Reverting to the origins of the human being, where better can we see the very notion of the group and its nature; the co-existence of charisma and authority, and the impassable frontier of the individual? The door to the mystical is closed and the sociologist will explore only the environment. He knows his bounds and his limits, but within his realm the structures—hierarchies and companies—are

[63] Puech and Vignaux giving an account of the Science of Religions in a section of *Sciences socials en France*, 1937.

[64] See P. M. Schuhl, *Essai sur la formation de la pensée grecque*, preface to the second edition, Paris, 1949, and for Catholicism, Mgr. Andrieu, *Les Ordines romani du haut moyen âge, II. Les textes*, Louvain, 1948, pp. xiii–xiv. In the *Revue des sciences religieuses*, 1948, P. Nedoncelle invites the historian of dogmas to follow the social and popular evolution of words (*Prosopon et persona*, pp. 277–99) and L. Bouyer (pp. 313–33) points to a "supernatural sociological creation" in the theology of the mystical body.

These four appeals come only from the University of Strasbourg, but if we were to look further afield we would hear them repeated.

Schöllgen (1953) and, later, Geck discussed the relation between religious sociology and Catholic ethics.

present in the cities and the fields which urban and rural sociology are trying to penetrate.

Ontology, social psychology, in this brief survey we have encountered all the areas of science. Dominating them is epistemology. Religious sociology has no pretensions of erecting an arrogant awning over other branches of sociology—it has no illusions about the nearness of heaven. But embracing all mankind and all gods as it does, its scope is exceptional and its subjects incalculable.

The frontiers between the religious sciences and their lay auxiliaries may be eased, but a well-defined barrier separates this condominium from the applied sciences which exploit it. Impartial investigators are often united, in the interest of pure science, with those engaged on this legitimate exploitation. And the two meet at times beyond the frontiers of pure science. We feel it necessary to point out the distance which separates the pure science of religious sociology and the applied sciences, which are an extension of it. By excluding them from the scope of this Review we are not denying their legitimate existence and the valuable service they perform.

Let us first consider the science of government and administration of religious groups, whether large churches or local communities. Intelligent direction implies an adaptation of religious society to lay society—that is, a methodical knowledge of the structure and the life of the secular world on which to base the administration and methods of the religious world. The Catholic hierarchy is not alone in appreciating this necessity. Other Christian confessions are preoccupied with it,[65] as are Moslems

[65] It is natural for militant Catholics, clerical or lay, to desire a clearly defined apostolate; they are constantly justifying their searching in order to convince or to disarm the sceptics. The same preoccupations are found among Protestants (Leenhardt, Ellul). *Économie et humanisme* (R. P. Lebret), the C.P.M.I. (R. P. Motte), Canon Boulard and J. Labbens produce periodic lists of works completed in France and these help us to follow the progress of very active teams, grouped in a Catholic Centre with its headquarters at 282 rue Saint-Honoré. Every country is today competing to form a pastoral sociology. The first manuals have already appeared (Banning).

who are aware of the blow inflicted on the Five Pillars of Islam by contemporary civilization, and learned Bikkhus concerned for the future of Buddhism. In the Christian world it results in a mound of useful statistics and annotated graphs, whilst other religions merely collect analyses and predictions.

Political science is inclined to regard religious sociology as one of its departments. Do not all states regard religion as a source of support or as a threat? The whole history of Islam is illustrated in this situation which is apparent in Europe where Christianity, formerly a force of unity, is now either the support or the enemy of republics. When religious and lay societies are closely linked, the sociology of religion is at the same time a political sociology. Where they are distinct, as in France today, the object is to reconcile them. Is it not one of the problems of every present-day state to delimit religious society, either to secure its decline as in the peoples' democracies, or its restriction as in Egypt?[66]

It would be necessary to recapitulate on all the chapters on the relations between the two worlds on earth, the religious and the secular, in order to show the benefits which knowledge of religious societies offers to a state—their material resources, their family attitudes, their economic practices.[67]

Political parties, too, take into account the data of religious sociology for their propaganda, whether favourable or hostile, which explains the reservations of the Holy See and of certain Bishops, who are hesitant to use information calculated to encourage or prepare the way for actions harmful to the Church.[68]

[66] A policy of hostility or rivalry—there is no lack of examples both in the past and the present—implies a deep knowledge of religious societies. Many governments have failed in the past through ignorance. Experience may concern a limited section of ecclesiastical power, as, for instance, jurisdiction in Egypt today.

[67] Classic problems of the effect of different religions on the frequency, stability and fertility of marriages; on supplies, trade and distribution of goods. Demographers and economists alike encourage the work of sociologists. The great debate about the role of Protestantism in the growth of capitalism continues.

[68] The hierarchy's reserve in Italy and Belgium turned on the suitability of publishing the findings.

Might I add that even the methods of religious sociology have been adopted for the benefit of pure politics?[69]

The changes in religious societies are not unimportant to the various trade associations which feel the effects. Certainly they can restrict themselves to elementary forecasting, but trade, transport and town planning would welcome a more open outlook.[70]

We have justified our aims by necessity, means and end, but they can only be fully justified by the results.

As mentioned earlier, the first number is divided into three sections. By honouring Joachim Wach we are expressing the affection in which so many of us held this friendly and warm-hearted man and, more especially, our admiration for his work and our respect for his far-reaching method, which at the time of his death he was endeavouring to extend still further.[71] Our last contact with him leaves us assured that he would have been interested in the thesis of a former pupil, Jacques Petit, which many of you requested us to publish because it introduces a method of inquiry since practised many hundreds and thousands of times—an unusual example of the success of a single manuscript from a private library.[72]

Lack of space has forced us to postpone publication of several accounts on the state of religious sociology in different countries. Out of the seven articles offered to us, we have retained only three under the heading "Notes and Documents".

Finally, the vitality of our science will be evident from the lists of French theses and diplomas in religious sociology, the bibliography of recently published books, and the book reviews.

[69] My colleague Ossowski has assured me that they have served to establish criterions of secular discrimination in the regions recovered by Poland.

[70] See the chapter on ecology in *La Sociologie au XXe siècle*.

[71] He spoke of his intention to devote a greater part of his research to history and practice.

[72] F. Isambert consented to the preparation of a shortened edition of the original document.

In subsequent numbers, articles on Buddhism, Islamism and African religions will widen still more our horizon, which we aim to extend to the furthest limits of time and space. All those who believe in the future of religious science for which sociology is like a receptacle, or better still a focal point, will wish to support us in a task whose reward, if deserved, will be the elevation of culture and, God willing, a degree of progress in human wisdom.

Religious Sociology and its Aims

E. Poulat

This article reviews the following books:

Gabriel Le Bras
  Études de sociologie religieuse, Presses universitaires de France, In–8°, Vol. I, 1955, xx–394 pp., Vol. II, 1956, 395–820 pp. (Bibliothèque de Sociologie contemporaine).
  Sociologie des religions, tendances actuelles de la recherche et bibliographie, Paris, Unesco, 1956. In–8°, 87 pp. (*Current Sociology* 5, No. 1).
  Sociologie religieuse, sciences sociales, Preface by Professor G. Le Bras, Introduction by Canon J. Leclerq. Les Éditions Ouvrières—Économic et Humanisme, 1956. In–8°, 270 pp. (Conférence internationale de sociologie religieuse, Actes du IVe Congrès international).

Fernand Boulard
  Premiers Itinéraires en sociologie religieuse, Les Éditions Ouvrières—Économie et Humanisme, 1954. In–8°, 156 pp.

Joachim Wach
  Sociologie de la religion, translated from English by M. Lefèvre. Payot, 1955. In–8°, 367 pp. (Bibliothèque scientifique).
  Archives de sociologie des religions, published by the Groupe de Sociologies des Religions. Éditions du Centre National de la Recherche Scientifique, No. 1, January–June, 1956. In–4°, 228 pp.

It would be excessive to say that religious sociology is currently experiencing a "crisis" analogous to that which modern physics has just recently passed through.[1] And yet, although its founders always have sought for it the status of a positive science, it has only with difficulty succeeded in breaking away from the metaphysics and theologies which wanted it as a subordinate branch. Being a science which relates to man, on the one hand, and

[1] A. Van Gennep's survey of 1920, *L'État actuel du problème totemique,* spoke of the "crisis of totemism".

sacred matters, on the other, it was threatened from both sides. However, its emancipation cannot be considered complete, in so far as it has not acquired an epistemology corresponding to its recent developments. And anyone realizing the need for this must at the same time see the inherent difficulties. This has led, in the general body of work, to a well-advised empiricism, whose fruitfulness stems from its care never to alienate its freedom of research.

Is it because of this that religious sociology often seems to be a hybrid being, even a parasite, which people are a little afraid to have dealings with? The experience of the great periodic sessions organized by the international congresses illustrates this point. The history of religions is scarcely ever concerned with sociology, while sociology, called upon by the multiple aspects of a world in the process of accelerated transformation, attaches hardly any importance to religious phenomena. Should religious sociology therefore insist on being acknowledged, substantiate its claims, and establish itself as a branch of one or the other discipline; or else take advantage of its autonomy to assert its specific character?

This is not all. Its strictly positive bias, before a domain which professes to be irreducible to pure objectivity, is liable to lead it into more serious conflicts. Does it not essentially imply a perpetual violation of the sacred, a consistent scorn for transcendence, which renders it powerless to understand the object it would encompass in its systems of determinism? As soon as it moves a little away from the ground and the traces which religion has left there, the phenomenologists reproach it for its leaden feet, in the name of humanity and conscience, while believers suspect it of sacrilege, in the name of their belief.

And yet religious sociology has a long history behind it, marked with illustrious names. How is one to explain this hesitation, displayed now even more acutely, with regard to its status? In fact, the essential problem is a concern, at several successive levels, with the *limits* of a sociology of religions—its place in the vast field of "religious sciences", the particular ability of its methods to grasp the religious reality of its object, its attitude to the institutionalized religions, which ambivalently reveal and conceal that object.

These questions are not new. The renewed interest in them comes precisely from the extraordinary growth in religious sociology over several decades, along with the other branches of sociology, while the stimulus given originally to the general body of religious sciences has still proved just as effective. This has been demonstrated in several recent publications. In the present article we will refer to the following works: the collective edition of the works of G. Le Bras, a selective bibliographical survey of the last fifteen years, compiled under the auspices of Unesco, a translation of a piece where J. Wach (1898–1955) has left us a synthesis of his life-work,[2] two volumes presenting the most recent results of Catholicism carrying out research on itself, and finally a new French journal, the only one in the world hitherto devoted to the sociology of religions, and whose first issue included an important memorial to Wach. Whether systematically or by inference, the three themes or questions we have just enunciated constantly recur in these works.

I

Research workers cannot be content with a formal definition of religious sociology, since they are well aware of how much the progress of work is always expanding the scope outlined by the pioneers of their discipline. A long way has been travelled since the famous works of Max Weber, E. Troeltsch, W. Sombart, who were stimulated more or less urgently by the problematics of German socialism to attempt vast frescoes on the connection between the evolution of economic structures and that of religious ideas; or since the pioneer work in the religions of primitive peoples, undertaken by the founders of sociology in France, E. Durkheim, L. Lévy-Bruhl, M. Mauss and others.

[2] Mircea Eliade mentioned the original edition, *Critique*, August 1949, pp. 718–20.

G. Le Bras's work, so original in its early stages, but not un-connected with that of these last mentioned, has itself progressed in successive jumps.[3] In 1924, M. Mauss had expressed the wish that greater attention should be paid to the present main religions of humanity. It was seven years later that his profession as a canon lawyer brought G. Le Bras in contact with this wish, which he set himself to satisfy. Living in contact with texts of canon law, he had acquired the conviction that over and above their abstract character he should seek the human reality which it was their role to guide: "there is no history of law fully intelli-gible without sociology". But sociology cannot be contented with an auxiliary role: the religious life of populations was quickly to become a subject for original research, while, in return, the sociological preoccupations of G. Le Bras preserved throughout their development a historical perspective, which not only broadened the field of research, but, through its possibilities for comparison, influenced the actual technique of research.

For about fifteen years, this was confined to religious observ-ance in rural areas of France, both in the present day and at the end of the *Ancien Régime*, involving both field-work and archive research. During the course of the investigation, there emerged with reference to religious observance a fourfold classification (devout, practising, conformist and lapsed); this made it possible in turn to compile in 1947, in collaboration with Canon F. Boulard, a religious map of rural France, where a tripartite division strikingly revealed the state of Catholicism in our rural areas.

As time has passed, this map has been perfected; the supple-mentary material necessary for the inevitable gaps in this vast work has gradually appeared, work which has entailed so much amateur collaboration. But as the work continued, it developed

[3] We will not re-state here what has been so well developed by H. Desroche, Domaines et méthodes de la sociologie religieuse dans l'oeuvre de G. Le Bras, *Revue d'histoire et de philosophie religieuses* (Strasbourg), 1954, No. 2, 128–58; and by F. A. Isambert, Développements et dépassement de l'étude de la pratique religieuse chez Gabriel Le Bras, *Cahiers internationaux de sociologie* **20** (July 1956), 149–69.

on new lines: there was the sociology of urban religious practice, which first of all required the invention and application of new techniques in order to give a valid approach to great anonymous masses (in this field, the way has been opened up by J. Petit, whose dissertation, hitherto non-edited, appeared in *Archives de sociologie des religions*); also the extension of research into the religious history of the French people; an attempt to assess, rather than the actual observance, the religious vitality of practising Catholics, through numerous indications of a more subtle nature; and, finally, there was the transition from French Catholicism to world Catholicism in general, and then from a sociology of Catholicism to a sociology of religions, for which was suggested in 1953 a wide-ranging and versatile questionnaire.

To define the limits and framework of such a diffuse field, one could only proceed empirically, though rationally something much more systematic was required. The provisional reconciliation of these two contradictory demands have been achieved through a procedure benefiting from experimentation: avoiding the difficulty of a general sociological theory of religion, the bibliographical survey compiled for Unesco by the Groupe de Sociologie des Religions (C.N.R.S.) has simply tried to assemble and classify the main world literature in this field in the course of the last fifteen years. The work could only be done by constantly bringing a relatively *a priori* attitude to bear on material that is necessarily formless. Naturally the survey is incomplete: not only by virtue of limited space, which confined it strictly to 891 titles out of the 4000 collected, but also of difficulties of information concerning certain countries, religions or periods. Such as it is, however, it offers a sufficiently comprehensive documentation for showing the principal fields.

There were two possible perspectives here: the one more empirical, referring to the main sociological lines of approach generally followed by research workers, without concern for homogeneity; or the other, concerned with the different levels of the research itself, at risk of doing violence to the whole work. In this case, they kept to the first perspective: general problems (particularly considerations of the methods employed and of the connection with related disciplines); a comprehensive outline of religions (by confessional classification, geographical distribution and inter-confessional relations), bringing out the problems relevant to each group; an internal analysis of religious communities (the morphology of groups, collective manifestations, religious evolution and vitality); the connections of the latter with the surrounding milieu (the multiple functions of society as a whole, its social differentiations and age levels).

This outline shows clearly the current state of research. The detailed headings, and the number of titles in each, indicate the dominant preoccupations, and their great variety, but also the sections omitted. In consequence, the levels of elaboration have been somewhat blurred; it is difficult to distinguish the successive stages of this pyramid which graduates from the statistical and descriptive research, currently so much in use, to the project of a general typology and etiology of religious facts, returning by the original paths to the ambition of a comparative history of religions, only to move beyond it.

As the price, moreover, of G. Le Bras's originally unhoped-for success, religious sociology has come, in one section of its opinion, to be identified with a simple sociography of religious practice within Catholicism. This unwarranted limitation not only betrays the efforts and work of the above mentioned, who, when renewing the methods of his masters and predecessors, never forgot either the tradition he had inherited, or the fruitfulness of the angle he had adopted, or the extent of the new ground to be broken; it also ignores the importance of the work undertaken in the most varied spheres, if only just recently in France, such as Africa, French Protestantism, Islam, the Far East, sects of Christian origin, classical antiquity, Jansenism, or even the less urgent problems of Catholicism.[4]

---

[4] The list is interminable. We will confine ourselves to the following references: E. G. Léonard, *Le Protestant français*, P.U.F., 1953; G. Balandier, *Sociologie actuelle de l'Afrique noire*, P.U.F., 1955; J. Berque, *Recherches sur les structures sociales du haut atlas occidental*, P.U.F., 1954; H. Desroche, *Les Shakers*

A number of these works, however, are only of a more or less directly sociological inspiration. In our opinion, this represents a regrettable shortcoming. On the other hand, it shows that the problems of the barriers between religious sociology and the neighbouring sciences should not present any difficulty, and that elucidatory theories are not a necessary preliminary. It is normal, even fruitful, for specialists of different training and disciplines to find themselves on common ground; research cannot fail to be stimulated by it. Sociology is based on precise factual knowledge: it relies, when necessary, on the research of historians and philologists, whose patient methods are alone capable of reproducing the features of past centuries and extinct civilizations; it does not try to replace this work; one man can be at the same time a sociologist and a canon lawyer: the one cannot act as a substitute for the other. Both G. Le Bras, long ago, and G. Gurvitch, more recently, have indicated what sociology expects from history: besides the work of the former, one could mention that of L. Febvre, or of E. G. Léonard. In other fields there is the work of geographers like Max Sorre or P. Deffontaines, or of ethnologists like G. Balandier.

II

There are, however, difficulties. They are not always attributable to prejudices or susceptibilities. The principal one lies in what one might call a *landslide* in connection with the methods introduced by G. Le Bras. In order to carry out the considerable research on religious practice in France, it was necessary to call upon numerous collaborators whose everyday professions belonged neither in the academic sphere nor in that of canon

américains, Ed. de Minuit, 1954; L. Goldmann, *Le Dieu caché*, Paris, Gallimard, 1955; Jacques Gernet, *Les Aspects économiques du Bouddhisme dans la société chinoise du Ve au Xe siècle*, Saïgon, 1956; H. Jeanmaire, *Dionysos, histoire du culte de Bacchus*, Payot, 1951; Robert Schilling, *La Religion romaine de Vénus, depuis les origines jusqu'au temps d'Auguste*, E. de Boccard, 1953; P. Droulers, *Action pastorale et problèmes sociaux sous la Monarchie de Juillet, chez Mgr. d'Astros*, Vrin, 1954.

law, and yet were involved with them in several ways. To obtain a scientific comparison between the two planes of reality, and bring the canon law texts to life, G. Le Bras turned to the members of the clergy, who, by virtue of their profession, possessed the experience and information he needed. The effect of his appeal was firstly to make them aware that they only knew their parish or diocese on the empirical level; and secondly that it was to their advantage to follow a more strictly methodical investigation.

But a collaborator is far from being a disciple. This is not surprising, nor indeed is it undesirable. G. Le Bras wanted specifically to widen the traditional field of religious sociology. This was not in fact what interested the new helpers, who, remaining within the limits of the field which was familiar to them, and in which a professional sociologist had declared his interest, were concerned with utilizing methods capable of raising the level of their activity. At the 4th International Conference of Religious Sociology at La Tourette (Rhône), it was declared that "Religious sociology should be at the service of the Church, in other words, the Apostolate", while, at a similar national congress in Italy, Cardinal Lercaro saw it as an "instrument of government".

In his preface to F. Boulard's *Premiers itinéraires en sociologie religieuse*, G. Le Bras opportunely reminded us that "one of the conditions of our success is that we should in no way confuse the spheres of science and of pastoral activity". Hence a tension between "the academics enamoured of method, and the apostles enamoured of action", or, in current terminology, between *pure* sociology and *pastoral* sociology.

This situation has certain consequences. In the first place, it is not only in their formal aims and initial purpose that these two "sociologies" differ, but also in the tasks they set themselves. The ambition of pure sociology is to develop, on a wider and wider basis of religious data, an ever greater degree of generality, if it is true that there is no science that is not general. For its part, by an apparent paradox, pastoral sociology tends to sidestep specifically religious phenomena, "religio-graphical research", or at least to reserve only a secondary place for them, in order to turn itself into a bureau of social studies and technical equipment, at the service of various ecclesiastical requirements. This is, at any rate, the direction taken in Holland by the Catholic Institute of Social–Ecclesiastical Research run by Professor Zeegers, who is at the moment trying to spread the network of his subsidiary branches over the whole world.

The secular world open to influence has thus become more interesting for pastoral sociology than for the religious body charged with its care. The example of Holland is certainly a border-line case (at the opposite end of the scale, there is France, and, in between, a wide network which is worth serious attention —the work of Fichter in the U.S.A. occupies an original position in this field). This case is not accidental: it arises from an inevitable duality, to which insufficient consideration has been given. If the religious community agrees to being the object of investigation, it does so rather from self-defence, against a situation which is especially perceptible in France. Surely there was, in fact, a danger that, under the pretext of developing its self-knowledge, the Church would ignore its fundamental work as an agent of transformation, and be tempted to question its own self-awareness, or, still worse, compromise its essential transcendence, accessible to faith alone?

So one cannot simply oppose or confuse these two elements— academic and confessional—in the sociology of Catholicism. One can no longer see the distinction as between an objective science and its applied forms, or as one inquiry orientated to the universal and one nearer to the concrete. In actual fact, there is no more pastoral sociology than pure: there is simply pastoral, on the one hand, well or badly informed, but mistress in its own domain, which emphasizes theology; and a sociology, on the other, which operates freely and positively, defining itself as it develops, accessible and available for all; while between pastors and research workers (neither excluding the other) there is developing a body of consultant sociologists, whose activity unfolds, as in other similar bodies, on the level of practical application. The disinterested character of sociology does not detract from its usefulness, and this usefulness does not imply any ancillary link. The discussion will therefore benefit here by dispensing with the theoretical and practical conclusions drawn from the results of a scientific approach, or the motivations which quite legitimately stimulate individual or collective research, in fact postulates of all kinds, declared or implicit, which support working hypotheses.

III

The debate is not exhausted here. Sociology is also called to order for its claims to self-sufficiency. In other words, can the essential nature of the Church and, more generally, of the "religious element", however one labels it, be the object of scientific understanding? If so, is sociology a medium adapted to this understanding?

For Durkheim and Lévy-Bruhl, the answer to these questions caused no doubt, and it was their partial but incontestable influence which caused the suspicion of sociology, current for a long time and still prevalent, among believers;[5] they failed to dissociate sociology, as a method, from the "sociologism" of its founders. The attitude of the many Catholics and Protestants who are working on it or show an interest in it manifests a positive reaction, but it always has an element of reserve, a limiting clause. G. Le Bras wrote: "The believer quite naturally objects to sociology interfering with the supernatural." Father Pin declared: "the universal Church cannot be a subject for sociology". According to R. Mehl, "Sociology can study Christianity, the *Corpus Christianum*, but the Church, the *Corpus Christi*,

[5] Recent foreign works, introductory to the sociology of Catholicism, nearly always have a section devoted to refuting objections, current among their readers, to religious sociology; such objections claim that it will destroy the supernatural character of Catholicism, naturalize the Apostolate, lead to determinism, depart from the concrete, act on the side of the enemy. . . . See, for example, Don Aldo Leoni, *Sociologia religiosa e Azione pastorale*, Rome, 1955.

will always elude it: in other words, the Church is only accessible to it insofar as it ceases to be the Church."

Such statements come from a justifiable anxiety for reciprocal autonomies, visibly seeking to reassure rather than to explain. They are made by those who nonetheless accept the situation. Basically, they express the conception of the tasks and problems which occupy these people; the implications of such statements remain empirical.

From this angle, G. Le Bras's work has a characteristic which seems never to have been emphasized. J. Wach stated: "Historically, religious sociology, like sociology in general, rises both from the awakening of social awareness with the arrival of large-scale industrialization in the West, and from the inability of official or academic philosophy and theology to explain this transformation." The sociology of religion was therefore first initiated and developed in lay circles, then among the different confessions, who felt threatened by the implied examination of the *religious element* in its historical expression and social conditioning, and, beyond this, of its more profound nature. However, G. Le Bras seems to display a complete immunity with regard to this general phenomenon, which has gained him so wide a readership for his studies. His efforts did not initially arise at the meeting-point of two worlds in conflict, but from within a world ruled by texts which he wished to bring back to life. His journey led him from the canon law regulation of the religious element to its human basis, and the further he went, the more he marvelled at the unexpected wealth of this humanization.

For him, as a sociologist, the religious element has therefore a sort of noumenal reality which does not concern him: that is, in his eyes the *constant* factor and science are concerned only with the *changeable*, in other words, all that indicates the *vitality* of a religious group. This is the master-word, a dynamic outline, rather than an elaborated concept, but unequivocal nonetheless. The sociologist does not here borrow his norms and values from the theologian; inversely, if he does not oppose social vitality and religious vitality, nonetheless he does not confuse temporal achievement with religious authenticity. Vitality does not differ from practice as the qualitative from the enumerative. The introduction of this more general category corresponds perhaps less to an idea of intensity than of organicism: it raises research, methodologically speaking, from a swarm of facts and figures to the dynamic structure which is the source of all these manifestations which need exhaustive study.

But the *changeable* is always defined empirically. Nobody knows its limits *a priori*. But certain theological principles, set up like the angel on the threshold of the Forbidden Land, are intended to establish an inverse procedure. One comes up against, not the opinion that a reality is eluding you, but a taboo which will not admit of discussion, and whose import remains in any case very imprecise. The very reasons for its existence are variable: sometimes a prudent desire to "black out", where the invocation of the supernatural serves as a sort of diplomatic bag, sometimes a more understandable fear of being the object of a learned incomprehension. G. Le Bras finally took up an intermediate position, between those who reduce religion to a mere product of society and those who refuse society the right to come too close to religion: he stops short of potential disputes, while at the same time seeming to open the way to moving beyond the concern with religious externals, of which his sociology of religious observance has been accused. But, opposed to the phenomenological conception of an essence which becomes degraded through historical documentation, he constantly puts forward the religious element as a potential source of unfailing sustenance of human activity.

It is difficult to elaborate this position further in the absence of authorized texts. However, it would seem by an inverse evolution to have gradually approached that of J. Wach. The latter, starting from theology and phenomenology, always preoccupied with "the original meaning of religious phenomena", came progressively to consider sociology indispensable. The concern to interpret religious experience sympathetically seemed to him in the end inseparable from the study of the infinitely varied relations between societies and religions.

From his early training, Wach had acquired a *hermeneutic* approach. Religion seemed to him an inexhaustible creative force, the matrix of all values. He praised his masters for having: "refused to allow their personal metaphysics to interfere", and denounced the illusions of those who "imagine that their studies can reveal for them the nature and essence of religion in itself". Even scientific objectivity seemed to him to impose an insuperable distinction between actual religious experience and its varying historical expressions: a middle way between those for whom to know one religion is to know them all, and those who identify the object of religion with the religious subject, be it individual or society.

Such a conception gives scope for research, and justifies the transition from phenomenology to a sociology which is no more hostile to phenomenology than the latter itself is to theology. The sociology of religion is a descriptive science, considering all religious manifestations, without jurisdictional powers: it can fulfil its role without danger of usurping anyone else's. The supernatural of the theologians is not the same as that of the sociologists and the phenomenologists. The latter will never come in contact with it, any more than a surgeon ever finds a soul on the end of his scalpel. The religious sphere does not have to be protected from sociological interpretation or understanding: both are secondary, reflexive operations, and their analyses of mechanisms and significance refer to its consistent forms of expression. What either one defends, often bitterly, is the significance it attributes to these forms in terms of the propositions they express. For man, the religious element is, by definition, one of participation and communion. In this respect, though differently situated, theology is no better than sociology or phenomenology: none of these approaches leaves the plane of conceptual mediation, always short of actual experience.

Because of this, J. Wach came to teach two theses often held to be irreconcilable: on the one hand, although there is, for example,

a Catholic and a Marxist philosophy of society, there can only be
one religious sociology; but, on the other hand, there is no
reason why the sociological apprehension of the origins and
different aspects of a religious group should shake the steadfast-
ness of its members' faith. There are two methods necessary
here: firstly, one must pay great attention to the way the group
in question interprets itself, without prematurely introducing
value judgements into the description; and simultaneously one
must specify the validity of expressions of religious experience.
The functional connections to be discerned between the teachings
of an Isaiah or a Luther and their social substructure in no way
detracts from their value. The analysis of these conditioning
factors can help in classifying a religious conviction more clearly,
but it cannot establish its general validity: it has no way of
bridging the gap between the ultimate nature of its object, real
or illusory, and the relative aspects with which it is involved by
vocation. The participation required of the sociologist in fulfilling his task is never of the same kind as the religious participation which gives the faithful their internal unity.

According to Wach, the acceptance of this relativity, imposed
by the entire development of religious sciences over a century, is
the first condition for preserving the absolute in faith. If religions
in *general* are to be explained by the differences in societies,
religions in *themselves* can only be explained by *religion*. After a
series of attempts at syncretism, whose juxtapositions only bring
more confusion, there was a period of ecumenicism, with its
concern tirelessly to restore the multiple forms, which it records,
to the original inspiration they represent.

Wach believed he had thus assured the reciprocal autonomy
of a positive sociology and its delicate object of research. It might
be said that, in fact, he stops halfway in this attempt, prisoner of
a personal theology which holds him back on the path of a
rigorous, epistemological consideration. Fearing any value
judgement which would falsify objective description, he still
terms an *impasse* any path he does not wish to follow. Rejecting
both an "excessive spiritualization" of history and a "superficial

materialism", he takes from materialism what saves him from being *excessively* spiritualistic, and condemns in it what prevents him, as he thinks, being spiritualistic at all; but this is still on the basis of general and empirical statements, which govern the research, instead of being tested and more clearly defined by it. In this way, he re-covers the phenomenon of religion with the protective cloak of his irreducible originality, at the very moment when one might have hoped for him to develop his own understanding of that originality. But could he do this, if he did not snatch at the moment in time? History is a river flowing away: Wach works on the actual river, but in order to extract, bit by bit, the materials necessary for his classifications.

So the reconciliation he wanted to achieve, between disciplines that had been hostile too long, was only realized by introducing their conflict into his own work. Religious sociology, the study of religions, seemed to him to be perpetually drawn between the study of religion and the study of society. He saw the only outcome of this dualism as being in the association of their methods, attempting to "combine a sympathetic insight into the meaning of religious experiences different from ours in time and space, with a critical understanding of their relation to life and contemporary problems". In fact, the two approaches occupying his mind co-existed without being theoretically united successfully. H. Desroche clearly demonstrated the hesitation one can perceive in his manner of expression, where two groups of terms overlap: "The first series presents the religious fact as the *example, illustration, concrete representation*, etc., of an abstract type previously described. The second series presents this fact—which might be the same—as the *reflection, product, effect* of a host of conditioning factors or of a social–historical situation."[6]

Have we arrived at a Gordian knot? Wach drew the first series from what he termed, in a narrow sense, the "sociology of religion", and he thought to refer to the social sciences when using the second. His eminently religious outlook, which made him see in religion "the sovereign force for social integration" and admire

[6] *Archives de Sociologie des Religions*, Vol. I, p. 56.

its "prodigious power of fomentation", also veiled from him the depth of the conflict he wanted to avoid by this division. Does religion influence society? Does society influence religion? The very formulation of this problem means one cannot solve it by isolating each one in itself; a comprehensive formulation of it means accepting the conflict between man and angel. J. Wach by-passed it, thinking to solve it by the loftiness of his approach. He could not escape it completely.

Who in fact could? It must be stated that the possibility of such a synthesis, its conditions and limits, remain the secret problem to be easily discerned at the heart of much current research. In spite of extreme resistance, religious sociology has won its case: nobody is surprised any more at seeing religion studied as a mode of social existence. It commands attention by the seriousness of its studies, and perhaps also by the fact that these last are concerned with the more external aspects of the great religions. Its tasks are hard; it must extend its research to all religions, explore more deeply the aggregate of their forms of expression, and simultaneously carry out an epistemological investigation of each of their claims. For this, it must have a sincere respect for its object of research, and abstain from any false complacency.

The Role of Reference Groups in the Integration of Religious Attitudes

H. CARRIER, S.J.

PRESENTATION OF THE PROBLEM

In reviewing recent progress in studies in the sociology of religion, there is one result in particular which stands out as especially significant and promising. This is the new sense of direction among researchers themselves. They share a common desire to progress towards an appreciation of the psycho-social significance of religious facts instead of mere sociographic description of them. Beyond simply enumerating the religious groups and analysing socio-religious structures, they are trying to probe the mentality and the psychology of participants (or non-participants). M. Gabriel Le Bras was surely speaking for a large number of sociologists when he stated recently: "Research in depth begins with psychology. The soul of the masses can be penetrated through psychology, and such, to my mind, is the ultimate aim of all sociology."[1]

From all quarters the same plea is heard. Religious officials and researchers alike are seeking to "penetrate the soul" of religious groups and are striving to gain a better understanding of collective mentalities and religious attitudes. Studies in this direction, particularly since the last war, have multiplied and a new interdisciplinary approach, which might be termed a

[1] G. Le Bras, La Sociologie religieuse parmi les sciences humaines, *Recherches et débats* **25** (Dec. 1958), 11–25.

psycho-sociology of religion, is currently developing. Briefly, the psycho-sociology of religion is the study of social frameworks as they affect religious behaviour. We have now provided a summary definition of the new approach and have suggested the place of this paper in relation to current work.

The theme "religion and social integration" raises numerous problems, of which we feel the two most obvious to be the following. Firstly, to what extent in a given milieu does a religious fact constitute an element of cohesion and social integration? Religion is here taken to be an integrating factor. Studies such as those of Wach and Yinger have investigated these problems and shown how the religions of mankind have brought to society either the benefits of cohesion and unanimity, or the torments of discord and tension. In this first case, in other words, it is the social consequences of religion which are under consideration. But our present approach is quite different.

We are mainly concerned with a second type of phenomenon. Instead of working from religion itself, we shall work from social integration. Instead of saying "religion and social integration", we shall say "social integration and religion". Our question is this: to what extent are our spiritual attitudes influenced by the groups (religious or secular) to which we are attached?

Immediately we have some idea of the serious problems to which this general question gives rise. What, for example, is the influence of the family group and the primary group on the formation of religious feeling? What part does school play in a child's spiritual education? To what form of behaviour is an individual prompted by his membership in a particular Catholic Action Group? What attitude develops from affiliation to a certain political, or professional, group?

This paper will not aim to answer all such questions. That can be left to empirical research. It is rather our intention to suggest an analytic model, or a scheme of analysis, which will allow the type of problems mentioned above to be realized and studied systematically. The line of research we propose was suggested to us by a methodical survey of current literature on the psycho-sociology of religion.[2]

First of all we wish to make it clear that our analysis is outside the scope of the discussions raised by the old sociological and psychological theories on "the origin" of collective religious sentiments. More and more researchers have come to realize that these are "false problems" and that the desire of early authors to find religious origins by sociological means and by starting with collective phenomena is an illusion and a trap, as Gernet recalled.[3]

If then we reject, as most objective sociologists do, the so-called "explanations" (socio-cultural, socio-economic, psycho-analytic) of religious sentiment, and assume as an element of intelligence in the religious life the absolute primacy of faith, we will then ask ourselves how the sociologist can observe the phenomena of the collective psychology of religion, how he can analyse the mentality and the singular spiritual behaviour of a given group.

The answer which we suggest is drawn essentially from two fundamental chapters of psycho-sociology—that introducing us to analysis of "collective attitudes" and that dealing with "reference groups". These two subjects are closely connected, as we shall see. After a formal explanation of the subject we shall go on to consider some practical applications.

I. PSYCHO-SOCIOLOGICAL STUDY OF ATTITUDES

What is a psycho-social attitude? How do sociologists define attitudes? How can the formation, progress and transformation of collective attitudes be studied? How important is it to study the

[2] Hervé Carrier, S.J., *Psycho-sociologie de l'appartenance religieuse*, Rome, Presses de l'Université Grégorienne, 1960 (2nd ed. 1964); see English translation—H. Carrier, *The Sociology of Religious Belonging*, New York, Herder & Herder, 1964. An English edition has just appeared, entitled *The Sociology of Religious Belonging*, Darton, Longman & Todd Ltd.

[3] L. Gernet, Histoire des religions et psychologie: confrontations d'aujourd' hui, *Journal de psychologie* 1, (47–51) 175–87 (1954).

attitudes? These are some of the questions we shall try to answer briefly.

Knowing the attitudes of a person or a group is to a large extent to know the secret of their behaviour and conduct. Let us suppose that we are told the particular attitudes of an individual —for example, of a Christian, who is also the father of a family, member of a certain association or political group—can we not guess from that what will be the direction of his opinions, of his obligations, of his behaviour? A person's attitudes reveal to us his behaviour; hence the great interest in the study of attitudes. The notion of attitude is right at the centre of psycho-sociology. Let us try to be more precise, firstly by saying what it is not.

Attitude is no mere psychological "preference" or "sentiment" or "interest". These states of mind can remain purely on the emotional plane without ever leading to concrete action. They are not "attitudes of behaviour".

Nor is attitude a simple psycho-social "motivation" or "inclination"; or a particular way of "discerning" social reality or of "aspiring" to a coveted status. These behaviour factors can in a sense remain ineffectual and of the platonic order.

Attitude is a "synthetic" and "dynamic" reality. Though it may not be possible to confine it to perception, motivation or emotional reaction, it does embody all these reactions and effectively predisposes the subject to act in one way or another.

Prompted by G. Allport and J. Stoetsel, the two authors who have contributed most towards defining the concept of attitude,[4] we would define attitude as an organization of the personality which orients behaviour, either positively or negatively, towards a psycho-social object. It is a "set", a "disposition to action" or, again, "dynamism preparatory to action". To give it a more elaborate formulation we might describe it as a disposition

---

[4] G. W. Allport, Attitudes, in C. Murchison (Ed.), *A Handbook of Social Psychology*, Worcester, Mass., Clark University Press, 1935, pp. 798–844. J. Stoetzel, La Psychologie sociale et le théorie des attitudes, *Annales sociologiques*, Section 4, 1941, pp. 1–24 (cf. the Symposium of the Association de Psychologie Scientifique de Langue Française: *Les Attitudes*, Paris, Presses Universitaires de France, 1961).

esulting from relatively durable configurations of our perceptive, emotional, and motivational processes being exerted in
respect of a psychological object. For instance, when we speak of
our attitude to foreigners, to politics, to a particular religious
group, we are using a synthetic formulation to show our way of
seeing, feeling, and reacting towards a social object. This stereotyping of our mentality forms a kind of predisposition which
commits us to a form of behaviour, either favourable or un-
favourable, towards foreigners, the political party, religion, etc.

Straight away the manner in which the idea of attitude can be
applied to religious behaviour becomes apparent. The theologian
will not fail to realize the advantages of the theory of attitudes.

1. Attitude embraces the "whole of behaviour", thus avoiding
arbitrary distinctions like those sometimes drawn between
religious behaviour and moral behaviour. Religious behaviour
will not therefore be treated as an autonomous and hermetic
compartment of our psychological life. On the contrary, religious
conduct will embody the whole of behaviour.

2. With the idea of attitude we go beyond social behaviourism,
for we find that we are giving to the "cognitive and perceptive"
aspect of psycho-social behaviour a fundamental role. It is
useless to dwell on this advantage when one understands the role
of knowledge and belief in ethico-religious behaviour.

3. The idea of attitude is inseparable from that of psychological disposition and stereotyping; that is, in stressing the early
socialization and psycho-social experience of the subject, we are
postulating a "substratum of the personality" which can
possibly be treated as such by the moralist or the metaphysicist
(cf. the idea of "person"). The theologian can easily reconcile
the data of psycho-sociology and his own explanations of religious
behaviour.

4. Likewise it will be seen that attitude analysis is at a level
which "transcends the antinomies of psychologism or sociologism". No longer is it merely a matter of comparing irreducibly

the individual's liberty and the sociological conditioning he undergoes. Our attitudes express equally our own personality and the milieu and culture of which we are a part. Thus two sources of our attitudes are shown: one derives from individual psychology and the other is inspired by the social environment. But, while we take into account these two specific factors, we must not neglect the interactions which are set up between them. Certainly it is "we" who react in such and such a way, according to our inner psychology, but also according to the influence of the groups with which we are identified. Moralists and theologians will be ready enough to welcome this type of explanation, being accustomed to interpret religious behaviour precisely in terms of personal responsibility and socio-religious regulations. This leads us to consider in more detail the connections between our attitudes and the groups with which we are associated.[5]

II. THE CONNECTIONS BETWEEN OUR ATTITUDES AND OUR REFERENCE GROUPS

Sociologists have always been intrigued by the fact that our fundamental attitudes are influenced by the groups to which we are attached. Moreover, this phenomenon is heavily underlined in popular psychology in such expressions as "like father, like son", or "you can tell a man by the company he keeps".

William James long ago pondered at length on the ambivalence of our feelings in relation to our various social allegiances. On this point he quoted the words of a magistrate condemning the conduct of a criminal: "As a man I pity you; in my official capacity I must show you no mercy."

These examples reveal to what extent our attitudes reflect a psycho-social context; and this context, we can well imagine, is

[5] Several practical methods of observing collective attitudes are used. For instance, consult; L. Festinger and D. Katz, *Research Methods in the Behavioural Sciences*, New York, The Dryden Press, 1953; A. L. Edwards, *Techniques of Attitude Scale Construction*, New York, Appleton–Century–Crofts, 1957.

no static or fixed reality. It exists, as we shall see, in numerous points of reference between our attitudes and the groups around us. Albert Einstein remarked humorously at a conference in the Sorbonne: "If my theory of relativity is accepted, Germany will claim me as a German and France will declare me a citizen of the world. If my theory is rejected, France will call me a German and Germany will say I am a Jew."

From these examples let us take the obvious data. Our attitudes are to be found in a social framework of reference; our behaviour relates to the groups to which we are psychologically bound. But how have sociologists managed to make a methodical analysis of these data? Three stages of their research may be indicated briefly.

In the first stage sociologists shook themselves free of the Durkheimian positivism in which absolute, sacred values, one might even say unilateral values, are imposed on the individual by social pressure. These theories have been superseded by the more pliable and realistic concept of psycho-social dynamism. Without neglecting sociological influences on the individual a person's original function and specific contribution in collective life have been reaffirmed. "This", wrote Lawrence Frank recently, "simply brings to light the reciprocal relationship between the individual and society. This binary relationship today seems evident."[6]

Once the theses of social determinism had been rejected, the second stage entailed a closer analysis of the reciprocal relations of the person and the groups to which he belongs. For instance, take a man, father of a family of five children, working in a technical team, active member of a political party, and belonging to an urban parish, and so on. How does the sociologist envisage the network of influences at work on the psychology and the behaviour of this individual? One simple way of conceiving this network of psycho-social interactions is to liken the groups to which we belong to a small social universe, a miniature society

[6] K. L. Frank, Psychologie et ordre social, *Esprit* (Jan. 1959), 23–44.

with its own norms, its own hierarchy, its means of communication, codes of behaviour, and sanctions. Examples of similar small social universes would be a trade union, a professional group, a group of friends, or a group of militants. If one of these groups accepts me as a member, by that very fact it imposes its values on me; in a sense I must conform to its norms, whether implied or formal, otherwise I expose myself to the censure, verbal or tacit, of the other members; sanctions are reserved for any serious deviation or lack of discipline. Final condemnation would be expulsion and loss of membership. If I accept the group's regulations, I am rewarded; my participation in the communal life becomes narrower, my behaviour receives the approbation of collective opinion, my prestige increases and promotion within the hierarchy of the group may perhaps recognize the fact that I have fully identified myself with my group.[7] The relations which exist between a member and his group may be described then as a sort of "social system" or social microcosm reflecting the individual's psychology, his attitudes and his behaviour.

These explanations of the psycho-sociologists are suggestive, but require amplification, for they only concern the groups to which we belong physically and ignore all the other groups to which our behaviour can be referred without our actually being effective members—for instance, a social class to which we aspire or a prestige group on which we model our behaviour without being in fact a member of it.

This brings us to a third stage in the scientific analysis of collective attitudes, a stage tackled by Hyman in his early work on reference groups. The concept of the reference group is far wider than that of membership groups. The reference group covers any group to which the individual is connected psychologically, whether because he is already a member, or would like to be included in it at some future date. It contrasts the individual's

[7] We are summarizing here, broadly speaking, explanations given by such social psychologists as G. Mead, F. H. Allport, T. Parsons, and J. Stoetzel.

psychology and practical interest. It may be an actual membership group like our family, our religious or professional group; but it may also be a group to which we aspire without being a member of it, as, for example, a certain social group, or an association whose prestige to our eyes is immense.

The theory of "reference groups" is relatively recent. Hyman put forward the concept in 1942 and the idea was taken up again and made more specific by the research of Sherif and Cantril (1947) and Newcomb (1950) and by a large number of articles which have appeared in recent years in reviews of sociology and social psychology.[8] Those of Sherif (1953) and more especially those of Merton (1957) are the most comprehensive presentations we have.

The original and specific nature of the new theory does not lie in explaining the link between our attitudes and our membership groups (that had already been done), but in emphasizing that our behaviour, our attitudes, and our judgements are influenced by the groups of which we are not true members. This discovery seems essential for us to understand such ambivalent phenomena as social aspirations[9] and mobility between classes[10] and to analyse on a more general plane the conflicts of allegiance which threaten individuals living in a very specialized society in

[8] The bibliography on reference groups is already ample; the following are some references which seem to us most useful: R. Girod, *Attitudes collectives et relations humaines*, Paris, P.U.F., 1953, Ch. 2; M. and C. Sherif, *Groups in Harmony and Tension*, New York, Harper, 1953, Ch. 7; R. K. Merton, *Social Theory and Social Structure*, Glencoe, Ill., Free Press, 1957, Ch. 8—Contributions to the Theory of Reference Group Behavior, and Ch. 9—Continuities in the Theory of Reference Groups and Social Structure; S. M. Eisenstadt, Studies in Reference Group Behaviour, *Human Relations*, 7 (1954), 191–213; E. L. Hartley, Psychological Problems of Multiple Group Membership, in S. Bahrer and M. Sherif (Eds.), *Social Psychology at the Crossroads*, New York, Harper, 1951.

[9] E. Stern and S. Keller, Spontaneous Group References in France, *Public Opinion Quarterly* 17, 208–17 (1953).

[10] E. Bott, The Concept of Class as a Reference Group, *Human Relations* 7, 259–83 (1954).

which social integration implies options which at times are contradictory.[11]

To sum up, the theory of reference groups shows that our attitudes are influenced by the values and norms of the groups to which we are psychologically bound, either on the plane of actual membership or that of simple identification.

This analysis seems to us very useful in the interpretation of the psycho-social behaviour which can be observed in our complex societies. Because of the division of labour and extreme specialization in the functions and groups around us, the individual finds himself faced with competing, even conflicting, affiliations.

Several types of reference group may be distinguished. We shall describe some of them before proceeding to the section on socio-religious applications. The reference group may arouse loyalty, just as it may inspire a desire to break away and escape. The group which is simply a reference group may, in cases of conflict, offer the possibility of evasion, polarize a desire for social promotion, or nourish a hope of change and mobility. There are reference groups to which an individual conforms, and there are those against which he rebels. There are reference groups with which he fully identifies himself, whether to find norms of behaviour (or justification), to define or assert himself, or simply to develop his aspirations.

Immediately numerous applications of this analytical scheme in the field of religious sociology come to mind, particularly for the study of the attitudes, the mentality and the behaviour of the faithful.

III. APPLICATION TO SOCIO-RELIGIOUS BEHAVIOUR

It is not our intention to put forward overall explanations of the psycho-social significance of religious affiliation. We have had occasion elsewhere to consider these questions and indicate in

---

[11] S. Stouffer, An Analysis of Conflicting Social Norms, *American Sociological Review* **14**, 707–17 (1949).

what psycho-sociological context the religious attitudes of a person are formed and develop in a specific direction.[12]

At this point we will confine ourselves to illustrating the method of analysis proposed above and suggesting some possible paths of inquiry.

1. *The Religious Sentiments of the Young*

In the first case let us take the religious attitudes of the child. The priest of a not very Christian parish told us how the children attending his catechism classes were invariably punished and held up to ridicule the next day by the schoolmaster, a militant Communist. How can the behaviour of these children be understood unless we take into account the deep conflicts arising from their desire to participate fully in both the religious group and that of their classmates? Two psycho-social systems are demanding the child's allegiance and at the same time are dividing him within himself. The religious instructor can only take this young Christian as a sociologically isolated person. His inner psychology is as though it were divided between two reference groups, the one favourable to religion and the other hostile. The conflict is not only in external facts, but is engraved in the child's attitudes. It is by taking into consideration the concrete fellowships into which the behaviour of the young is placed that we can succeed in binding them to the church in a lasting way. It is necessary, we realize, to make an intensive pedagogical effort fully adapted to the many milieux of life.

Serious conflicts may equally arise in the child's psychology after the time of holy communion. In many regions it is claimed that religious practice declines rapidly after the twelfth or thirteenth year.[13] The adolescent detaches himself from the religious group at this time and is absorbed into competing

[12] See reference 2, p. 168.

[13] In this connection Desabie's study is characteristic: J. Desabie, *Le Recensement de la pratique religieuse dans la Seine*, Paris, I.N.S.E.E., 1958.

groups whose norms in practice exclude fidelity to the church
(e.g. groups of friends, leisure groups, work groups, etc.). Here
again pastoral action should take into account the concrete
references which serve as a psycho-social framework for the
behaviour of the young Christian.

If we take the analysis further we shall see by what process the
child's religious attitudes, which at the beginning are as if they
were "anchored" in the parental group, undergo during adoles-
cence a sort of institutional transfer in such a way that the
adolescent identifies himself more and more consciously with the
ecclesiastical group as such. The sociologist Harms described
this type of socio-centric evolution in the psychology of the child,
so confirming in a sense the more general propositions of Piaget,
Murray and Bossard.[14] More thorough studies should be made
on this aspect of institutional transfer, which in the child corresponds to the personal discovery of the ecclesiastical community.
Perhaps we would find that the religious sentiments of the young
who reject the church so soon after holy communion had had no
psychological reference to the church group. It would be worth
while verifying this hypothesis by empirical research.

Examples illustrating the theory of reference groups could be
multiplied. A study of religious vocations would furnish ample
subject matter for our observations. It would show how the
young candidate for the religious life detaches himself from his
membership groups (parents, friends, colleagues, etc.) and
turns towards a spiritual group which gives him a point of
reference. To be able to understand to what extent the values,
norms, traditions and spirituality of a religious order may inspire
different spiritual attitudes, we need only to consult the very
provocative study by Francis on types of religious communities.[15]
But we do not wish to dwell any longer on this question of

[14] E. Harms, The Development of Religious Experience in Children, *American
Journal of Sociology* **50**, 112–22 (1944).

[15] E. K. Francis, Toward a Typology of Religious Orders, *American Journal
of Sociology* **55**, 437–49 (1950); cf. French translation Pour une typologie des
ordres religieux, *Chronique sociale de France* **63**, 37–50 (1955).

vocations and we shall consider our second subject of application immediately.

2. *Attitudes of the "Modal" Catholic*

Let us consider, in the same perspective of the reference group, a slightly more complex problem, whose importance will not escape responsible members of the church. Let us ask how the adult Christian's attitude refers to religious groups or secular groups acting as a framework to his behaviour. Let us take as our central point of comparison the "parochial group".

If we consider the parish within the sociology of groups, we shall ask how the attitude of parishioners is susceptible to variation according to differences of status and role within the local Christian community. Likewise we shall ask ourselves if there are not, alongside religious groups, certain secular groups which integrate the Christian's status and roles and whose values more or less polarize the customary behaviour of the faithful.

It is of some importance, as far as our first question is concerned, to ask whether the parish always constitutes a true "sociological group". Contrary to Nuesse and Harte, who show the Catholic parish as a formal group, Fr. Fichter maintains that large parishes no longer show the strict characteristics of the actual social group. They lack the minimum interpersonal interactions and participation which are required to constitute a true community life on the psycho-social plane.[16]

If the parish is sufficiently confined and constitutes a living group, identification with the immediate community is easier, participation is encouraged by interpersonal relations and membership in a religious group takes on direct local references. If, on the other hand, the parish is vast and anonymous, participation among individuals becomes practically impossible for the majority; psychologically the faithful no longer tend to refer their membership to "an immediate context"; only "universal"

[16] J. H. Fichter, S.J., *Social Relations in the Urban Parish*, Chicago, Chicago University Press, 1954, pp. 18 *et seq.*

links hold good. One belongs to the Church, but less and less has the feeling of belonging to a particular local church, to a particular immediate community which in the long run is bound to affect the more "universal" sense of belonging.

Fr. Fichter's research, as we know, led him to develop a typology which allows the different levels of participation in parish life to be studied. He recognizes four types of parishioner— the nuclear, the modal, the marginal and the dormant. Let us consider the most common type, the modal parishioner. What is the psycho-social significance of his religious membership? How are his various roles integrated in his religious behaviour? How does his overall conduct refer to the spiritual group of which he is member?

To answer these questions would, in the words of G. Le Bras, mean "measuring the vitality of Catholicism" in a given environment. We are not trying here to reach a universal answer; each Christian community must take its own soundings. But with the aid of results given by Fr. Fichter in his report of 1956,[17] we shall suggest some lines of approach which may facilitate research.

With the modal Catholic three levels of behavioural value-norms are found, each referring either to the religious system, the secular system or an ambivalent ill-defined system. The first level of reference comprises stable values (for instance, fundamental beliefs, moral norms, well established through habit and conviction). The second comprises more or less fluctuating values (for example, moral standards adopted in less stable fashion). At the third level values are confused (for instance, the norms dictate attitudes in social, economic and racial affairs; these norms are obscurely connected to the socio-religious system).

From this outline of the system of values it appears that the religious role has no unifying effect on the other roles and is not the integrating element in the social personality or the "social character". In his complete social personality the modal Catholic greatly resembles the non-Catholic; however, his behaviour is

[17] J. H. Fichter, S.J., Religious Values and the Social Personality, *American Catholic Sociological Revue* **17**, 109–16 (1956).

not entirely "secularized". His specifically religious role distinguishes him from the non-Catholic. But the influence of that
role is limited.

In short we may say that for this type of Catholic religious
affiliation remains a firm and stable attitude towards absolute
values; but an understanding of the religious attitude does not
embrace all values. "Secular" areas appear which in practice are
considered more or less autonomous in relation to religious
norms. Some of the values which inspire customary behaviour
have no concise psychological reference to the religious membership group. There is a conflict between the reference groups and
the membership groups.

If, like Spengler and Allport, religious feeling is shown ideally
as unifying all the values of a person, one might say here that the
spiritual attitude does not take in every interest. There are some
left out which are not integrated into the psycho-religious
systems. Membership of the church has become institutionalized
and tends to become parallel, if not marginal, to the other social
membership groups.

Morris even spoke of alienation in connection with these
phenomena of institutional selection.[18] From this it would seem
that participation by these individual members of the faithful is
ambivalent. Their behaviour reveals a true fidelity to the
fundamental values of the religious group; but, on the other
hand, one finds behaviour more or less consciously withdrawn
from the norms of the church. Their behaviour stems from values
which co-exist but are not integrated. In sociological language
there is an "adaptation" to the cultural and moral pluralism of
the milieu.

From all this there emerges an important pastoral application.

In each environment one must observe the customary behaviour
of the "modal" Catholic in order to determine which values of
behaviour he firmly refers to the religious membership group, and

[18] R. E. Morris, Problems concerning the Institutionalization of Religion,
American Catholic Sociological Review **17**, 98–108 (1956).

which values remain ambiguous or confused, that is, more or less tied to secular reference groups.

We would point out, in passing, that such observations will help especially to explain the behaviour of a Catholic minority living among a non-Catholic majority. The study of Mayer and Marx on the moral transformations undergone during the course of several years by a Polish community living in the suburbs of Detroit might to some extent serve as a model for this type of observation.[19]

3. *Institutional References of Religious Conversion*

We should like to end this paper with one last case, that of religious conversions. This example was deliberately chosen to bring out a vital point, namely the irreducible and specific nature of religious behaviour. If the theory of the reference groups happens to be applied in the field of religious attitudes, it is only with considerable amplification and modifications, and by observing religious conversions this point can be driven home.

Starting with a simple observation, there is sooner or later in every Christian conversion a psycho-social link between the convert and the church. It is an institutional aspect of behaviour which one can attempt to study within the perspective of the reference groups. Approaching the institutional aspects of conversion raises the more general problem of religious identification. As the phenomena of identification overlap the field of conversion we shall only consider two points which are of immediate interest to us—the "psycho-social reference" of the convert to the religious institution and his "integration" into the church society.

In acknowledging an element of identification in the conversion, we are led to wonder how, in the course of the development of the new religious attitude, the reference between the candidate and the church is formed. In fact, the church should

[19] A. J. Mayer and S. Marx, Social Change, Religion and Birth Rates, *American Journal of Sociology* **62**, 383–90 (1957).

be recognized, at least as a reference group, if not as a true membership group, according to the distinction explained above.

If the church seems in the candidate's experience to be a group to which he "wishes access", the institutional reference which we are discussing here is established and the behaviour is relatively easy to understand. The convert adheres to a church which is known and desirable.

Analysis, however, is not always that simple. Autobiographical accounts of conversions reveal cases where the church seems to have no place in the conscience and where no institutional reference is apparent in the psychology of the convert. The church, apparently, seemed to be neither a possible membership group nor a simple reference group. Yet there was a sudden conversion to the church. How, in this case, can the sudden identification with the religious group be explained?

Sociologists have noted that beyond an individual's attitude of indifference there may exist a reservoir of institutional influences which condition, perhaps unconsciously, his behaviour and his psychological references. Cuber[20] in his study on religious "marginality" succeeded in demonstrating that the cultural impact of the church cannot be reduced to a process of dichotomy: real influence or no influence. To say of a person that he is on the fringe of the church's "culture" does not mean that his participation in this culture is non-existent. Marginal participation is still a form of participation.

Merton[21] goes further and stresses that the influence of religious values may continue to be felt with astonishing persistence even in an environment where the theological bases which formerly justified this order of values have been rejected. In this context he quotes Troeltsch: "There is no more logic in the behaviour of today than in yesterday's; spiritual forces can exert a powerful influence even where they have been publicly repudiated."

[20] J. F. Cuber, Marginal Church Participants, *Sociology and Social Research* **25**, 57–62 (1940).

[21] R. K. Merton, *op. cit.*, p. 583.

It is for cultural sociology to determine the areas of collective psychology in which the influence of these values is felt; but analysis of individual behaviour has already revealed their tracks. Penido[22] quotes the evidence of an English convert in which the "effect of marginality" is apparent in the institutional reference of conduct: "My liberal Protestant leanings, which the Anglican influence secretly and unknown to me was undermining, became more pronounced, at the same time as my hostility towards Rome. I felt, no doubt unconsciously, a need to defend myself against the Catholicism which in certain aspects had attracted me since I had come to know the Anglicans. This was the period when I wrote articles in the *London Signal* which were very hostile to the church and which I would never have written at all if I had remained indifferent to Catholicism."

This example brings to light the phenomenon of "cultural marginality". Our convert felt, he said, a need to "defend himself unconsciously" against the influence of the church and he confesses afterwards that Catholicism did not leave him indifferent.

The observer must take these phenomena into account when looking for institutional references in conversions. One sees that the influence of religious values at times is exerted conversely. Merton speaks of "dysfunctions". An institution, in this case the church, will be present at some time even in the psychology of an indifferent person or of an opponent. According to Jung, radicalism or fanaticism often will serve as over-compensation for secret doubts and uncertainties.

In certain cases it even seems that no explicit reference exists between a convert and the church; but one cannot deny that the very fact of being "on the fringe" of the church already involves a certain form of participation, negative perhaps, but real, in the diffuse religious culture of a milieu. The case will become quite clear if the opposite process to identification is examined, namely "projection", which consists of rationalizing one's behaviour

[22] M. T. L. Penido, *La Conscience religieuse*, Paris, Téqui, 1935, p. 69.

whilst attributing to "another" one's own dispositions, especially the most trying ones. Stoetzel[23] pointed out that projection is directly connected with lack of self-knowledge. If projection is exercised within the church it is explained by saying that in a sudden conversion spiritual reunification of the personality is accompanied by a sudden transfer from projection to identification. The convert discovers himself whilst discovering the church. He sees a "close resemblance". Allport defines identification as "affective imitation". The convert "gets to know himself" and joins the church. He accepts the new role and status offered by the religious institution to which henceforth his behaviour will explicitly refer.

Religious conversion, which at first sight seems to be a strictly individual act, involves relationships with a community. Is that all? Does the final explanation lie in integrating the new religious attitude? It is necessary to go on and add an essential complement to the first indications suggested by the reference group theory. Affiliation with the religious institution supposes not only psycho-social adherence, but also "integration of worship".

Religious integration, beginning with the decision to "make oneself" a member of the church, is only achieved from the religious and psycho-social standpoint in that integrating process *par excellence*, the rites of the church. We are only considering specifically at this point the adult convert joining the church for the first time. His specific attitude as "member of the church" will not be perfectly integrated until after his baptismal rites. Integration of worship will then round off his institutional behaviour.

Studies on the sociology of ritual reveal clearly the integrating role of acts of worship. In a recent review of the question[24] Fr. Gordon George showed that ritual may be considered as a form of symbolic communication. It is a pattern of ceremonial behaviour expressing community religious life and relating to a

[23] J. Stoetzel, *Théorie des opinions*, Paris, P.U.F., 1943, p. 304.

[24] G. George, S.J., The Sociology of Ritual, *American Catholic Sociological Review* **17**, 117–30 (1956).

reality which transcends gestures and words. Ritual has a cohesive power; it is the opposite of *anomie*; it creates the feeling of "we" in that it identifies. Over and above the theological functions of ritual, the author recognizes in it a latent sociological function; integration with a social structure as also the difference of the statuses and roles within the heart of the community of the faithful. If, like Zetterberg,[25] we compare conversion with a socio-religious change of role, we could say that the baptismal ritual plays an important function in the candidate's sacramental integration with the structure of the church and assignment to him of the definitive status of a Christian.

In summary, there is a profound identification between the "reference group" (the church which nourishes the aspirations and hopes of the neophyte) and the affective "membership group" (the church which has accepted him definitively).

CONCLUSION

Two complementary remarks may serve as conclusion for this paper. The first underlines the relative and functional aspect of every method of research, particularly in the socio-religious field. The second observation touches more closely on the theological relations between the individual and the member of the community and their consequences for studies in pastoral sociology.

1. *Functional Value of the Research Method*

We have attempted here to describe a method of research which would allow systematic examination of collective religious attitudes. The theory of reference groups has seemed of particular use to us in this field. We feel we must stress the relative nature of any method employed in the observation of human behaviour, particularly religious behaviour.

[25] H. L. Zetterberg, The Religious Conversion as a Change of Social Roles, *Sociology and Social Research* **36**, 159–66 (1952).

Any method of research is merely a practical means of discovering a social reality and it is this reality itself which should attract the observer's attention. Otherwise there is a danger that the method may become a futile and superficial systematization.

We have tried above to describe the "psycho-social references" of religious behaviour, but we might easily remain on the surface of reality were we not to make an effort to site these "references" of religious conduct in the perspective of our "spiritual relations" with the church.

For this we must realize that psycho-social references to the church are themselves of a religious nature. In our relations with the Christian community there is a reality which comes from faith and charity; this dimension should not be disregarded by the sociology of religion. Otherwise religious behaviour might be confused with secular forms of behaviour. Religion will have lost its specific character.

Even non-Catholic and non-Christian social psychologists would be willing to recognize this original and this specific nature of religious behaviour. A phenomenologist such as Van der Leeuw[26] has often said as much: "The typology of Christianity", he wrote, "can be described in a single word—love; love responding to that of God assumes a form—the church; the church demonstrates its irreducible unity with love." An author like Freud, whose studies in the psychology of religion are normally so ambiguous, recognised the religious depth of the spiritual references in the church of Christ. "Not without reason", he says, "do we stress the analogy between the Christian community and a family and do the faithful consider themselves brothers, that is, brothers through the love with which Christ bestows upon them. It is undeniable that the link which binds each individual to Christ is the cause of the link which binds one individual to all others."[27]

---

[26] G. Van der Leeuw, *La Religion dans son essence et ses manifestations: phenomenologie de la religion*, Paris, Payot, 1955, pp. 630–3.

[27] S. Freud, *Psychologie collective et analyse du moi*, Paris, Payot, 1953, p. 42.

2. *The Individual and the Community*

The social psychology of religion endeavours to study the community aspects of spiritual behaviour; we stress the factors of solidarity which act as points of reference in moral behaviour; we take out the groups, that is the data of collective psychology, which point out the attitudes of an environment, of a group, or of individuals.

The Christian community as such is holy: it is a mystical reality and one should work for enlightenment. But the indications of the sociology of religion would be misunderstood were we to make it a pretext for centring too exclusively the pastoral programmes on collective values, on community aspects as such, at the expense of the interpersonal apostolate.

The sociologist should double as a theologian and affirm that, beyond the essential work on the groups, it is necessary wholeheartedly to support pastoral action on its fundamental principle, which is always the same: "the primacy of personal formation by word and grace". This was Pope Pius XII's directive to sociologists. "In caring for whole communities," he wrote, "we will never lose sight of the importance of individual contact and guidance of souls; a just appreciation of the facts about the milieu to be evangelized could not overshadow the sovereign efficacy of grace, the power of the word of God and the supernatural richness of sanctity."[28]

[28] His Holiness Pius XII, Letter to S. Exc. Mgr. Renard, 30 March 1956, quoted in the Preface to *Sociologie et pastorale coutances*, 1957, p. 6.

2. INSTITUTIONAL ANALYSIS

The Urban Parish as a Social Group

J. H. FICHTER, S.J.

IT HAS always seemed strange to me that the principal aim of scientific sociology—the study of social groups—has been so neglected by the sociologists of religion. The greater part of research in this field has emphasized the demographic, sociographic and statistical aspects. Even here, the phrase "social structures" is interpreted in the sense of social stratification, and religious observances are measured on criteria of profession, age, matrimonial status and place of residence.

The concentration on finding census material has been the dominating concern of sociologists of the parish, in Europe and America alike. National, diocesan and parish statistics have been studied in order to show the proportions of Catholics and non-Catholics, the proportion of active observance, attendance at Mass, the proportion of baptisms, communions, marriages, etc. Elaborate graphs, some of them, indeed, very ingenious and enlightening, have been presented to illustrate the comparisons and tendencies among forms of religious practice. All this fundamental work is extremely important, and should be continued, even if we begin to carry out true sociological research within the religious groups and institutions.

Demography, sociography and statistics should be appreciated for what they are: a valuable preliminary for sociology, and a basis of information on which the sociologist can work. We should not confuse this preliminary research with the central object of scientific sociology: the types of attitudes, the functions, relations and processes of group life. The statistical studies of Catholic populations are not, strictly speaking, the scientific study of the Catholic socio-cultural system.

The principal objective of our research, *Southern Parish*,[1] was introduced in a completed volume of these preliminary details relating to religious observance. The three following volumes, which are concerned with sociological analysis, have not yet been published. In the book *Social Relations in the Urban Parish*,[2] attention was especially drawn to the different aspects of parish social groups. Our research in Germany, which will be published under the title *Small Groups in a German Parish*,[3] is an attempt to study this complicated question of the social relations existing between parishioners. A further research project, on which we have yet to embark in the Middle-West, will concentrate on the parish school as a form of social group.[3a]

On analysing the literature—both European and American— dealing with the sociology of religion, I could find no reference to study of this type. Professor George Homans of Harvard University is undertaking the supervision of a small group of studies in the United States, but the work is limited to non-religious and non-Catholic groups. The range of the present article is not, however, historical or comparative. We will deal with the American urban parish, starting from the sociological perspective of the group.

It is a commonplace in sociology that every social organization should fulfil two basic requirements for it to remain in existence. The first is to maintain a minimum level of co-operation among its members; and the second is to justify its existence by satisfying certain social needs of its members.

---

[1] *Southern Parish*, University of Chicago Press, 1951.

[2] *Social Relations in the Urban Parish*, University of Chicago Press, 1955.

[3] To appear in the *Institut für Kristliche Soziale Wissenschaft* of Munster.

[3a] Subsequently published as *The Parochial School*, Notre Dame, 1958.

If, at this point, we apply these fundamental principles to the normal American urban parish, we see that these parishes have a real solidarity, that some of them are even flourishing. The parishes satisfy the religious needs of the parishioners in a particular way; and there is sufficient collaboration between some of the laity and the clergy to ensure success.

However, our problem here is not simply to stop at the fact of the existence of the parish as a social organization. Indeed, the bishop can guarantee this minimum requirement by demarcating a territory on which some Catholics are dwelling, and nominating a parish priest to build a church there and take the faithful under his care. Our problem is to analyse this urban parish organization and see if the technical definition of the social group can be applied to it. In our bibliographical research, we find Cooley, who has treated at length of the primary group. Further, McIver has written a good deal on association and secondary groups. In each case, the definition of the group is the following: a community of people in reciprocal communication, fulfilling communal functions, having a body of common values, showing evidence of a certain solidarity, and acknowledged by the non-members as constituting a group in itself.

It is evident that these characteristics can be found in varying degrees, and give rise to different combinations, wherever social relations are formed.

The more pronounced these features are, the nearer it is to being a primary group. If they are not so defined, it will be more a case of a secondary association. Empirically, however, this is an excessive schematization. Large secondary associations harbour within them a number of primary groups, which ultimately enable the two basic requirements of the secondary association (i.e. maintenance of co-operation, and response to social needs), to be realized. This is true of a large industrial company, a political party, a system of education; and it is true also of the Church and the parish. This sociological generalization is a fundamental law in sociology, and it is universally applicable.

The American urban parish, when it is carefully studied and analysed scientifically, cannot as a total community present the features of a primary group. The European parish priest can think of his parish as a Christian community, and the American parish priest can look on his as a "large, happy family". These two assessments refer to the life of an integrated group, and neither the one nor the other can be confirmed in the American urban parish.

The ordinary urban parish can be studied from different points of view, each of which has a certain degree of validity, in terms of the investigator's intention. A sociological line of approach, which is fruitful and technically applicable, distinguishes four general functions in the parish. These are: (a) the types of religious activity revolving immediately round the Church and the priests, and in which practically every parishioner is required to participate at one moment or another of his life; (b) the numerous parish associations of lay people, directed by the priests, which fulfil various roles, but are supported by relatively few parishioners; (c) the parish primary school, run by nuns under the general supervision of the parish priest, where the majority of children receive their first education; (d) and finally, the Catholic families of the parish, in whose life every parishioner must of course take part.

In the ordinary run of everyday life, there generally prevail two interpretations of the urban parish: that of the laymen and that of the priests. When questioned on the importance of his parish, the priest tends to quote the number of families living in his parish. The average parishioner, however, tends to believe that it is individuals rather than families which comprise the parish. This indicates two different aspects of the same social phenomenon. When considering the parish as a layman would, from within the family, one envisages the different members of the community. When approaching it as the priest does, from the standpoint of the Church, directed towards the rest of the parish, one tends to see groups of members rather than individual ones.

These two different attitudes contribute to the continued confusion of the sociologist studying the urban parish. Which of these two conceptions ought the sociologist to adopt when analysing the concrete data? If he takes on the priest's mentality, he will tend to interpret the parish as a social group; if he adopts the layman's outlook, he will tend to interpret the parish as a secondary association.

It is only by considering the present social situation that the social investigator can come to a valid conclusion.

Neither an urban parish priest nor any one urban parishioner can be personally acquainted and have reciprocal contacts with every baptized Catholic in the parish. Since many priests are very practical men, they tackle the analysis of their parish on a basis related to their experience. They have better relations with those families which send their children to the parish school, or have one or several members involved in the parish organizations, or whose members receive the sacraments more frequently and regularly. Consequently, their perspective for classification tends to fix their attention on their relations with families, as a means of getting to know and remembering the individuals who live in their parish. The priest is acquainted with the families, above all, through the intermediaries of the sacraments, the parish school, and the parish associations.

On these grounds, reciprocal communication and social relations are established, and communal functions are carried out. These points of contact and their regularity are what develop a whole network of mutual relations between the parish priest and the families. Up to a certain point also, it is through the same channels that parishioners come to know each other. As far as types of religious and sacramental activity are concerned, it is mostly a question of one parishioner observing another. It is in the school activities and the parish societies that individual parishioners actually co-operate with each other, in communal functions.

But the core of the sociological problem rests in the number of participants and frequency of participation. It is at this level that the sociologist begins his most penetrating research into the social life of the parish. The problem is to see whether the parish is a group, as the priest sees it, or just a simple association of individuals, as laymen think of it. The usual method in social science is relevant here. A strict statistical check will show that less than 6 per cent of adult parishioners take part in parish associations, that around 12 per cent of them receive Holy Communion every Sunday, and that less than 25 per cent of the parents of schoolchildren take an active interest in the parish school. If widespread participation and the regularity with which functions are fulfilled are significant for sociologists as criteria of group life these minimal percentages indicate that every parish does not function as a single group.

This does not mean, however, that the social group is entirely absent from the American urban parish. In fact, at the heart of any urban parish the sociologist will discover a category of "nuclear" parishioners, which one can call a social group in the strict, technical sense of the term. They form a parishional or religious group because their activities are directed towards religious ends, and they can be identified by a religious criterion. People of this category answer to the definition of a social group, because they can be identified as members, because they show evidence of solidarity, share common values, act together and are in reciprocal communication. It is this low percentage of parishioners—and only these—which forms this collective unit, such as makes it possible to call a parish a social group, in the technical sense of the term.

What then is to be said of the remaining large number of parishioners, the great majority or perhaps 90 per cent of those who count as members of the urban parish? The most that can be said is that they constitute the units of a social category of persons, who, in an organized parish, are beneficiaries rather than participants. These persons do not constitute a social group, and it is easy to prove this by referring to the characteristics of a social group.

1. IDENTIFICATION THROUGH THE GROUP

The majority of people do not identify themselves in relation to strangers as members of a certain parish, and others do not recognize them as such. It is only occasionally that the inhabitant of an American town uses his place of residence or the name of his district as a form of identification. Only in rare cases, where a parish of nationality coincides with a certain district, can one find a reference to the name of the parish. This is true only where large numbers of immigrants live together, and this kind of community is rapidly tending to disappear in the United States.

2. SOCIAL SOLIDARITY

Every social group, if well defined, should present a certain degree of social unity, and this unity is expressed by the ability of people to co-operate in a close circle. In the large urban parish (since the Catholic Church is open to all), parishioners are from varying social levels, and they differ by education, race, wealth, and profession. We have often had categorical proof that parishioners tend to co-operate more with non-Catholics of the same cultural and professional level than with parishioners from different social and professional classes. Social solidarity, therefore, as based on the condition of members of the same parish, is not very real.

3. COMMON VALUES

It was formerly a tradition among sociologists to put very strong emphasis on common adherence to the same scale of values as the principal factor in group life. There are indeed groups which show this characteristic, but this is not the case with the American parish. Religious values differ in intensity and significance, and other types of values—political, economic, recreational, racial—carry more significance, as it turns out, than religious values. The United States is pluralist in its systems of values. Catholics, like other Americans, differ considerably in their attitude to the important question of social morality. It is unlikely that, in large parishes, people could rise above these divergences by virtue of their common religious beliefs.

4. COMMUNAL FUNCTIONS

The most adequate means of measuring the solidarity of the group is to see if the people who comprise it work together with the intention of achieving common aims. We have seen that a minimum of co-operation on the part of a limited number of persons allows the social organization of the parish to exist. It is a well-known fact that American parishioners make generous monetary contributions to the material needs of the parish, and, moreover, that they hear Mass on Sundays with a high degree of regularity. These two attitudes are both praiseworthy and religious, but they tend to be exemplified by individuals. The communal functions of co-operation, in many urban parishes, are the feature of a small group and not of the general body of parishioners.

5. RECIPROCAL COMMUNICATION

The application of the four other criteria of group life shows clearly that, as far as parish life and religious interests are concerned, numerous persons do not communicate with each other in the urban parish. The anonymity of urban life, along with the pursuit of other interests, largely accounts for this lack of communication. Some of them certainly are associated in particular groups of political clubs, recreational activities and so on, but this association does not embrace the entire community: these people do not come together as parishioners or with the furtherance of parish aims in view.

Unfortunately, I cannot know whether a similar analysis of the lack of social cohesion could be applied to the European urban parishes. The research I carried out in a German parish in 1953–4 indicates both similarities and differences in relation to the typical American parish. It seems to me, however, that the European parish comes nearer to the technical definition of the social group than do the American parishes, with which I am more familiar.

Certain factors and conditions peculiar to the American socio-cultural system should be kept in mind when one attempts to explain the lack of social cohesion of the urban parish.

We cannot accept the oversimplified sequence of causalities, which asserts that industrialization caused urbanization; that urbanization entails secularization, and that secularization kills religious life. This may be true, but it does not explain very much. Certain other aspects of American culture and society enable us to explain why Catholic urban parishes do not and probably never can constitute complete groups.

(a) The American social system as a whole tends to develop *secondary associations*. This comes out clearly in economic and political functions, in educational and recreational activities. Given this tendency, it is only to be expected that family and religious groupings should be affected. One can only assume that primary groups are in danger of dying out. Every social research worker is aware of the fact that society cannot exist without foundations or primary social relations. The closed, personal and informal relations of the former village parish have been necessarily replaced by the formalist and impersonal relations of the large urban parish.

(b) *Organized giganticism* is also characteristic of American culture. Large-scale industry and large universities, for example, are considered by the population to be desirable. They are not, however, considered effective until they embody a balanced system of particular departments functioning interdependently, with a view to achieving higher output. The urban parish has been affected by the tendency to giganticism, but it has not yet introduced the systematization of structures and functions.

(c) *Efficiency* is another characteristic highly valued in the American culture. This is most commonly measured by productivity, that is, by production in relation to the human effort and costs allowed for that production. One can see a sign of this preoccupation with efficiency in the religious services and the Mass and the rapid sermons, the provision for parking-space for cars on Sunday mornings, the elimination of the little-appreciated evening services, the use of air-conditioning, mechanical devices and various systems for saving time. However, an efficient administration has not yet been introduced in the most complex relations of parish groups and secular parish functions.

(d) *Responsibility and authority*, at several levels, is another almost imperceptible but extremely important aspect of the way American society works. This complex system of roles and chains of subsidiary functions could probably not exist without an effective decentralization. Up till now, for different reasons, this conception has not been successfully introduced into the large urban parishes. The parish priests, on the whole, have not been drawn in the direction of efficiency; they still fear "trusteeism", and the laity is either uninterested or incapable of participating in the responsible and authoritative aspects of religious life.

(e) *Social mobility* is another important value in the American culture. Among the various criteria of a rise in social status, the most important is generally the professional function, whereas the religious role tends to have less and less place. In the minds of lay people, these two criteria seem to act in opposite directions. The professional function is often dissociated from sacred and religious ideas, and does not allow of serious participation in religious and parish functions. On the other hand, the hierarchical structure peculiar to the Church leaves little opportunity for laymen to obtain a social rank within the framework of religious activity. Consequently, there is missing one of the most powerful forces capable of driving the American layman to participate in the internal sociological administration of the urban parish.

The pivotal institution of the American culture is of an economic type, whereas the religious institution is largely peripheral. This does not signify that religion is completely subordinate to economy, or that religious groups tend to imitate the manner of behaviour of the economic world, even to assimilate its ethics, values and ideals. But it is obvious that people themselves are influenced by this tendency. The parish should in their eyes meet with success, and this success is related to material criteria: a modern church building, a convent without debts, an up-to-date school. There is an odd contrast here: the laymen make generous financial contributions to a social organization over which they have no control, and in which the majority of them take no active part.

This series of observations does not claim to be a detailed analysis of the socio-cultural factors in the work of the large urban parish. It will, however, serve to show the importance of the sociological aspects, beyond the simple statistical and demographic aspects of the urban parish. This will prove to us also that the concept of the parish community—the parish as a primary group or a large family—is out of date in the American society.

In the intention of the author, the point of this article is not to suggest reforms, or even to list the defects of the urban parish, but simply to describe sociological phenomena actually in existence. It does not come into his province to judge whether the disaffection with regard to primary relations is good or bad. In the United States, we hear much of the European efforts to "restore the Christian community". This often seems to us to be a reversal, a resurrection or revival of traditional ways of life. American efforts will be directed more towards continual adaptation of religious groups and institutions to the American socio-cultural system, in perpetual evolution.

o

Religion in a Secularized Society

W. Herberg

SOME ASPECTS OF AMERICA'S THREE-RELIGION PLURALISM

The basic fact defining the contemporary religious situation in this country is the transformation of America, in the course of the past generation, from a Protestant nation into a three-religion country. It is necessary to examine somewhat more closely the nature of this transformation, and its concomitant circumstances.

Writing just about thirty years ago, André Siegfried described Protestantism as America's "national religion", and he was largely right, despite the ban on religious establishment in the Constitution. Normally, to be born an American meant to be a Protestant; this was the religious identification that, in the American mind, quite naturally went along with being an American. Non-Protestants felt the force of this conviction almost as strongly as did the Protestants; the Catholic and the Jew experienced their non-Protestant religion as a problem, perhaps even as an obstacle, to their becoming full-fledged Americans; it was the mark of their foreignness. In a very real sense, Protestantism constituted America's "established church".

This is no longer the case. Today, to be born an American is no longer taken to mean that one is necessarily a Protestant; Protestantism is no longer the obvious and natural religious identification of the American. Today, the evidence seems to indicate, America has become a three-religion country: the normal religious implication of being an American today is that one is either a Protestant, a Catholic, or a Jew. As I have already suggested, these three are felt, by and large, to be three alternative forms of being religious in the American way; they are the three "religions of democracy", the "three great faiths" of America. Today, unlike fifty years ago, not only Protestants, but increasingly Catholics and Jews as well, feel themselves to be Americans not apart from, or in spite of, their religion, but in and through it, because of it. If America today possesses a "church" in the Troeltschean sense—that is, a form of religious belonging which is felt to be involved in one's belonging to the national community—it is the tripartite religious system of Protestant–Catholic–Jew.

This transformation of America from a Protestant into a three-religion country has come about not as the result of any marked increase in Catholics or Jews—the Protestant–Catholic ratio has not changed drastically in the past half-century, and the proportion of Jews in the general population has probably been declining. It has come about as a consequence of the process discussed in the first lecture whereby the socioreligious group has emerged as a primary subcommunity in American society, replacing the older ethnic group in that capacity. I will say no more about the process itself, but I do want to explore certain aspects of the three-religion pluralism to which it has given rise.

SECULARIZATION AND RELIGIOUS GROUP TYPES

The sociology of secularization has been widely discussed, and many attempts made, since Troeltsch, to relate degree of secularization with organizational type. Professor Harold W. Pfautz has suggested a series of five organizational forms, in order of increasing secularization, as follows: the cult, the sect, the institutionalized sect, the church, and the denomination. Understanding by secularization the widening gap between conventional religion and operational religion, there is much to be said for this series of organizational types. I think, however, that the present-day American situation suggests certain qualifications and elaborations.

The cult, to begin with, seems to exhibit the lowest degree of secularization possible in modern society. For the member of the cult fellowship, there is a minimum distinction between conventional religion, operative religion, and existential religion, though it may be noted that in this country cult members are sometimes members of established denominations as well. The cult is not so much at war with the world and its ways as outside of them.

Cults suffer a high degree of mortality. If a cult survives, it becomes a sect, and undergoes the familiar sociological changes in size, leadership, associational structure, and the like. The sect follower has already advanced on the road to secularization, but it is hard to say how far since the sect too is not very stable. Sooner or later, it either disappears, or else develops into something quite different: in Europe, it generally became a church; in this country, however, the line of development has been toward the denomination, which, in America, has come to mean something quite distinctive. A variant is the institutionalized, or "established", sect.

In the strict Troeltschean sense of the term, this country has not had a church since colonial times. The church, in this sense, is essentially the national community on its religious side, the national community religiously organized. Even where the transplanted religious bodies set up in the English colonies on the Atlantic Coast were churches to begin with, widespread religious dissidence, coupled with the diversity of population, soon broke the formal religious unity and induced an incipient denominationalism. Denominationalism became the established religious pattern in the wake of the great revival movements; and in denominationalism we have a further and very advanced stage of secularization. For denominationalism, in its very nature, requires a thoroughgoing separation between conventional religion and operative religion, and this is the mark of secularization.

The denomination, as we know it in this country, is a settled, stable religious body, very like a church in many ways, except that it sees itself as one of a large aggregate of similar bodies, each recognizing the proper status of the others in legitimate coexistence. The denomination in America is not at all the "nonconformist sect" that it is in Europe; or rather, it is the "nonconformist sect" become central and normative. It differs from the church in the European acceptation of the term in that it would never dream of claiming to be the national ecclesiastical institution; it differs from the sect in that it is socially established, thoroughly institutionalized, and nuclear to the society in which it is found. So firmly entrenched is the denominational idea in the mind of the American that even American Catholics have come to think in such terms; theologically, the Catholic Church, of course, continues to regard itself as the one true church, but in their actual social attitudes American Catholics, hardly less than American Protestants or American Jews, tend to think of their church as a kind of denomination existing side by side with other denominations in a pluralistic harmony that is felt to be somehow of the texture of American life.

Obviously, the denominational system implies the emergence of a "common religion" distinct from the conventional religion of the denominations, for without such a "common religion" the society in which the denominations find their place in mutual legitimation would hardly be able to hold together. Denominational pluralism, on the American plan, means thoroughgoing secularization.

It is interesting to observe the process by which the successful sect becomes a denomination, and to follow the corresponding stages of secularization. Long ago, John Wesley, who was a keen observer of religion as he was a powerful evangelist, noted the forces that were at work undermining the religious revival he had launched.

> Wherever riches have increased [Wesley pointed out], the essence of religion has decreased in the same proportion. Therefore, I do not see how it is possible in the nature of things for any revival of religion to

continue long. For religion must necessarily produce both industry and frugality, and these cannot but produce riches. But, as riches increase, so will pride, anger, and love of the world in all its branches. How, then, is it possible that Methodism, that is a religion of the heart, though it flourishes now as the green bay trees, should continue in this state? For the Methodists in every place grow diligent and frugal; consequently, they increase in goods. Hence they proportionately increase in pride, in anger, in the desire of the flesh, the desire of the eyes, and the pride of life. Is there no way to prevent this—this continual decay of pure religion?[1]

What Wesley was here describing was not only the inner contradiction in every revival of religion; he was also describing the dynamics of the transformation of the sect into a denomination. For the sect is essentially an "outsider" group: it is largely composed of elements who see themselves "disinherited", outside the culture, with no stake in it, with no participation in its values. The sectarian ethos and the sectarian ideology reflect this "outsider" stance. This was substantially the position of the mass of the early Methodists, as it still is the condition of the "fringe" groups in this country today. But in a mobile society, "outsiders" do not long remain "outsiders". Within a generation or two, encouraged by the very virtues which religious sectarianism breeds, many of the sect following grow prosperous, gain economic substance, and thus improve their social status. Their hostility to the culture diminishes as they move closer to the center, and they begin to share many of its values: they send their children to college, their preachers to seminary; they build impressive churches, with a more or less elaborate institutional superstructure, including Boy Scouts and Sunday schools. Their sectarian ideology grows mellow, loses its rough edges, and becomes little more than a set of ritualistic formulas. Their ministers sometimes even join the local ministerial association. In short, the sect is well on the way toward becoming a denomination, a small denomination, usually, but a denomination nevertheless.

It should be noted that, despite Wesley's account, this process

[1] Quoted in Robert Southey, *Life of Wesley and the Rise and Progress of Methodism* (2nd Amer. Edition; Harper, 1847), Vol. II, p. 308.

is not simply one in which "pure religion" is corrupted by economic prosperity, itself the consequence of the "industry and frugality" which, according to Wesley, "religion must necessarily produce". It is rather that economic prosperity, in modern Western society, brings its beneficiaries closer to the nuclear culture and its values, thus undermining their "outsider" stance and the extremism and hostility it breeds. Thus the movement from sect to denomination is a movement from the margin to the center of society, and therefore a movement from the sectarian ideology to the "common religion" of the society. The movement from sect to denomination is therefore a movement of rapid secularization.

Actually, what happens is much more complicated than this account would suggest. Economic prosperity and cultural advance appear to exert a double effect: on the one side, they impel better advantaged members of the sect to leave the sect and join a recognized denomination; on the other side, they tend to raise the entire sect in the sociocultural scale on the way to denominational status.

The first movement is difficult to document since it is composed of millions of unrecorded personal or family decisions; yet every observer is well aware that it is going on. As to the second movement—the elevation of the entire sect to denominational status—the evidence is easily at hand. Such great denominations as the Baptists and Methodists in this country came out of sects in precisely the way described; and somewhat later, the Campbellites, against their own intention, gave rise to the Disciples of Christ. Because it emerged so late, the Disciples became only a small denomination by American standards; the field had already been well charted out by the others.

Exactly the same process is taking place before our very eyes today. The Nazarenes, over a large part of the country, are indistinguishable from small Protestant denominational churches. The Assemblies of God have their liberal arts colleges and graduate schools of religion; their men's associations, their women's councils, and their Sunday schools; their publicity, promotion, and public relations agencies, including an international radio program. But the most astonishing illustration is provided by the Jehovah's Witnesses. The Jehovah's Witnesses would certainly seem to constitute the model sect group: a "disinherited", "outsider" group, militant, growing, arrayed against the culture and its values, promoting a typically sectarian ideology. Yet in a recent issue of a Witnesses journal there appeared an article on "How to Dress Well". In this article, the Witnesses are told that neatness is the first requirement, that they should never wear a patterned sports jacket with patterned slacks, that shoes and socks should complement, not clash with, clothes, and other such bits of esoteric wisdom. This article, I think, is of immense significance. It shows several things: it shows that large numbers of Witnesses are now able and eager to dress well, but simply do not know how since they come from strata of society where such things are not learned at the mother's knee; it shows also that the Jehovah's Witnesses leadership is very much concerned that they learn what they want to know, and in general that Witnesses learn to fit into lower-middle-class suburbia and be accepted by it. Obviously, the sectarian "outsider" stance is beginning to give way, some of the values of the culture at least are being accepted, and others will be at an accelerating rate. Jehovah's Witnesses do not yet constitute a denomination, not even in the sense in which the Nazarenes or the Assemblies of God do; but the Witnesses are on their way, and the way is the way of growing secularization.

This way leads from the cult, to the sect, to the denomination. With the denomination, secularization reaches its most advanced stage. But, in the American system, denominations have their groupings within a scheme of mutually legitimated coexistence: specifically, they group themselves into the three great socio-religious subcommunities known as the "three great faiths". We can thus carry the series further: *cult—sect—denomination—socioreligious community*. Despite denominational rivalries at top administrative levels, American Protestants and American Jews—Catholics do not enter the picture here since their "denominational" lines are within the one church—American Protestants and American Jews, especially the younger people, are becoming less denominational-minded, tending to identify themselves as Protestants or Jews rather than by denominational labels, choosing where they can "united" or "community" churches, or converting existing churches along such "non-denominational", "ecumenical" lines. This process—in which denominations are increasingly being articulated within the religious community—seems to be already well under way.

Now I want to get back to the trifaith system. What I should like to suggest is that, whereas America does not have a church in the Troeltschean sense as an organized institution, America does possess an overall religious entity that corresponds to the Troeltschean church, and that is the trifaith system of Protestant–Catholic–Jew. This is the kind of religious belonging that today, normally and naturally, goes along with being an American; it is, in a real sense, the nation on its religious side.

If there is any truth to this view at all, it would seem that there is still a further stage of secularization beyond the religious community. The series can now be completed: *cult–sect–denomination–socioreligious community–trifaith system*. Beyond this, secularization cannot go. In the trifaith system, conventional religion and operative religion have been almost completely separated and almost completely syncretized.

THREE-RELIGION PLURALISM AND RELIGIOUS GROUP TENSIONS

The transformation of America from a Protestant nation into a three-religion country has also exerted a far-reaching influence upon the patterns of religious group tension in this country. Let us examine some aspects of the situation, with an eye to the problem of secularization.

It is my contention that the transformation of America from a Protestant nation into a three-religion country, along with the concomitant upward movement of the Catholic population in the sociocultural scale in the course of the past generation, has had a double effect: in the short run, it has tended to exacerbate and sharpen Protestant–Catholic tensions; in the long run, however, I think, the very same process will tend to alleviate these tensions and mitigate their sharpness. And this duality of operation is closely connected with significant generational differences in outlook and attitude.

It is not difficult to see why the processes we are considering should make for a certain exacerbation of tensions. Protestants in this country are now faced with the prospect of the loss of accustomed status. The mass of the older Protestants have had their attitudes formed in an America that understood itself as a Protestant nation; the country, in a very real sense, was theirs, belonged to them, was their home. Now, within one generation, their own generation, the country has, almost literally, been taken away from them, to be parcelled out among the "three major faiths": what was once their own home they are now being compelled to share with two interloper groups. No wonder they feel dispossessed; no wonder they feel threatened. There was a time, not so long ago, when the middle-class Protestant in this country hardly came across a Catholic in those community institutions and organizations that really counted. There were, of course, many Catholics around, but they were largely at the margin of society, laborers and servant girls, hewers of wood and drawers of water. But within the past generation American Catholics have advanced dramatically from a peripheral, foreign, lower-class group to a nuclear, middle-class American community. Today, the Protestant, wherever he turns in community life, confronts Catholics on every side; no wonder he is convinced that Catholics have multiplied enormously and are taking over the country, whatever the statistics may say. Once, too, the general American institutions were simply Protestant institutions. Protestants did not need any separate organizations of their own, because the general community organizations and institutions were Protestant and obviously theirs. Jews and Catholics, on the other hand, and incidentally Negroes, too, had begun their very existence in

American life as minority groups, requiring special institutions, organizations, and agencies to represent and protect them, and these institutions, organizations, and agencies they rapidly built up. Today, Protestants, in most parts of the country, can no longer take the general community institutions for granted as theirs; but (aside from the Negro group) they have not managed to develop any significant institutions of their own, or at least did not get to developing these till very late. As a consequence, they frequently find themselves at a great disadvantage and are very resentful at the "separatism" of the Catholics and Jews, whose institutions they denounce as "divisive" and "un-American". All in all, the older Protestants in most parts of the country find themselves in a very frustrating position; it is no wonder that they have tended to develop an outlook that the editor of the *Christian Century* has very aptly, and with not too much exaggeration, described as "Protestant paranoia".

Where the older Protestants are faced with the grave threat of loss of accustomed status, American Catholics, on their side, are exceedingly anxious over their newly acquired status in American society; they are status-anxious. They feel that their recently achieved status as Americans, and as good middle-class Americans, is not being adequately acknowledged by the older masters of American society, the Protestants; and they therefore tend to be belligerent and resentful. They are suspicious and touchy, easily tempted to self-assertiveness and to gross overcompensation. But, above all, they feel hampered and closed in, denied their proper recognition; they see themselves ever anew threatened with exclusion and segregation. They therefore tend to develop what the editor of the *Christian Century*, to match the "Protestant paranoia", has called "Catholic claustrophobia".

Aside from these quasi-clinical designations, it is not difficult to see why, in this transition period from a Protestant to a three-religion country, there should be a certain exacerbation of Protestant–Catholic tensions, and of Protestant–Jewish tensions, too, in those places where Jews have made a sudden appearance in significant numbers in an older Protestant community. But, by the same token, there is every reason to expect an alleviation of tensions in the longer run.

We already have sufficient evidence to suggest that there are significant generational differences in attitudes that relate to religious group tensions. Younger Protestants tend to take a very different view, and to respond very differently, from the older members of their group; and this is true, though not so markedly, for the younger Catholics as well. It is well known, for example, that on the so-called "Jack Kennedy" question, which the Gallup organization has been asking for the past twenty years—I mean the question: "If your party nominated a generally well-qualified man for the presidency this year, and he happened to be a Catholic, would you vote for him?"—the younger voters have uniformly taken a far less anti-Catholic attitude; and this attitude they have tended to retain as they have grown older, so that there is a marked long-range trend in the same direction. Whereas in 1940, 31 per cent of the respondents answered "no" —they would *not* vote for a Catholic, even though he was a well-qualified man and a member of their party—by 1956, the proportion had fallen to 22 per cent. In that year (1956), the "no" vote was 31 per cent for respondents 50 years of age and over, 17 per cent for those between 30 and 49, and only 14 per cent for those between 21 and 29. This pattern is borne out by every other available bit of information, including community studies.

Again, it is not difficult to see why this should be so. The younger Protestants have not had their attitudes formed in an America that was a Protestant nation, but rather in an America that was emerging as a three-religion country; consequently, they do not feel particularly dispossessed, threatened, or overwhelmed. On the contrary, to them Catholicism is a legitimate part of American religion, one of the "three great faiths", while Catholics are just good, middle-class Americans, an integral part of the American people. The response one gets from these younger Protestants—I am thinking of a community survey of a New England town not yet published, a town once entirely Protestant, now about half Catholic—the response one gets from these younger Protestants is something sociologists ought readily to understand. It runs something like this: "What's all the excitement about? So they *are* Catholics! But they're our kind of people, and after all, we're all Americans, aren't we?"

As Catholics become more obviously "our kind of people", and equally Americans with the rest of us, as American opinion becomes more and more defined by the generation that has grown up in a three-religion country, the group tensions that now disturb us will tend to allay. This would appear to be a safe prognostication.

It seems worth noting, I think, that this analysis of Protestant–Catholic tensions proceeds without any reference to the social and religious issues that are alleged to divide the two communities. This is not because I regard these issues to be of no importance; on the contrary, I think they are issues of great importance, which deserve careful consideration on their own account. But I do not believe that they are so much the source of the tension as the expression of it. They become issues precisely because they arise in an already established context of tension and become vehicles of this tension and antagonism. Moreover, even though they have become issues in Protestant–Catholic conflict, they are not usually questions on which Protestants are aligned all on one side, and Catholics all on the other; on the contrary, on every one of these questions there are differences and divisions within both communities, with sizable minorities in each group crossing the lines.

However that may be, it will be observed that the better relations emerging between Protestants and Catholics are grounded in the "common religion" of American belonging— "After all, we're all Americans!"—and its predominance over the conventional religions of the three groups, not in opposition but in comprehension. In other words, the promising alleviation of religious group tensions would appear to be due to the advancing secularization of American life and religion. However we may feel about secularism, this should be noted and appreciated. It is the advanced state of secularization in the three-religion pluralism of contemporary America that is the decisive factor in the emergence of better religious group relations in this country.

Yet there is another side to the story, which may not be ignored. If, for the great mass of Americans, the new tolerance is a by-product of the emerging solidarity of the secularized "common religion", for a small group of theologically concerned people, something very like it comes from the opposite direction. Of recent years, we know, there has been a *rapprochement* in America as in Europe, between theologically concerned Protestants and Catholics, even between theologically concerned Christians and Jews, precisely as a consequence of their theological concern. It is not the "common religion" of the American Way that binds them; it is rather their common Christian, their common Biblical, faith and understanding. Indeed, suspicion of the American Way as a substitute-religion serving Americans as their ultimate context of meaning and value is a common premise. Whereas, for the great mass of Americans, the operative formula is "After all, we're all Americans", for the theological *élite* it would run something like, "After all, we're all Christians, standing on the same Bible", or, where Jews are included, "After all, we acknowledge the same God and recognize in Abraham our common father in the faith". The two attitudes are often confused under the vague rubrics of "tolerance", "unity", and "ecumenicity"; but they are very, very different and ought to be carefully distinguished.

The intergroup situation in this country at the present time is thus a very complicated one. There is a significant sweep toward better understanding as a result of extensive secularization at one end, and of a theologically oriented reaction against secularization at the other. In between are masses of Americans caught in the grip of the transition from the old America to the new, from the Protestant nation to the three-religion country, and driven to fear, hostility, and a kind of defensive aggressiveness as a result. For completeness, we ought to mention small groups of anti-religious secularists and self-styled "liberals" who find in anti-Catholicism a more viable, and even more respectable, form of anti-religion. As Peter Viereck has well pointed out: "Catholic-baiting is often the anti-Semitism of the liberals." But these elements are dwindling, and the prospect is definitely for a steady improvement of intergroup relations among the religious communities. And largely this is the result of increasing secularization, either directly, or indirectly by way of reaction.

THREE EMERGING GENERALIZATIONS

How shall we evaluate the sweeping secularization of American life and religion? No theological assessment will here be attempted. But there are certain things that will occur to every serious observer of American religion who has reflected on recent developments.

Secularization, which has been advancing at an increasing pace in Western society ever since the high middle ages, has taken a special and characteristic form in the United States, reflecting the special and characteristic pattern of acculturation of the many diverse groups of immigrants who have come to make up the American people. First, the emergence of the well-known system of multidenominational pluralism; then, the recasting of American society in terms of the socioreligious community, in which the denominations are typically grouped: these are the two major phases of the structural development of American religion since the early nineteenth century. Each of these phases marks a further stage of secularization.

The restructuring of American society along the line indicated has transformed America from the Protestant nation it has been since its beginning into a new kind of socioreligious entity—a three-religion country, in which social identification takes place by way of religious belonging. This transformation has obviously had far-reaching consequences, which are by no means all of one piece.

1. Religious belonging has become a mode of defining one's American identity. In this way, the two great non-Protestant

religions—Catholicism and Judaism—have acquired American status and been granted a place in the three-religion system. Catholics, Jews, Lutherans, and others, who remember how formidable an obstacle to the preservation and communication of their faith the taint of foreignness once was, will not be altogether ungrateful for what has happened. And all Americans may be thankful for the new spirit of freedom and tolerance in religious life that the emergence of the tripartite system of the three great "religions of democracy" has engendered: it makes increasingly difficult the sinister fusion of religious prejudice with racist or nationalist chauvinism. But these gains have come out of a thoroughgoing secularization of religion, in which conventional religion—Protestant, Catholic, and Jewish—has been integrated into the "common religion" of the American Way and made to serve a nonreligious function. As a result, American religiousness has been growing increasingly vacuous—a religiousness of belonging, without religious commitment, religious concern, or religious passion. To many religiously concerned people, this seems a very high price to pay.

2. Religious belief today tends to be assimilated to the ideas and values of the American Way. The conventional religions—Protestantism, Catholicism, and Judaism—are typically understood as variant expressions of the "common faith" which all Americans share by virtue of their participation in the American Way of Life. Consequently, religion enjoys a high place in the American scheme of things, higher today, perhaps, than at any time in the past century. But it is a religion thoroughly secularized and homogenized, a religion-in-general that is little more than a civic religion of democracy, the religionization of the American Way. Here, too, the price may be a very high one to pay.

3. Religious group relations in this country, despite a certain exacerbation for the moment, seem headed for a very considerable improvement in the foreseeable future. Every American will welcome this prospect, and will welcome it without qualification.

P

But again, it is coming largely, though not entirely, as the consequence of a secularizing evacuation of conventional religion. The price here, too, is a heavy one.

It is not my purpose to draw any balance sheet. All I have attempted to do is to call attention to certain aspects of the secularization of religion in contemporary America that may help illumine the paradox with which we began our discussion, the paradox that America is at once the most religious and the most secularistic of nations. I hope it is now possible for us to see in what way this paradox is true, and what this paradox has come to mean for the social and religious life of America.

Religion's Impact on Secular Institutions

G. LENSKI

DURING the last decade the subject of religion has received considerable attention both in popular and scholarly circles. Much of this has been devoted to the recent religious revival and its causes. Little attention has been devoted to the consequences of religious belief and practice in the everyday lives of the masses of men. Yet from both the sociological and religious standpoints, these could be of crucial importance.

Such interest as there has been in this latter problem stems chiefly from the work of Max Weber half a century ago. In his many writings on the sociology of religion, Weber set forth the thesis that each of the major religions of the world has developed its own distinctive orientation toward all aspects of social life, and, furthermore, he asserted, these differences have had profound consequences for the development of human societies.

Not all social scientists have shared Weber's views, by any means. On the contrary, if we may judge from the literature, most modern social scientists regard religion as a matter of minor importance, at least in contemporary society. Frequently the subject of religion is ignored entirely in their analyses of major social institutions, and, when it is mentioned, it usually receives no more than passing comment.

Several years ago it was my good fortune to obtain the resources necessary to explore the relevance of Weber's thesis for a portion of contemporary American society. At that time I was named principal investigator for the Detroit Area Study for the academic year 1957–58. This organization is a research facility of the Sociology Department of the University of Michigan and each year conducts a systematic survey of some sample of the population of the Detroit metropolitan area, utilizing formal interviews. The results of these surveys have been shown to be highly accurate when compared with known characteristics of the population sampled (e.g. the age composition of the population and other characteristics reported by the Bureau of the Census.

Each year a different problem is studied, depending upon the interests of the principal investigator. In my year I chose to study the impact of religion on three crucially important areas of life in our society: politics, economics, and family life.

The opportunity provided by the Detroit Area Study to investigate this subject was unique for two reasons. In the first place, it provided an opportunity to study the impact of religion in the context of a modern metropolis. This seemed important since the American population (together with that of the world as a whole) is becoming increasingly concentrated in such communities. Also, thanks to the influence of the mass media which are dominated by residents of these communities, the influence of the metropolis is penetrating and transforming the smaller cities and towns, and even the rural areas. Hence, the metropolis is clearly the community of crucial importance for the future.

In the second place, the Detroit Area Study provided me with a unique opportunity to follow up on one of the really important insights of Weber. Far too often, in attempting to assess the influence of religion on society, scholars have limited their study to investigations of the sporadic efforts of churches, acting as pressure groups, striving to reform society in some way, or striving to advance their own peculiar organizational interests (e.g. the efforts of certain Protestant groups to outlaw the manufacture and consumption of alcoholic beverages, or the efforts of Protestant and Catholics alike to eliminate the seven-day work week in the steel industry some years ago).

Weber was largely unconcerned with these rather obvious, deliberate, and calculated efforts to influence secular institutions in which most religious groups occasionally indulge. Rather, he was concerned with the fact that all religious groups are *continuously* shaping and molding the personalities of their adherents who then, as private individuals, staff the economic, political, educational, and other institutional systems of society. This he felt to be the far more influential process by which religious groups influence secular life.

Since the Detroit Area Study provided a means of studying the lives of a cross-section of the residents of a modern metropolis, it provided an ideal facility for my purposes.

IS RELIGION A MAJOR FACTOR?

With this by way of background, let me turn now to some of my findings.[1] For those who regard religion as a factor of minor importance in the life of our society, there will be many startling findings. However, none will be more startling than the basic conclusion to which I ultimately came as a result of my study. This was the conclusion that religion is a factor *comparable to social class* in its influence on the behavior of individuals and hence on the life of society as a whole.

Those of you familiar with current sociological research and writing will recognize that this is an extremely strong statement. It is safe to say that there is no other factor which sociologists have found to have greater influence than class. The class position of individuals influences everything from the political party for which they vote to the types of recreation in which they engage. In short, it is regarded as a factor of major importance both because of the *range* of behavior influenced by it, and because of the *magnitude* of the influence exercised.

My data indicate that religion is a factor of comparable importance in *both* respects. It influences an equally wide range of

---

[1] A more detailed summary of my findings may be found in *The Religious Factor: A Sociological Study of Religion's Impact on Politics, Economics, and Family Life* (Garden City, N.Y.: Doubleday, 1961).

behavior, and the magnitude of the influence exercised is comparable.

At one point in my analysis I divided the white Christians in my sample into four categories: (1) middle-class white Protestants, (2) working-class white Protestants, (3) middle-class white Catholics, and (4) working-class white Catholics. These four categories were then compared with respect to thirty-five different matters pertaining to politics, economics, and family life. Included here were such things as party preference, attitudes toward labor unions, attitudes toward work, number of children, frequency of visiting relatives, attitudes toward the kin group, beliefs concerning the political rights of Communists and Fascists, and similar matters. Taking all thirty-five items together, the differences between religious groups with class level held constant were slightly greater on the average than the differences between classes with religion held constant.

This does not mean that there are not some areas of behavior which are more strongly influenced by class than by religion. However, for each such area, there was another for which the reverse proved true. In short, far from being a factor of minor importance in the most highly urbanized segments of our population, these data indicate that religion is a factor of major importance—equal, in fact, to social class.[2]

POLITICS AND THE THREE RELIGIONS

To become more specific, let me cite the case of party preference. Prior to my study, a number of other studies had shown that there are differences in party preference linked with socio-religious group membership. White Protestants (everywhere

---

[2] It has just come to my attention that a recent test of my finding by Professor Charles Westoff of New York University provides additional support for my conclusion. Using data from the Princeton study of fertility, gathered in twelve metropolitan centers, Westoff found the differences between religious groups (with class held constant) as great as the difference between classes (with religious groups held constant) for a range of 25 variables pertaining to politics, economics, and family life. These results have not yet been published.

except in the South) have always been found to be the strongest supporters of the Republican Party. Catholics, Jews, and Negro Protestants have just as consistently been found to lean toward the Democratic Party.

For a time it was argued that these differences were merely reflections of differences in the class composition of the several groups. However, the work of Lazarsfeld and his colleagues at Columbia proved decisively that, even when comparisons between Protestants and Catholics were limited to persons similar in class position, substantial political differences remained.

The skeptics then retreated to the argument that these differences were due to nineteenth-century patterns of immigration. After the Civil War, the white Protestants of the North came to control the Republican Party, and hence newer immigrant groups were driven into the Democratic Party in order to find a vehicle for political action. Since party preference, like religious preference, tends to be handed down within families from one generation to the next, present-day Jews and Catholics tend to be Democrats, since they are the children and grandchildren of the immigrants who came after the Civil War. By contrast, white Protestants tend to be Republicans, since they are the descendants of the earlier immigrants.

In an effort to test this very plausible hypothesis, I inquired into the party preferences of the fathers of the Detroiters whom I interviewed. I was interested to see whether it could be shown that, when the political preference of the *fathers* of Catholics and Protestants was held constant, religion would still make a difference. I found that clearly it does. For example, among the sons and daughters of *Republican* fathers who were interviewed, only 13 per cent of those who were white Protestants had become Democrats, compared with 44 per cent of those who were Catholics. Similar differences were found both among the children of Democratic fathers and among the children of fathers with no political preference. From this it seemed clear that the current differences in party preference between Catholics and white

Protestants represent something more than a lingering heritage of the nineteenth century.

In the political area differences were not limited merely to party preference. Significant differences were found in many other areas of political life as well. For example, I found significant differences in the interpretation of the Bill of Rights as it applies to the area of freedom of speech. White Protestants and Jews were somewhat more likely than Catholics to put a liberal construction on the Bill of Rights and see it as protecting the rights of Communists, Fascists, and atheists to express their points of view. These differences were especially marked among *middle*-class members of these groups, a fact of great significance since most government officials, both elected and appointed, are persons recruited from the middle class. It is also noteworthy that differences were much more marked when comparisons were limited to those who were regular participants in the worship services of their respective groups. All of these differences were found when comparisons were limited to persons of similar class level.

ECONOMIC BEHAVIOR AMONG THE FAITHS

A second major area I explored was that of *economic* behavior. Here I found, as have others previously, that there are significant differences in the degree to which members of the several groups have gotten ahead in our competitive economic system. Jews were the most successful, both in terms of income and in terms of the percentage in business or professional occupations. White Protestants ranked second, white Catholics third, and Negro Protestants last.

Here again, these differences have been explained away on the grounds that they reflect the influence of factors other than religion. Often it is argued that the relative lack of success of Catholics and Negro Protestants is a function of their late arrival in the urban centers of the North. Coming as immigrants long after many of the white Protestant families had established themselves, they were obliged to take the least desirable positions.

Hence, present-day Catholics and Negro Protestants are more often manual workers with limited incomes than are white Protestants, simply because their fathers were not able to give them the same advantages as the sons and daughters of most white Protestants.

Again this is a very plausible argument, particularly if you do not examine it too closely. However, critical examination of this argument should lead one to ask why the Jews have fared so well. While they are not as recent migrants to the urban North as the Negro Protestants, they are generally more recent immigrants than the Catholics. Hence, one would expect them to rank behind the Catholics, when in fact they rank ahead of even the white Protestants.

When the argument is subjected to an empirical test, still further weaknesses become apparent. For one thing, my own research and that of one of my former students indicate that, when you compare white Catholics and Protestants whose fathers were in comparable occupations, the sons of white Protestant fathers have fared better than the sons of Catholic fathers. For example, if you compare the Catholic and Protestant sons of unskilled or semiskilled manual workers, the Protestants are more likely to have risen to the ranks of business or professional men. Or, if you compare the sons of business and professional men, Catholics are more likely to have dropped into the ranks of the semiskilled and unskilled. Differences were most evident at the upper-middle-class level.

The explanation for these differences proved to be rather complex. It is not simply a matter that Protestants and Jews have more ambition or drive than Catholics or that they value material success more. So far as my evidence indicates, differences in these respects are not great. Rather, a series of other, less obvious, factors seem responsible.

In view of the limitations of space, I shall attempt to describe only two of the lines of analysis which proved profitable in my study of this problem. One of the questions which I asked all of the men we interviewed was whether they would quit their work if suddenly they were to become financially independent. Regardless of how they answered, I then asked them to explain why they felt as they did.

The answers to these questions proved extremely interesting. Basically, responses fell into three major categories. First, some men told us that they would never quit work if they could avoid it since they enjoyed it so much. Some of these men said life would hardly be worth living if they were not able to work. A second category of men told my interviewers that they would quit work immediately if they were able to do so: they worked only because they had to for financial reasons. Finally, some men expressed an ambivalent attitude toward work.

When the several religious groups were compared, it was found that, among whites, Jews were the most likely to have a positive attitude toward work, while Catholics were the least likely. But what proved even more important, those Protestants and Jews in responsible positions were the members of their groups who were most likely to have a positive attitude toward work, while among Catholics those in responsible positions were the most likely to have a negative attitude. Among Catholics, those in menial occupations were more likely to have positive attitudes toward work than those in responsible positions. This was surprising.

The significance of this finding became clearer when I analyzed the responses to a further question. Each person interviewed was asked which of the following was most important for a child to learn to prepare him for life: (1) to obey, (2) to be well liked, (3) to think for himself, (4) to work hard, or (5) to help others when they need help. They were then asked which they thought was next most important, and so on until they had ranked all five.

The most important differences involved the relative ranking of the first and third items—those involving obedience and intellectual independence. To begin with, there were marked differences between the several *classes* in their ranking of these two items. The higher the class position of individuals, the more likely they were to regard it as important for the child to learn to think for himself. The lower the class position, the more likely they were to regard it as important for the child to learn to obey.

Equally important, however, was the finding that beliefs on this subject are strongly linked with religious preference, even when comparisons are limited to persons in the same class. White Protestants and Jews are a good bit more likely than Catholics to rate intellectual independence ahead of obedience.

On the basis of all we know about the more responsible positions in our society today, it is extremely important for a person to be able to think for himself. This is especially true in the rapidly expanding fields of science. The person who can only obey and follow instructions will not advance far. *Creativity* is the quality most in demand, and creativity presumes a capacity for autonomous thought. What is true in science is also true to nearly the same degree in the free professions such as law, medicine, and architecture. Even in the middle and upper levels of management, far more is required than mere obedience to orders. Initiative and imagination are qualities still sought and valued, William Whyte notwithstanding.

Yet these are qualities which Catholics apparently bring to the job world somewhat less often than either white Protestants or Jews. This, I believe, explains in part why Catholics are less likely to rise to the more responsible positions in our economy, and why also, when they do, they are less happy in them.

This is a matter which has profound implications not only for the individuals involved, but for the society as a whole. At the present time, our society is engaged in a deadly competition with Soviet Russia for world supremacy and influence. The outcome of this struggle may well depend on the quantity and quality of our scientists. Repeated studies have shown that Catholics are far less likely to enter careers in science than Protestants and Jews, and Catholic institutions of higher education produce only a small fraction of the number of scientists produced by non-Catholic institutions even when numbers of graduates are held constant.[3] Catholic leaders are aware of these studies and in recent years have taken certain steps to remedy the situation. However, my findings suggest that the differences between Catholics and non-Catholics in this area cannot be entirely eliminated merely by administrative reforms in Catholic colleges. Rather, the root of the problem seems to lie in fundamental differences in basic values which separate Catholics and non-Catholics and which are internalized in individuals early in life.

DIFFERENCES IN FAMILY LIFE

In my attempts to understand why Catholics were less successful in competition for the better jobs in our society, I was inevitably led into an examination of the area of *family life*, following up a clue provided by Max Weber. In one of his later writings on the interrelations between religion and economics—a comparison of Puritanism and Confucianism—Weber developed the thesis that one of the reasons Puritanism gave rise to the spirit of capitalism was because it succeeded in "smashing the fetters of the sib", or the extended family system. He argued that Puritanism replaced the community of blood with the community of faith. It placed the ties of faith ahead of the ties of kinship. Thus it was possible for new patterns of social relations to emerge—patterns in which the ties of kinship were wholly ignored.

In seeking to follow up on this thesis, I inquired into the place of the kin group in the lives of those whom I interviewed. It quickly became apparent that the kin group is more important to Catholics and Jews than to Protestants. Catholics and Jews visit their relatives more often, and see less of neighbors and co-workers in the off-the-job relations. Furthermore, they are less likely to migrate and thus break their ties with kith and kin. Finally, they are less likely to become divorced.

[3] See, for example, Robert Knapp and H. B. Goodrich, *Origins of American Scientists* (Chicago: The University of Chicago Press, 1952); Francis Bello, The Young Scientist, *Fortune Magazine* June, 1954, pp. 142 ff.; or S. S. Visher, *Scientists Starred*, 1903–1943 (Baltimore: Johns Hopkins Press, 1947).

More interesting than this was the relationship between church attendance and these indices of kin-group loyalty and involvement. Not too surprisingly, I found that the more faithful Catholics are in their attendance at Mass, the stronger is their tie with the kin group. By contrast, among Protestants just the reverse proved true. The more faithful Protestants were in their attendance at worship services, the weaker were their ties with their kin group. In short, my data led me to the conclusion that church and family stand in a rather different relationship among Protestants than among Catholics. Whereas these two important institutional systems appear to be mutually reinforcing agencies in the lives of Catholics, there is evidence that they conflict with one another to some degree in the lives of Protestants.

This is not to say that the Protestant churches criticize or demean family life—far from it. However, it does appear that Protestant churches with their intensive programs of organizational activities throughout the week compete with the kin group for the time, energies, and loyalties of men.

It is my conclusion that to the degree that the Protestant churches weaken the hold of the kin group on the individual—especially the extended kin group—to that degree they aid their members in rising in the job world. Success in the job world increasingly presupposes a willingness on the part of the individual to migrate and leave family and friends. In many of the large corporations, with plants scattered around the country, it is standard policy not to promote executives within the same plant. Every promotion is accompanied by a move to another plant and another community. The individual who is tied too closely to his family thus operates at a serious disadvantage. Even in less bureaucratized fields of endeavor such as medicine, law, and small business, the job competes with the kin group for men's time and energy. Once again, the individual who has strong family ties is not likely to get ahead in these fields as readily as the individual whose ties are weaker. In fact, if he knows something about the demands of various jobs, he is likely to prefer some 40-hour-a-week white-collar job in preference to law, medicine, or business. In brief, it appears that the vitality of Catholic family life and the relative lack of success of Catholics in the job world are two sides of the same coin.

INFLUENCE OF PAROCHIAL SCHOOL EDUCATION

In the course of my study I was interested not only in comparisons between Catholics, Protestants, and Jews; I was also interested in intra-group comparisons of various types. One of these of special interest was that concerning the influence of parochial school education. Some of my findings in this area were not too surprising, but others were.

One of the less surprising findings was that those Catholics who have received all or most of their education in Catholic institutions are more faithful in their observance of Catholic norms than those who received all or most of their education in non-Catholic institutions. For example, 86 per cent of the former claimed to attend Mass at least once a week compared with 71 per cent of the latter. How much of this difference is attributable to the influence of Catholic schools and how much to the influence of parents is difficult to say, but there is probably some residue of school influence operative here.

I found that, the further one moves from the more visible, outward aspects of religious practice to the more inward and private, the smaller the differences between the two groups became. For example, whereas there was a difference of 15 percentage points between the two groups with respect to attendance at Mass, there was only an 8-point difference in frequency of daily prayer. In view of the secondary character of social relationships in a school setting, this difference is not too surprising, but I suspect it is important.

One of the great fears of non-Catholics concerning the Catholic school system is that it fosters intolerance and prejudice toward non-Catholics. On logical grounds there is good reason for expecting this, since ethnocentric attitudes frequently flourish where there is an absence of primary-type relations. However, despite the reasonableness of the logic, I could find no evidence that exposure to the Catholic educational system produces intolerance toward Protestants, Jews, or Negroes as individuals. At least it had no influence which could be detected when the adult graduates of these schools were compared with Catholics who had attended non-Catholic institutions.

However, while attendance at Catholic schools did not seem to foster intolerance of non-Catholic *individuals*, it did appear to produce intolerance of non-Catholic religious *groups*. This was especially evident when I analyzed the responses of Catholics to the question of whether ministers of other faiths should be permitted to preach publicly (as on the radio) things contrary to Catholic teaching. Fifty-five per cent of the Catholics who had received all or most of their education in non-Catholic schools felt that ministers of other faiths should be permitted to do this, but only 31 per cent of those who had received all or most of their education in Catholic institutions shared this view.

On a more encouraging note, the Catholic school system seems to stimulate an appreciation of the democratic process. Or at least, this is suggested by the fact that those who have attended Catholic schools are more likely to vote than those who attended non-Catholic schools.

Not only does attendance at Catholic schools stimulate voting—it also has an impact on party preference. It creates converts to the Republican Party. The basis for my statement is this: among those Catholics who received all or most of their education in non-Catholic institutions, there were just as many Democrats with Republican fathers as there were Republicans with Democratic fathers. In other words, there was no net shift among these Catholics. However, among those who had attended *Catholic* schools, only 11 per cent had fathers who were Republicans, but 27 per cent of the children were. In other words, there was a net shift of 16 percentage points, or a net gain of one child out of six for the Republican Party. No wonder President Kennedy was opposed to federal aid for parochial schools!

Another important difference linked with attendance at Catholic institutions was the attitude which men developed toward work. This difference was especially evident among the middle-class Catholics whom we interviewed. Only 6 per cent of those with all or most of their education in Catholic institutions expressed a positive attitude toward work. By contrast, 28 per cent of the middle-class Catholic men with a non-Catholic education expressed such an attitude. I also found that, among middle-class Catholics, attendance at Catholic institutions was linked with a greater appreciation of the value of obedience and less appreciation of the value of intellectual autonomy. Finally, I found that ties with the kin group were stronger among those who had received most of their education in Catholic institutions than among those who had attended non-Catholic institutions. In short, the Catholic school system seems to foster this interesting and important cultural syndrome which simultaneously results in strong familial ties, on the one hand, and limited enthusiasm for the job world and relative lack of success in it on the other.

THREE MORALITIES CONSIDERED

By now I suspect that some may be thinking, "This is all well and good to show that religion is a factor influencing the outcome of elections, the production of scientists, and similar matters, but this is not what really concerns us. We are concerned with religion as a regenerative force in society. We are chiefly concerned with whether the various religious groups are influential in this respect."

This is surely a legitimate and proper interest of clergymen—and of social scientists as well. However, I would insist that we cannot ignore the fact that religion has consequences other than those which it deliberately seeks to produce or those which are socially beneficial. More than that, the clergy bear some responsibility for the former. Religious leaders and religious groups cannot claim credit for the good which results from their efforts if they are not prepared to answer for other consequences as well. Yet it is my impression that, by and large, this is precisely what is usually done.

As a sociologist it seems to me to be the height of folly to pretend that religious groups are not in part, at least, human institutions and reflect human nature in all of its varied aspects. Thus religious groups are not merely vehicles for the expression of divine grace, they are also vehicles for the expression of human ambition, avarice, and folly. This is a point to which I shall return shortly.

If one searches for evidence of the regenerative influence of religious groups, one can surely find it. However, the churches are not the powerful force one might wish them to be, as can be seen when comparisons are made between those persons who are most active in the churches (and hence presumably most exposed to their influence) and those who are marginal. Let me cite a few examples.

In the course of the interview, two of the questions asked dealt with what might be designated *personal morality*. First, we asked whether our respondents would return change at a supermarket if they received a bit more than was due them. Second, we asked whether they would pay the fine if ticketed for parking overtime in a strange city. If they said "Yes" to this question, we then asked whether they would pay if they were in a hurry and knew that they would never be caught if they ignored the ticket.

On the question concerning the supermarket, Catholic and Negro Protestant churchgoers were somewhat more likely to say they would return the change than marginal members of the same groups. Among white Protestants there was no difference associated with church attendance. On the question concerning the parking ticket, Negro and white Protestant churchgoers were more likely than non-churchgoers to say they would pay the fine regardless. Here there was no difference among Catholics. However, among whites, both Catholics and Protestants, the differences between churchgoers and non-churchgoers were so small that it is difficult to say that involvement in these churches has any great effect on personal morality. Only in the case of the

Negro Protestants was the difference great enough to assume any real social significance.

I also explored the area of what might be designated as *social* or *group* morality. By this I mean the attitudes of individuals with regard to the moral standards of the groups to which they belong—especially the community and nation. For example, I asked Detroiters whether they believed that our country should spend money abroad even when it could not be justified in the interest of national defense. In all of the groups, churchgoers were more likely than non-churchgoers to take the humanitarian position and advocate foreign aid even if it could not be justified on the grounds of national defense. Similarly, churchgoers were more likely than non-churchgoers to favor racially integrated schools. I was especially interested to find that this was true even among the Southern-born white Protestants, who are rather numerous in Detroit. However, except in the case of these Southern-born Protestants, differences were not large in any of the groups.

I also explored a third area which, for lack of a better term, I have designated as *sectarian morality*. By this I refer to those moral standards, both personal and social, which some one religious group supports in the face of the opposition of most other groups. For example, many Protestant denominations have long been opposed to drinking and gambling and have sought to discourage their members from engaging in these practices but have found no support for this from Catholics or Jews. Similarly, Catholic teaching with regard to birth control might be designated as sectarian morality, since almost all Protestant and Jewish groups have conflicting views.

This is the one area in which the churches clearly make a powerful impact on their adherents. Differences between church-goers and non-churchgoers on questions dealing with these matters are extremely large. For example, 70 per cent of the active Catholics expressed the belief that the practice of birth control by married couples is always or usually wrong from the moral standpoint. By contrast, only 25 per cent of the Catholics who did not attend Mass regularly shared this view. Or, in the case of white Protestants, 70 per cent of the regular churchgoers believed gambling is always or usually wrong from the moral standpoint, but only 45 per cent of the marginal members shared this view.

There is, of course, an obvious logic to the practices of the churches as revealed by these findings. Each church feels it can leave the problem of reinforcing the basic moral standards of society to other agencies since, after all, it has no monopoly on such things as the belief in the rightness of honesty and social justice. However, since only one's own group is aware of the rightness of certain sectarian moral standards, these are the ones which must be supported by all available resources. Thus, while striving to be a regenerative force in society, the churches often come to be divisive agencies concerned far more with sectarian morality than with the more basic problems of personal and social morality. In this connection, it is interesting to speculate whether the pressures of intergroup competition and conflict have not led American religious groups to stress certain aspects of their message out of all proportion to their true importance.

TRUE NATURE OF RELIGIOUS GROUPS

These findings which I have sketched in so briefly raise almost as many questions as they answer. For one thing, if religion has as important an influence on secular institutions as I indicated earlier, why is it that the experts have so frequently underestimated it? Furthermore, how is it possible that religious groups have as much, or more, influence on job careers, voting behavior, and similar matters than they have on basic individual and social morality?

The answers to both of these questions are, in my opinion, tied together. In both instances our difficulties arise out of our failure to comprehend the true nature of religious groups. This applies to social scientists and religious leaders alike.

Far too often religious groups have been equated in our minds with the churches. In other words, far too often they have been thought of as merely one more type of specialized, formal association—the counter-part of the corporation, the labor union, the Kiwanis Club, or the P.T.A.—except, of course, that the religious group is thought to be far less influential than most since it brings its members together for only an hour a week and even then attracts only a minority of the population.

This view corresponds with certain obvious facts but ignores others. It is the truth, but not the whole truth. The crucial fact which it ignores is that religious groups are basically endogamous —their members normally marry within the group. As a result, interaction among the members of a family also normally involves interaction among members of the same religious group, with all that this implies.

This is not to say that Catholic families, for example, are *merely* subunits of the Catholic church, any more than we would say that American families are merely subunits of American society. However, just as American families function as subunits of our society, reinforcing by rewards and punishments those societal norms which they adopt for their own, so, too, religiously homogeneous families serve as subunits of religious groups, reinforcing their norms. In this connection it should be noted that the special interdecennial population survey of the Bureau of the Census in 1957 revealed that more than 93 per cent of the American families are religiously homogeneous.

What is true of the great majority of American families is also true of a very large number of other primary groups. They, too, are often religiously homogeneous, and, when this is true, they also tend to function as subunits of religious groups.

As a consequence, most individuals are exposed to the influences of their religious group every day of the week and in a variety of social relationships—especially those they cherish most. Not only are they exposed to the influences of the religious group on Sunday morning or Friday evening—they are also exposed to these influences in most of the more intimate social relationships in which they are involved. On the basis of all we know about the socialization of the individual and the process by which the personality of the individual is shaped and molded, this is largely accomplished through just such relationships as these.

Because of this, it is a serious mistake to equate the religious group with the churches or synagogues. The churches and synagogues are only a part of the social system constituting any major religious group. Religious movements normally give rise to *communities* of persons united by ties of kinship and friendship as well as to the associations formally established for specifically religious purposes. Too often we ignore or overlook the communal aspects of religious groups and thus are led to underestimate their power and influence.

This brings me to a second major point. Though the interest of religious associations are often somewhat limited and circumscribed, the interests of religious communities typically encompass all phases of human life. Religious communities are vitally concerned with such mundane matters as politics and economics, even though the religious associations with which they are linked may have but limited interest in such matters. What is more, they are often concerned about these matters in basically selfish terms. In a pluralistic society such as our own, religious communities easily become embroiled in a not very attractive competition for political power, social status, and the other rewards society has to offer.

As a consequence, each of the major religious groups tends to develop a rather complex subculture. These subcultures include secular as well as sacred elements. Far too often we make the mistake of thinking that religious groups are only concerned with theological doctrines, ritual practices, and matters of church government. Nothing could be further from the truth. The subcultural heritage of modern Judaism contains countless elements of a strictly secular nature. The same is true of the subcultural heritage of contemporary Protestantism and Catholicism.

Once these facts are recognized, we can more easily understand why it is that scholars have so often underestimated the influence of religion in contemporary society. Once these facts are recognized, we can also more easily understand why religious groups often have so much more influence on partisan politics and other mundane matters than on matters of basic morality. These things cease to be such a mystery once we grasp the complexity of the network of social relationships which constitutes the typical religious group, and once we grasp the corresponding complexity of the cultural heritage which these groups preserve and develop.

Biographical Notes

BANKS, J. A. Senior Research Lecturer, Department of Social Science, University of Liverpool.

Major publications include:

Prosperity and Parenthood 1954; Industrial Participation 1963; Technical Change and Industrial Relations (with W. H. Scott, et al.) 1956; Feminism and Family Planning in Victorian England (with O. L. Banks) 1964.

BROTHERS, Joan, B.A., Ph.D. Research Officer, University of London Institute of Education's Centre for the Study of Educational Policies 1966.

Major publications include:

Church and School (with J. D. Halloran, eds.) Liverpool 1964; Sociology London 1966; and numerous articles in the sociology of religion.

CARRIER, Hervé, S.J. Pontifica Universita Gregoriana, Rome. Professor of Sociology and Secretary of the Faculty of Social Sciences.

He is the author of several books on religious sociology and a contributor to scientific journals in Canada, France, Belgium, Italy, and the United States.

FICHTER, Joseph H., S. J. Chauncey Stillman Professor, Harvard Divinity School, Cambridge, Massachusetts.

Major publications include:

Priests and People 1965; Cambio Social en Chile 1962; Religion as an Occupation 1961. Parochial School 1958; Soziologie der Pfarrgruppen 1958; Sociology 1957; Social Relations in the Urban Parish 1954; Dynamics of a City Church 1951.

HERBERG, Will. Graduate Professor of Philosophy and Culture, Drew University, Madison, New Jersey, U.S.A.

Major publications include:

Judaism and Modern Man: An Interpretation of Jewish Religion 1951, 1959; Protestant–Catholic–Jew: An Essay in American Religious Sociology 1955, rev. ed. 1960. He has edited The Writings of Martin Buber 1956, Four

Existentialist Theologians 1958, and *Community, State and Church: Three Essays by Karl Barth* 1960; and has published three monographs: *The Jewish Labor Movement in America* 1950, *The Political Theory of American Marxism* 1950, and *Religion and Education in America* 1961.

LE BRAS, Gabriel. Director of Studies, École Pratique des Hautes Études, Sorbonne.

Major publications in the sociology of religion include:

Études de sociologie religieuse, 2 vols., 1955, 1956. Numerous articles on religious sociology and on the history of the Catholic Church in France.

LENSKI, Gerhard. Professor, Department of Sociology and Social Anthropology, The University of North Carolina.

Major publications include:

Principles of Sociology 1956; *The Religious Factor* 1961.

PARSONS, Talcott. Professor (formerly Chairman), Department of Social Relations, Harvard University.

Major publications include:

Protestant Ethic and Spirit of Capitalism (trans. of Max Weber), 1930; *Structure of Social Action* 1937; *Toward a General Theory of Action* 1951; *The Social System* 1951; *Essays in Sociological Theory* revised 1954; *Structure and Process in Modern Societies* 1959; Co-author: *Working Papers on the Theory of Action* 1952; *Family, Socialization and Interaction Process* 1955; *Economy and Society* 1956.

POULAT, Emile. Director of Studies, École Pratique des Hautes Études, Sorbonne.

Major publications include:

Les Cahiers manuscrits de Charles Fourier 1957; *Alfred Loisy, sa vie, son œuvre,* 1960; *Le "Journal d'un prêtre d'après-demain" de l'abbé Calippe* 1961; *Histoire, dogme et critique dans la crise moderniste* 1962; *Naissance des prêtre-ouvriers* 1965; contributor to *Priests and Workers* an Anglo-French discussion, edited by D. L. Edwards, London, 1961.

SIMEY, Thomas Spensley (Baron Simey of Toxteth). Charles Booth Professor of Social Science, University of Liverpool, since 1939.

Major publications include:

Principles of Social Administration 1937; *Welfare and Planning in the West Indies* 1946; *The Concept of Love in Child Care* 1960; *Charles Booth, Social Scientist* (with Mrs. M. B. Simey), 1960.

VOGT, Edvard D. Sentrum for Kultur og Religionsforskning, Bergen, Norway.

Major publications include:

Problemi di Sociologia Religiosa, Ed. Internazionali, Rome, First part 1958, Second part 1959; *Le leggi sociologische*, Ed. Giuffre, Milan, 1958; *Freidrich Engels and the Dialectics of Nature*, Academic Diss., 1962; *The Catholic Church in the North*, Bergen, 1962.

VRIJHOF, Dr. Pieter Hendrik. Sociologisch Institut van de Rijksuniversiteit, Utrecht, Netherlands.

Publications include:

Articles mainly on sociology of religion, social work and community organizations and some theoretical and psychological subjects. He contributed to the *Manual of Religious Sociology of the Netherlands*, edited by W. Banning, and wrote a book on the religious sociology of Utrecht.

THE COMMONWEALTH AND INTERNATIONAL LIBRARY

Joint Chairmen of the Honorary Editorial Advisory Board

SIR ROBERT ROBINSON, O.M., F.R.S., LONDON

DEAN ATHELSTAN SPILHAUS, MINNESOTA

Publisher: ROBERT MAXWELL, M.C.

Read

A